Confronting the Cyber Storm

A Coercive Cyber Strategy to Defend the Nation

Ronald Banks

Confronting the Cyber Storm

A Coercive Cyber Strategy to Defend the Nation

Disclaimer:

The content provided in this book is for educational and informational purposes only. While best efforts have been used in preparing this book, the author/publisher make no representations or warranties of any kind, express or implied, and assume no liabilities of any kind with respect to the accuracy or completeness of the contents and specifically disclaim any implied warranties of any kind. Neither the author nor the publisher shall be held liable or responsible to any person or entity with respect to any loss or incidental or consequential damages caused, or alleged to have been caused, directly or indirectly, by the information contained herein. Every attempt has been made to provide truthful, accurate, reliable and up to date information and to give credit where credit is due. By reading this document, the reader agrees that under no circumstances is the author /publisher responsible for any losses which may occur as a result of the information contained in this document, not limited to errors, omissions or inaccuracies.

Acknowledgements

I would like to thank several individuals who substantially contributed to my exploration and debate of the concepts within this book. From the start, Anthony Bishop, Jason Jordan, Mark Butt, Steve Luczynski, and the team of NPLI at Harvard, all helped advance the constructs presented here, as well as challenged me to dive deeper into the various aspects of the government and private industry organizations and their capabilities which are required to make this strategy executable.

Next, I wish to thank my handful of wise mentors and counselors who spent many hours reading, editing, and advancing my thoughts and writing style: Pano Yannakogeorgos, Rick Bailey, Eric McNulty, and Chris Watt. Without their tireless effort, this book would not have been as meaningful a contribution to the broader academic literature of national coercive cyber strategy.

Finally, and most importantly, I am tremendously grateful to my daughter Jessica for her magnificent design of the cover of this book, as well as my loving and patient wife Kathy who spent an incredible amount of time and energy reading, editing, and challenging the narrative, logic and content of the book. With her non-cyber perspective, Kathy was instrumental in the construction of a far better final product. She is the love of my life and I am extremely appreciative of her support!

Table of Contents

CHAPTER ONE

RAISING THE ALARM: THE NEED FOR A NATIONAL CYBERSECURITY STRATEGY

On December 7, 2014, 73 years after the attacks on Pearl Harbor, a team of seven newly acquainted executives from government and private industry assembled at Harvard to debate a new concept for a much-needed national cybersecurity strategy. This concept was one that I conceived to ensure the United States would never experience a Cyber "Pearl Harbor." At the same time this debate was occurring, Sony Pictures Entertainment received a note from the Guardians of Peace (a cyber hacktivist group) threatening Sony that the "world will be full of fear. Remember the 11th of September 2001."[1] This note, which drew my group's attention along with that of the United States' security agencies, was in relation to an earlier cyber-strike against Sony on November 24, 2014, that included the theft of confidential and proprietary information (47,000 social security numbers, executives' emails, and unreleased movies), the wholesale erasure of internal data centers, and the destruction of 75 percent of Sony servers. The United States later publicly accused North Korea of sponsoring the cyber-

1

strike.[2] North Korea has since compromised more than sixteen other organizations in at least eleven different countries, sometimes simultaneously, to steal an estimated $1.1 billion.[3] The invaluable discussion at Harvard would launch several years of my research and thought in order to understand and overcome the challenges and complexities involved in the development of a holistic national cybersecurity strategy for the United States…an issue of great concern for both government and private industry leaders.

Since 2014, government and private entities around the globe have experienced significant cyber-attacks from a multitude of threats. The targets have been entities such as Home Depot (2014), eBay (2014), major Indian banks (SBI, HDFC Bank, ICICI, YES Bank and Axis Bank) (2016), Equifax (2017), Under Armour (2018), Marriott (2018), and Facebook (2019) just to name a few. Furthermore, these cases represent examples of criminal and state-sponsored coercive cyber-enabled malicious activity (CEMA)[4] targeting national critical infrastructure in ways that are not clearly acts of war.

Today's malicious cyber actors continually and repeatedly assault national critical infrastructure sectors, each time with increasing sophistication and devastation, leaving national populations stunned by this raging cyber storm. United States' Critical infrastructure sectors– including financial, energy, tele-communications, technology, and retail sectors – are routinely the targets of ever-increasing nefarious activity in and through the virtual domain. In fact, very few modern nations can claim that they have not fallen victim to significant cyber-enabled malicious activity. In 2017, the global malware campaign "NotPetya" impacted the Ukraine, Russia, Denmark, the United Kingdom, and the United States. In 2018, "WannaCry" ransomware disrupted countless organizations including the UK's National Health Service (NHS), U.S. hospitals, Nissan, and Russian banks. North Korea has been accused of attacking and stealing money from banks in South Korea, Mexico, and Bangladesh. In 2016 and 2018, the United States accused Russia of interfering in

U.S. elections. In 2019, more than half of the United Kingdom firms (55%) reported falling victim to cyber-attacks,[5] more than 100 German politicians at all levels, including Chancellor Merkel were victims of a massive data breach.[6] The near ubiquity of CEMA highlights the fact that nations of the world are not keeping pace with cyber threat actors, who enjoy the fruits of their labor without fear of repercussion.

The Cyber Landscape – A Cause for Alarm

In cyberspace, new antagonists are now able to establish dominance regardless of their relative power in the physical domain. The comparatively low cost to enter this new form of conflict presents a window of opportunity for previously inferior actors to deliver a devastating blow to the exposed underbelly of a nation's key cyber terrain: its critical infrastructure, which the U.S. Department of Homeland Security (DHS) defines as those components of national industry "whose assets, systems, and networks, whether physical or virtual, are considered so vital to the United States that their incapacitation or destruction would have a debilitating effect on security, national economic security, national public health or safety, or any combination thereof."[7] DHS goes on to further define fifty-five "national critical functions" which include such things as: Provide Internet Based Content, Information, and Communication Services; Provide Internet Routing, Access, and Connection Services; Provide Positioning, Navigation, and Timing Services; Distribute Electricity; Conduct Elections; and Public Works and Services.[8] The United States' key cyber terrain includes both its national critical infrastructure and functions, and will be referred to in this book as either *key cyber terrain* or *critical infrastructure* interchangeably for ease of explaining relevant concepts.

With low risk and high reward, cyber-enabled malicious events are "virtually" the perfect crime and method of attack. They are inexpensive, distantly modifiable, and do not fit neatly within most nations current models of law enforcement or national defense policies.[9] They are also extremely profitable. Conservative estimates in "The Web of Profit" research show cybercriminal revenues worldwide of at least $1.5 trillion. This includes: $860 billion from illicit/illegal online markets; $500 billion from theft of trade secrets/IP [Intellectual Property]; $160 billion from data trading; $1.6 billion from crimeware-as-a-service; and $1 billion from ransomware. [10] This is an industry that exceeds the Gross Domestic Product of Russia, and that is reinvesting up to twenty percent of its profit into recapitalization. It is an industry that had more than the combined revenues of Facebook, Amazon, Apple, Netflix, and Google in 2017.[11] It is an industry that offers nearly unlimited capital with virtually no fear of imposed consequence, and whose targets provide a lucrative motive for continued nefarious cyber exploits and cybercrime industry growth. Malicious cyber actors now probe networks to exploit vulnerabilities in every critical infrastructure sector in the United States – from power grids, to water supply systems, to retail, healthcare and financial institutions. This rapidly increasing cyber threat trend must be reversed.

In addition to national security concerns, the constantly evolving cybersecurity threat landscape generates enormous costs for every modern state and industry involved. In 2018, the United States White House reported that the national economic costs of cyber-enabled malicious activities were between $57 billion and $109 billion in 2016 alone. Furthermore, it was estimated that global cybercrime extracts $375 billion or 15-20 percent of the value created by the Internet.[12] Despite the nontraditional notion of conflict in the virtual domain along with the exorbitant costs involved, the net negative impact to the United States (should they fail at securing the nation against cyber-attacks targeting its critical infrastructure) could spell catastrophe for its national and economic security. CEMA produces high returns at low risk and comparatively low cost for the threat actors. "The two most common exploitation techniques—social engineering, where a cybercriminal tricks a user into granting access; and vulnerability exploitation, where a cybercriminal takes advantage of a programming or implementation failure to gain access—are both surprisingly cheap."[13] Cyber threat actors understand that risk and cost are minor while payoffs are enormous. The rate of return on cybercrime favors the adversary and provides ample incentive to continue pilfering. Not surprisingly, numerous U.S. Presidential cybersecurity orders and directives opine a comparable theme – the cyber threat to critical infrastructure continues to grow and represents one of the most serious national security challenges that the nation must confront, and the United States' national and economic security depends on the reliable functioning of the its critical infrastructure in the face of such threats.[14]

Securing the Nation

National cybersecurity has been an emphasis item for every United States Presidential Administration since Ronald Reagan. In response to the evolving cyber threat, in February 2016, the White House released a "Cybersecurity National Action Plan" in which it indicated that cybersecurity is one of the most important challenges faced by the United States.[15] However, despite the Presidential emphasis over the last three decades, the cyber threat facing the nation's critical infrastructure remains undeterred. Former President Obama recognized this in calling for both the government and private entities to increase their cybersecurity efforts to defend the nation's critical infrastructure against CEMA.

Although the current and past U.S. governmental leaders have made efforts to promote national cybersecurity, in general they have supported a more a traditional hands-off, corporate-centric approach that relegates cybersecurity to the critical infrastructure owners and operators and requires them to secure their own networks and firms. Unfortunately, this approach by national leaders fails to address the new reality: the national protections, once afforded to the corporations and infrastructures by our nation's physical borders, national defense and law enforcement institutions, and are provided for in our constitution, either do not exist or are ineffective in deterring or preventing threats within and through the virtual domain. The global cyber landscape has changed the security paradigm to where threat actors now have direct access to American citizens, corporations, and infrastructure via the Internet without facing national defenses.

In this new world landscape, the removal of the government as the responsible agent for national defense and law enforcement (the disintermediation of national governments as the middleman between threats and the citizen) has left the United States and other governments struggling to deter cyber threats that routinely target national critical infrastructure. More importantly, the United States labors to define its role or achieve measurable success in securing the homeland against cyber-attacks, especially related to privately owned and operated critical infrastructure. One could ask why that may be when the United States, for example, possesses some of the most sophisticated cyber capabilities in the world? Or, why does the United States not have an effective strategy to contend with the cyber threat? Does the nation need to better integrate with private industry to defend the nation? The answers to these and other related questions are not straight forward nor easily answered. Consequently, America is at a noteworthy inflection point in its national cyber defense, largely because of the evolving nature of conflict in and through the virtual domain.

As the world's cyber threats grow unchecked, national leaders ask that "top strategic, business, and technical thinkers from outside of government…study and report on what more we can do to enhance cybersecurity awareness and protections, protect privacy, maintain public safety as well as economic and national security, and empower Americans to take better control of their digital security."[16] In light of these challenges, this book builds upon previous work across security and political studies to provide important answers and new measures to appropriately confront today's cyber storm.

Strategic Coercive Cybersecurity: A Better Deterrent against Malicious Cyber Activity

There is overwhelming evidence that the nation's cybersecurity efforts are not keeping pace with the cyber threat. Then Chairman Devin Nunes (United States Congressman) lamented to the House Permanent Select Committee on Intelligence in March 2015, that

"[l]ast April Home Depot was breached, compromising tens of millions of credit card accounts and email addresses. In November [2014], in an attempt to intimidate Sony Pictures from releasing a movie, intruders attacked the company and gained access to employee emails, confidential corporate information, and copies of unreleased films. This past January [2015], Anthem announced it had been hacked, potentially jeopardizing the personal information of 80 million people. And just a few days ago, Premera Blue Cross revealed that its systems had been compromised, possibly exposing the medical and financial information of 11 million customers… As a result, Congress urgently needs to strengthen the security of our nation's digital infrastructure…"[17]

In response to the cyber threat, contemporary research examines well-known security concepts as ways to help mitigate the growing negative cyber trend. Several scholars have been studying the application of coercion in the cyber domain as a method to curtail the threat. What is the relevance of deterrence in the virtual domain? Noted national security scholar William Kaufman articulated, "[d]eterrence consists of essentially two basic components: first, the expressed intention to defend a certain interest; secondly, the demonstrated capability actually to achieve the defense of the interest in question, or to inflict such a cost on the attacker that, even if he should be able to gain his end, it would not seem worth the effort to him."[18] Coercion and deterrence in the physical domain are designed to alter the cost-benefit calculus of the nation's adversaries. Respected RAND researcher Martin Libicki further stated, "Deterrence is anything that dissuades an attack, it is usually said to have two components: deterrence by denial (the ability to frustrate the attacks) and deterrence by punishment (the threat of retaliation)."

Coercion occurs in the minds of both the intended target and the attacker. Any potential malicious cyber attacker is bound to weigh the effort required to make an attack against the expected benefit of that attack – a function of how likely it is to work and what happens if it does. In this book, I do not seek to argue the empirical question of how decision making is influenced through coercion, but rather to demonstrate that coercion is underutilized at the moment, and can contribute to the cost-benefit calculus of the malicious cyber actors as part of a more effective national cybersecurity strategy. The objective of a coercive strategy is to increase the considerations of the attacker's decision calculus in a meaningful way, which is a function of whether the attacker believes the threat to retaliate will be carried out and the potential damage that will result when the retaliation occurs.[19]

More About Coercion In Geopolitical Conflict

Studying and understanding coercion is of great consequence to political leaders given that successful coercion can result in noteworthy changes to the distribution of power between nations in conflict.[20] For example, Germany's successful coercion to induce Austria and Czechoslovakia to bow to German rule provided the Axis powers[21] with a powerful military advantage over the European Allies during the early stages of World War II, which proved instrumental in the defeat of Belgium, France, and Poland.

Coercion as a form of human influence and control is not a modern concept, but rather a means of asserting power that has been documented over thousands of years. "Manipulating another's behavior through threats is a natural phenomenon."[22] Short of "brute force" (the taking of something by strength without bargaining or persuasion), adversaries have been threatening force or punishment for some desired aim throughout mankind's history. Coercion, influence, manipulation, persuasion, leverage, pressure, and sway are words that describe getting people, organizations, and states to do something they would not otherwise do.[23] Coercion also describes a *causal* relationship among at least two actors, in which actor A takes an action to *cause* actor B to act for actor A's gain. Coercion does not always mean that actor A will completely reverse its policies, act against its own interests, or alter its core preferences.[24] Coercion also does not necessarily mean the total control of another. Coercion can involve threats of force to manipulate the decisions of an opponent in favor of the coercer's aims. Coercion can be viewed as a spectrum of activity to influence others that ranges from the subtle to the overt.

A review of the vast coercion literature reveals several terms used synonymously (and incorrectly) with coercion, which include: deterrence, coercive diplomacy, compellence, military coercion, coercive military strategy, and strategic coercion. In actuality, each term means something very specific; however, when one distills the plethora of authors' definitions, one overarching foundational theme appears: *coercion is the use of threats or punishments directed at the adversary's strategy and/or pressure points along with inducement to influence his decision making.* I will leverage this definition in greater detail in later chapters.

During and following the Cold War, the United States engaged in several coercive political conflicts against weaker states and non-state actors (asymmetric threats such as extremists) in which those asymmetric threats were not intimidated nor swayed by the power and military might of the United States (e.g., Cuba, Haiti,

9

Iran, Iraq, Libya, Pakistan, and the former Yugoslavia).[25] Credible capabilities are an essential element in a successful coercive conflict; however, much more is necessary if the state is to influence or manipulate the decisions of its adversaries. As Byman and Waxman articulate, "success in coercive contests seldom turns on superior firepower. If that were the case, the United States would never lose such struggles, as its military forces outclass those of any conceivable rival."[26] However, the United States often appears to have the most difficulty with its least powerful adversaries. Today and despite its tremendous military might, the United States continues to struggle against "lessor powers" - the asymmetric threats in the cyber domain. To overcome the conundrum of effective national cybersecurity, this book applies coercion in national cybersecurity to illustrate how 'influence' may lead to preventing and resolving cyber conflicts of national significance.

Intent of the Book

This book answers the call for academic thought on cyber strategy and provides the United States, and other likeminded nations, with alternative cybersecurity political and strategic concepts intended to advance the defense of national critical infrastructure against CEMA. I present a new conceptual paradigm and specify a vernacular for securing a nation from its most significant cyber threats. Although the focus of the book is on the United States, every nation may learn from and apply the concepts presented here. Because so much has been written on the United States, it represents an ideal case study from which other nations may learn.

One only has to look at the daily headlines to see that coercion, influence, persuasion, and intimidation already exist in national and international competition and will likely continue to appear in the strategic relationships and interactions of states and non-state actors that operate in and through the virtual domain. Coercion in and through the virtual domain is not as revolutionary or as unusual as it may initially appear. Consequently, this book seeks to clarify coercion's applicability in international conflict in cyberspace and then apply coercion as part of a broader national strategy to alter the risk calculus of potential attackers to reverse the negative trend of cyber threats facing the nation's critical infrastructure. It addresses to what extent a nation, and more specifically the United States, can use coercion to influence the decision-making of state or state-sponsored malicious cyber actors in cases where they threaten a nation's economic and national security. To answer this fully, however, requires addressing the following questions. What is coercion and how can coercion influence the decision making of the nation's adversaries? Who are the state or state-sponsored cyber threat actors and how can they threaten economic and national security in or through cyberspace? What are the cases in which the United States' economic and national security could be threatened (not all CEMA rises to a level of national significance)? What is the role of the private owners and operators of United States' critical infrastructure in the cybersecurity of the nation and how well does the private industry secure its networks and systems? How, when, and why should the United States get involved in critical infrastructure cybersecurity? What is the threshold for government involvement/action? In addition, how does traditional coercion apply to cyber conflict and what constitutes an effective national coercive cybersecurity strategy?

Through my research, I conclude that there are three primary reasons why the United States does not effectively use coercion to influence malicious cyber actors who threaten its economic and national security: the United States does not possess the necessary political will, has a dearth of tangible national cybersecurity strategy, and lacks an effective cybersecurity organization/framework that truly integrates and synchronizes all of the government disciplines together with that of the vital private critical infrastructure entities. We will explore each of these shortcomings throughout this book. Remedying each of the three deficiencies individually is necessary, but not sufficient for the successful application of coercion in the effective defense of United States' critical infrastructure against CEMA. All three must be advanced and synchronized in order to influence malicious cyber actors' decision making.

Above all else, I believe that *leadership*...effective national leadership in government and private industry...is vital to navigating through the complex and nuanced enigma of national cybersecurity. National leaders play a central and prominent role in twentieth century conflict in and through the virtual domain. Leaders are not only vital decision-makers who dominate government and private industry strategies, but they also are the critical integrators, the main communicators of actions and intentions, and the primary sources of public and private trust and confidence. At no time has the significance of leadership been more obvious and needed than during the current national cybersecurity dilemma. The present-day cyber crisis is in many respects made worse by the current political chaos and both political parties' inability to unify government and private industry behind a comprehensive plan, which in turn creates a crisis of leadership. Although the primary focus of this book is not on leadership, I ask that the reader keep the essence of leadership in mind as you dive into the contents of this book. Effective national leadership is an unmistakable prerequisite for whether or not the United States effectively contends with the pervasive cyber threat in order to maintain its desired global leadership position and its level of national and economic security.

This is a *policy-prescriptive* book that seeks to evaluate the United States' cybersecurity policies intended to secure the nation's critical infrastructure. It assesses that cybersecurity policy as articulated in several Presidential Executive Orders and so-called national strategies, while appraising competing solutions to the problem of securing United States critical infrastructure. Additionally, it demonstrates that within the United States' cybersecurity policy and actions intended to defend the nation, either coercion was not used or not applied in ways that influenced the decisions of the malicious cyber actors in courses favorable to the United States. I believe that coercion can be useful in raising costs and/or probability of costs (as is accomplished in the physical domain) on malicious cyber actors, which is a necessary step to reversing the negative CEMA trend for any nation.

Throughout the book, several case studies were chosen to explain incidents of intrinsic importance to both the defining of the relevant high-end threshold for government involvement, and for evaluating the effectiveness of United States cybersecurity policy and use of coercion. Although there are a great number of examples of documented CEMA, only a scant few rise to the level of *cyber incidents of national significance* (CINS)[27] where the government should take an active role in the cyber defense. A note of caution is cited here regarding the number of case studies presented. Given the paucity of documented CINS examples, there are limitations to the conclusions that may be drawn. Were there a greater number of cases, then the significance of the conclusions may be starker. Nevertheless, the cases presented are adequate to support the assertions offered.

This book, for obvious reasons, is unclassified and does not focus on technical solutions. Given the rate at which cyberspace evolves, it is counterproductive to discuss the technology that constitutes the domain or the conflict within it. Conversely my goal was to write a book that articulates the complexities of cyber conflict while examining when, where, and how coercion may influence adversary decision-making. This book focuses on how coercion can raise the costs in an adversary's decision calculus and then articulates how to incorporate coercion into nation cyber strategy. This book springboards from the initial Harvard dialogue I led with national leaders in the both the public and private sectors from 2014 to 2017, and is the result of several years of research along with my unique, three-plus decades of military and corporate operational and cyber strategy and security experiences, observations and conclusions to create a ground-breaking national cybersecurity strategy. Changing the current national cyber strategy paradigm requires the effective integration and synchronization of the full might of the government with the emerging and competent capabilities of private industry. I offer a detailed explanation of that new strategy along with the vernacular and constructs necessary to carry it out. The book does not offer all of the answers, but is the beginning of the national dialogue to securing the United States' critical infrastructure and functions against cyber incidents of national significance. The United States must clarify its vision now for global cyber leadership with new, digital-age options in order to contend properly with the cyber storm facing the modern world. My intent is that this book will educate multiple audiences and build a ground swell of support to substantially transform national cybersecurity, not just for this generation, but also for our children, grandchildren, and beyond.

---

[1] Michael Cieply and Brooks Barnes, "*Sony Cyberattack, First a Nuisance, Swiftly Grew Into a Firestorm*", The New York Times, Dec 30, 2014, accessed online 15 Oct 2015, found at: http://www.nytimes.com/2014/12/31/business/media/sony-attack-first-a-nuisance-swiftly-grew-into-a-firestorm-.html?_r=0

[2] Ibid

[3] Cristina Maza, "North Korean Hackers Stole Over $1 Billion and Destroyed Computers around the World, Report Reveals," *Newsweek*, Oct 3, 2018, found at: https://www.newsweek.com/north-korean-hackers-stole-over-one-billion-dollars-and-destroyed-computers-1151198.

[4] I define cyber-enabled malicious activity (CEMA) as any type of unauthorized programming code, software or information manipulation(syntactic or semantic attacks), employed by individuals or whole organizations, that targets the confidentiality, integrity, or authenticity of data within computer information systems, infrastructures, computer and/or computing devices by various malevolent means and that steals, alters, or destroys a specified target.

[5] "More than half of British firms 'report cyber-attacks in 2019'," BBC News online, 23 April 2019, found at: https://www.bbc.com/news/business-48017943.

[6] "German politicians targeted in cyber-attack," Financial Times, accessed online on July 15, 2019, found at: https://www.ft.com/content/00954878-0ffa-11e9-a3aa-118c761d2745. See also "Massive data breach targets German politicians at all levels," *Aljazeera News*, Jan 4, 2019, found on-line at

https://www.aljazeera.com/news/2019/01/massive-data-breach-targets-german-politicians-levels-190104134236529.html.

[7] DHS identifies sixteen critical infrastructure sectors: chemical; commercial facilities; communications; critical manufacturing; dams; defense industrial base; emergency services; energy; financial services; food and agriculture; government facilities; healthcare and public health; information technology; nuclear (reactors, materials, and waste); transportation systems, and water and wastewater systems. See Critical Infrastructure Sectors, United States Department of Homeland Security, Washington D.C., found on line at: https://www.dhs.gov/cisa/critical-infrastructure-sectors.

[8] For more on "national critical functions" and to see the entire list, see: "National Critical Functions Set," U.S. Department of Homeland Security, at: https://www.dhs.gov/cisa/national-critical-functions-set.

[9] David N. Lawrence, Jay Clayton, and Frances Townsend, "We Don't Need a Crisis to Act Unitedly Against Cyber Threats", found at: http://knowledge.wharton.upenn.edu/article/we-dont-need-a-crisi-to-act-unitedly-against-cyber-trheats.

[10] "This is one of the first studies to view the dynamics of cybercrime through the lens of revenue flow and profit distribution, and not solely on the well-understood mechanisms of cybercrime. The new research exposes a cybercrime-based economy and the professionalization of cybercrime. This economy has become a self-sustaining system – an interconnected Web of Profit that blurs the lines between the legitimate and illegitimate. The platform criminality model is productizing malware and making cybercrime as easy as shopping online. Not only is it easy to access cybercriminal tools, services and expertise: it means enterprises and governments alike are going to see more sophisticated, costly and disruptive attacks as The Web of Profit continues to gain momentum." Dr. Michael McGuire, "Into the Web of Profit – Understanding the Growth of Cybercrime Economy," April 2018, pg. 4, found at: https://www.scribd.com/document/377159562/Into-the-Web-of-Profit-Bromium-Final-Report.

[11] Ibid.

[12] Center for Strategic and International Studies (CSIS), *Net Losses: Estimating the Global Cost of Cybercrime*, June 2014, found at: http://csis.org/files/attachments/140609_rp_economic_impact_cybercrime_report.pdf.

[13] Ibid.

[14] Barack Obama, "Executive Order- Improving Critical Infrastructure Cybersecurity," EO 13636 (Washington DC, Feb 12, 2013) found at: https://www.whitehouse.gov/the-press-office/2013/02/12/executive-order-improving-critical-infrastructure-cybersecurity.

[15] Barack Obama, "Cybersecurity National Action Plan," (The White House, Washington DC, Feb 9, 2016), found at: https://www.whitehouse.gov/the-press-office/2016/02/09/fact-sheet-cybersecurity-national-action-plan.

[16] Ibid.

[17] Opening Statement of Chairman Devin Nunes, House Permanent Select Committee on "Intelligence Hearing on the Growing Cyber Threat and its Impact on American Business," March 19, 2015, found at: http://intelligence.house.gov/sites/intelligence.house.gov/files/documents/NunesOpening0319201 5.pdf.

[18] William Kaufmann, "The Evolution of Deterrence 1945–1958," unpublished RAND research, 1958, pg. 8.

[19] Kauffmann, pg. 8. Robert Pape calculates Coercion this way: (Probability of benefit times benefit) minus (probability of cost times cost) gives you your expected gain…where greater than zero, there is expected profit. If one can increase both the cost and the probability of cost to the cyber attacker, one can make it a bad investment for the adversary.

[20] Maire A. Dugan, "Coercive Power", *Beyond Intractability*, (The Beyond Intractability Project, The Conflict Information Consortium, University of Colorado, Sept 2003), accessed online 22 Dec 2015, found at: http://www.beyondintractability.org/essay/threats .

[21] For more on the Axis Powers, see Dr. William Roger Townshend Ph.D., *Axis Power: Could Nazi Germany and Imperial Japan have won World War II?*, Sept 2012.

[22] Lawrence Freedman, *Deterrence*, Cambridge, Polity Press, United Kingdom, 2004, pg. 6. Also see Daniel Byman and Matthew Waxman, *The Dynamics of Coercion: American Foreign Policy and the Limits of Military Might*, (RAND, Cambridge University Press, 2002), pp. 3-6, 10, 124.

[23] David A. Baldwin, "Power and International Relations," Walter Carlsnaes, Thomas Risse, and Beth A. Simons, eds Handbook *of International Relations* (SAGE Publications, Ltd. London, UK, 2004), pp. 177-91. "Brute force succeeds when it used, whereas the power to hurt is most successful when held in reserve. It is the threat of damage, or of more damage to come, that can make someone yield or comply." Thomas C. Schelling, *Arms and Influence*, (New Haven, CT; Yale University Press, 1966), pg. 3.

[24] Jason U. Manosevitz, "Bolstering Analytic Tradecraft – Needed: More thinking about Conceptual Frameworks for Analysis – The Case of Influence," *Studies in Intelligence*, Vol. 57, No. 4 (December 2013), pg. 16.

[25] For more on this discussion see: "Economic Sanctions and American Diplomacy," *Council on Foreign Relations*, accessed on-line Nov 24, 2019, at: https://www.cfr.org/excerpt-economic-sanctions-and-american-diplomacy.

[26] Byman and Waxman, pg. 229.

[27] A cyber incident of national significance – CINS – is defined to be any national or regional strategically momentous cyber-enabled malicious activity intended to impair substantially the vital function(s) of an organization's cyberspace for a political, economic, or national security purpose

Ronald Banks

CHAPTER TWO

UNDERSTANDING THE CYBERSPACE DOMAIN AND THE CONFLICT WITHIN

If we continue to develop our technology without wisdom or prudence, our servant may prove to be our executioner.

—Omar N. Bradley

Any nation as reliant upon technology as the United States, is a nation equally vulnerable and ripe for cyber conflict – and a state in need of effective national cybersecurity. The technological advances seen over the last four decades exposed the American people and the homeland to conflict from and in the virtual domain. This relatively new form of conflict presents an unusual and complex international consideration for all technologically reliant states. In fact, as Michael Dell (of Dell Computer) said recently, cyberspace is the domain that see "the defining battle for the next 10 years."1 Understanding the domain in which cyber-enabled malicious activity exists and the malicious cyber actors who prey upon others in that domain is critical for developing strategies to outpace the cyber threat – and is essential for the United States' continued vitality and prosperity.

It would be inexcusable if the United States was brought to its knees by the same technology responsible for its economic advancement and global power.

One of the issues for unifying the United States' national cybersecurity effort is that there is a gulf between definitions and actions taken in response to *malicious cyber acts* and definitions and actions that constitute an act of *cyber war*. Most of the cyber incidents of national significance fall short of an act of war on the spectrum of conflict and consequently do not fit neatly within current national security policy. The Department of Defense (DoD), one of the numerous Federal government organizations responsible for protecting America in cyberspace, struggles to respond to malicious cyber activities that do not equate to a "use of force" or "act of war." The DoD defines cyberspace as: "a global domain within the information environment consisting of the interdependent networks of information technology infrastructures and resident data, including the Internet, telecommunications networks, computer systems, and embedded processors and controllers."[2] Other definitions of the domain are provided below. To contend effectively with the ever-growing cyber threat and to alter the path modern nations find themselves, requires new definitions for cybersecurity professionals and national security policymakers' use in designing a national cybersecurity strategy.

With the proper and complete understanding of cyberspace and its lingua franca, one may discuss cyber conflict and the corresponding appropriate responses to defend, deter, and/or influence decision making towards national objectives. With a thorough understanding of the malicious cyber actors, their motivations, and values, the United States will be able to adequately incorporate state actions in cyberspace, either individually or along with other instruments of national power, to influence the behavior of state or state-sponsored malicious cyber actors in cases where they threaten United States national security. Understanding the domain in which cyber-enabled malicious activity exists and the malicious cyber actors who operate within this realm is critical for developing strategies to outpace the cyber threat – and is essential for the United States' continued vitality and prosperity.

In the span of one generation, cyberspace has revolutionized the human interactive experience – and it is difficult to imagine life without it. Beyond dramatically improving and advancing a great number of aspects within our lives, cyberspace also creates a construct upon which we are vitally dependent. Currently, the United States is a country where businesses and processes are expected to be online; and consequently, is a nation extremely dependent upon cyberspace for its economic prosperity.[3] As an example, Fedwire, the Federal Reserve Bank's money movement system (just one of three primary money transfer systems in the United States), transferred on average over 3.3 trillion dollars daily in 2015 – and cannot accomplish that feat without cyberspace.[4]

In addition to Internet-based services, such as Fedwire, other technologies and services that are not connected to the Internet are also vulnerable to malicious cyber activity. For example, industrial control systems ICS (which include supervisory control and data acquisition (SCADA) systems) manage and control aspects of a nation's critical infrastructure (e.g., electricity, water, gas, etc.) and may not be connected to the Internet. However, several critical infrastructure sectors are networked internally together for greater corporate access and connectivity.[5] These control systems were not designed with security in mind or engineered for the Internet, but by being networked together, they are vulnerable to malicious cyber activity if a malicious actor is able to gain access to the network. Consequently, any nation that relies on technology for the proper functioning of vital services is a nation vulnerable to exploitation.

The United States' high-tech dependency has become its Achilles' heel. Unfortunately, portions of cyberspace do not have the proper security protocols designed into them for various reasons, including: a rush to send products to market, design oversight, a general ignorance of the impact of poorly secured technology, and expense for additional cybersecurity code.[6] Furthermore, vulnerabilities in network architectures may be created simply by inexperienced network engineers poorly configuring the organization's system, thereby introducing risk of exploitation that would not ordinarily be present. For software programmers, the notion of software assurance is growing in importance.[7] "The demand for constant online communication creates enormous opportunities for hackers to exploit weak vendor security practices as a point of entry into their ultimate target."[8] The corresponding vulnerabilities that exist when both hardware and software go to market without the proper cybersecurity create an open door for malicious cyber actors through which they may seize an opportunity to exploit those vulnerabilities. An exploited open door may become a catalyst for cyber conflict.

Cyberspace Defined

Cyberspace, as a term, has no universally agreed upon definition. The Merriam-Webster Dictionary defines cyberspace as: "the online world of computer networks and the Internet."[9] The White House refers to cyberspace as "networked technologies," "the digital world," and "networked information systems."[10] All of these descriptors are overly simplistic and do not capture the reality of what cyberspace is. The term information technology (IT) is oftentimes used synonymously with cyberspace, but is in fact a subset of cyberspace. Information technology "is the common term for the entire spectrum of technologies for information processing, including software, hardware, communications technologies and related services."[11] Examples of IT include computers, network routers, modems, etc.; and does not include technologies that do not generate data for enterprise use. IT should also be further distinguished from Operational Technology (OT), which is "hardware and software that detects or causes a change through the direct monitoring and/or control of physical devices, processes and

21

events in the enterprise."[12]   As an example, a power company's system for controlling the city's electrical grid is its OT. Cyberspace is much broader than IT and OT.

The widely accepted DoD definition for cyberspace does not fully portray the domain because it omits the electromagnetic spectrum. An alternative DoD definition found in *United States National Military Strategy for Cyber Operations* (MNS-CO) however overcame this distinction by defining cyberspace as a "domain characterized by the use of electronics and the electromagnetic spectrum to store, modify and exchange data via networked systems and associated physical infrastructures."[13] The advantage of the NMS-CO definition is that it suitably describes the domain and states cyberspace as not just a "virtual" domain but also as "physical" infrastructure which is necessary for the virtual application. The virtual and physical qualities of cyberspace may be described as layers of cyberspace and are further elaborated upon below. The physical layer of cyberspace is very real and tangible and can be referred to as the cyber environment.

For the purposes of this book, the NMS-CO definition is preferred because of its completeness and accuracy in describing the characteristics of cyberspace. The *cyber environment* is "a composite of the conditions, circumstances, and influences that affect the employment of capabilities and bear on the decisions of the [decision maker]. The information environment is the aggregate of individuals, organizations, and systems that collect, process, disseminate, or act on information, further broken down into the physical, informational, and cognitive dimensions."[14]

Information security can be further broken down into three distinct qualities: confidentiality, integrity, and availability (the CIA Triad). In this context, "confidentiality is a set of rules that limits access to information, integrity is the assurance that the information is trustworthy and accurate, and availability is a guarantee of reliable access to the information by authorized people."[15] Too often cyber experts talk of cyber defense but they are not specific as to what is to be defended. To further elaborate, defending the CIA Triad is concerned with protecting the purpose of and access to the data or information as it was originally intended.

It is critical to emphasize that a corporation's or government's cyber infrastructure is as important to protect as the tasks or missions which IT is meant to support. Operational technology (OT) is the subset of cyberspace that includes the components and systems that are used to execute the organization's missions or operations. OT is the "set of devices and processes that act in real time on physical operational systems, like electricity distribution networks, facilities or vehicle production plants."[16] Examples of OT elements include manufacturing systems, SCADA, meters, valves, sensors and motors. Furthermore, the broad vital functions of the organization that rely upon all layers of cyberspace and often encompass several networked systems must be understood so as to defend not only "what" the organization does, but also "how" it accomplishes its vital functions.

For the military, cyber defense would then also include the protection of its OT – the technology and software of its weapons systems needed to execute its defense missions (e.g., the software programs that support Naval Carriers, Fighter or Bomber Aircraft, Operations Centers, Satellites Constellations, etc.), as well as its IT and network, also referred to as the Department of Defense Information Network (DODIN). Put another way, cyber defense for the military can shield against cyber-enabled threats targeting its cyberspace (IT and OT), or cyber defense can be in support of physical domain operations such as critical infrastructure protection, national defense, or war in a foreign land. Cybersecurity occurs within and across both the virtual and physical domains of cyberspace.

The physical layer is concerned with the "transmission and reception of the unstructured raw bit stream over a physical medium."[17] It provides data encoding, physical medium attachment, transmission technique, and physical medium transmission. This layer includes physical security and controlled access spaces such as locked server rooms.[18] It is important to remember that items in the physical layer actually exist and therefore have a location.

The virtual layers of cyberspace function according to specified programming logic or code that defines "what and how" the various components interact and execute commands (see table 2.1).

Table 2.1 OSI Layer Model (Open Source Interconnection)[19]

Layer	Role	Application / Example
PHYSICAL LAYER		
	Transmission & reception of the unstructured raw bit stream over physical medium	**Physical structure**: cables, hubs, etc. Data encoding; physical medium attachment; transmission technique: baseband or broadband; physical medium transmission: bits and volts
VIRTUAL LAYERS		
Data Link	Provides error-free transfer of data frames from one node to another over the physical layer	**Frames** ("envelopes" – contains MAC address) Establishes & terminates the logical link between nodes; frame traffic control; frame sequencing; frame acknowledgement; frame

		delimiting; frame error checking; media access control
Network	Controls the operations of the subnet, deciding which physical path the data takes	**Packets** ("letter" – contains IP address) Routing; subnet traffic control; frame fragmentation; logical-physical address mapping; subnet usage accounting
Transport	Ensures that messages are delivered error-free, in sequence and with no losses or duplication	**TCP:** Host to host, flow control Message segmentation, acknowledgement, and traffic control; session multiplexing
Session	Allows session establishment between processes running on different stations	**Synch & Send to ports** Session establishment; maintenance and termination; session support: perform security, name recognition, logging etc.
Presentation	Formats the data to be presented to the application layer. It can be viewed as the "translator" for the network	**Syntax Layer:** encrypt & decrypt Character code translation; data conversion, compression, and encryption; character set translation

Application	Serves as the window for users and application processes to access the network services	**End User Layer**: Program that opens what was sent or creates what is to be sent Resource sharing; remote file access; remote printer access; directory services; network management

The most complex portions of the logical aspect (virtual layers) of cyberspace are the networked architectures, which are sometimes classified into two broad categories: open and fixed-function networks. Open networks are clearly defined by their open access within the Internet. Two common open networks are: client-server architectures[20] and peer-to-peer architectures.[21] Open networks are typically informational, commercial, and/or for profit. Fixed-function networks differ in that they are not accessible (easily) by the general public. Typically they perform some broader purpose or operational mission for a specified user (such as the Federal Aviation Administration's air traffic control system) and as such are not reachable through the Internet.[22] These complex layers represent the operating systems and OT used by the malicious cyber actor to exploit operational system weaknesses, vulnerabilities, security configuration and issues.

Each of the layers of the cyberspace exists to perform a function related to the adjacent layer which enables sending, receiving, applying, and understanding data. Too often cybersecurity professionals do not consider the totality of cyberspace when planning defensive activities or measures, and overly focus on just one or two layers. Each layer possesses its own set of vulnerabilities for which protective measures must be applied. Effective cybersecurity must account for all of the layers of an organization's cyber terrain.

Cyber Conflict

Cyberspace connects the functions and operations of commerce, critical infrastructure, government, and national security. Critical cybersecurity practices and business models rely heavily on global connectivity, which makes the "attack surface" (the portion of an organization's cyberspace that is exposed to outside penetration and exploitation by malicious cyber actors) much larger – especially through the use of cloud infrastructures, big data, mobile and social media.[23] Unfortunately, not everyone who uses cyberspace does so with peaceful intentions. In fact, the same technology that launched the information age has unfortunately also launched cyber conflict.

Today, the world is a volatile, uncertain, complex, and ambiguous (VUCA) environment with significant conventional (and unconventional…perhaps more important here) conflicts occurring in nearly every region of the world. The United States faces substantial cyber threats daily from a multitude of entities: state, non-state groups, criminal organizations, and individuals. A cursory glance at the news headlines provides the reader with a glimpse of the nefarious cyber incidents currently present which could lead to significantly greater acts of violence. Incidents such as hacking airplanes and cars, or intrusions into voting booths and medical devices, are scenarios which are ripe for exploitation and conflict initiation. Cyber-enabled conflict is not a new phenomenon however.

Throughout the latter years of the Cold War, nations witnessed the continued evolution of cyber-enabled malicious activity and the ensuing conflict. The first published account of a nefarious cyber incident occurred in 1982 when the United States' Central Intelligence Agency manipulated computer control systems which the Soviet Union bought and installed in their Siberian pipelines. According to a former Secretary of the Air Force, Thomas Reed, the altered computer control systems reset the pump speeds and pressures which caused the pipeline to explode...triggering the "most monumental non-nuclear explosion and fire ever seen from space."[24] Malicious cyber activity began in earnest in 1986 with the theft of thousands of documents from dozens of computers at the Lawrence Berkeley National Laboratory, other research institutions, and military facilities by former West German agents for sale to the Soviet Union's KGB. The information stolen contained data about President Reagan's "Strategic Defense Initiative" (also known as "Star Wars"), satellite specifications, and other secret information.[25] The espionage case exposed by astronomer Cliff Stoll and titled, "The Cuckoo's Egg," brought to light the vulnerabilities of Internet connected computers. From the earliest moments of cyberspace, states have endeavored to find vulnerabilities in other nations' cyberspace technology.

According to the Merriam-Webster Dictionary, *conflict* is a struggle for power, property, etc.; a competitive or opposing action of incompatibles; the opposition of persons or forces that gives rise to dramatic action. Cyber-enabled conflict juxtaposes malicious cyber actors, through the struggle of nefarious cyber activity, against end-users and network defenders. Conflict in cyberspace possesses similarities to and differences from conflict in the physical domain. Cyber conflict includes: cyberspace's dual-use (can be employed for both nefarious and beneficial purposes similarly to bioweapons) and borderless nature (similar to outer space) the difficulty in differentiating probe from attack and definitively identifying attackers (similar to counterinsurgencies) the relatively small-time interval between detection and attack the near scale-free and multiplicity of potential attack vectors, attackers, and motivations[26] Combine these predominantly Internet-centric characterizations of conflict with the vulnerabilities inherent in fixed-function networks and one quickly grasps the complexity of conflict in cyberspace.

Cyber-Enabled Malicious Activity

The term cyber-enabled malicious activity (CEMA) is presented here to describe the totality of nefarious exploits that occur in the cyber domain. All incidents, events, attacks, operations or any other descriptor used to label malicious cyber activity can be grouped under CEMA. "Cyber-enabled" is used to clarify the point that the activities on which this monograph focuses are executed or supported in and through cyberspace.

Cyber-enabled malicious activity (CEMA) is *any type of unauthorized programming code, software or information manipulation*(syntactic or semantic attacks), *employed by individuals or whole organizations, that targets the confidentiality, integrity, or authenticity of data within computer information systems, infrastructures, computer and/or computing devices by various malevolent means and that steals, alters, or destroys a specified target.*

There are two forms of CEMA: syntactic and semantic. Syntactic CEMA disrupts a computer's operating system, causing the network to fail. Examples include worms, viruses, Trojan horses and denial of service attacks. In contrast, a semantic CEMA does not affect the operating system, but attacks the accuracy of the information it processes. Consequently, a system under semantic CEMA operates and will be perceived to operate correctly . . . but it will generate responses that are no longer accurate.[27] There are an extraordinarily large number of cyber-enabled malicious activities that currently exist today…a number that grows constantly. The nefarious effects of CEMA range in severity from exploiting sensitive information, to disrupting or slowing down access to online goods and services, to degrading or destroying vital digital functions or operations. The Ponemon Institute previously released the 2018 Cost of Cyber Crime, which analyzes the cost of all cyber-crime for a variety of 58 U.S. organizations both public and private.[28] The U.S., in comparison with other nations in the Ponemon study, continues to rank highest in its cost of cyber-crime at an annual average of $21 million per company.[29] The annual cost for these companies grew more that 22.7%

over the previous year, and averaged $11.7 million. In 2017, there was an average of 160 successful cyber breaches.[30]

The former United States' Special Assistant to President Obama and the Cybersecurity Coordinator, Michael Daniels, defines malicious cyber-enabled activity (a derivation of CEMA defined above) as those events posed by

"the most significant cyber threats we face – namely, on actors whose malicious activities could pose a significant threat to the national security, foreign policy, economic health, or financial stability of the United States…and include: harming or significantly compromising the provision of services by entities in a critical infrastructure sector; significantly disrupting the availability of a computer or network of computers, including through a distributed denial-of-service attack; misappropriating funds or economic resources, trade secrets, personal identifiers, or financial information for commercial or competitive advantage or private financial gain; knowingly receiving or using trade secrets that were stolen by cyber-enabled means for commercial or competitive advantage or private financial gain; and attempting, assisting, or providing material support for any of the harms listed above."[31]

This definition is useful and provides several examples of nefarious activities as described by one of the United States government's leading cybersecurity experts. However, it shows that even the U.S. cyber leadership does not provide sufficient clarity (lacks defining method of attack) in their terms to accurately describe cyber-enabled malicious activity as does this book's definition of CEMA.

CEMA can be broadly thought of as a spectrum of activity with purposes ranging from gaining **access**, to **disrupting** data, services, or systems, to **attacking** systems to cause harm. CEMA can range from "virtually undetectable to merely annoying to destructive [and]…may be designed to gain access to a system for a variety of motivations, which could be to facilitate future criminal, espionage or military activities."[32] CEMA may even go unnoticed for months while others may never be noticed. In the most extreme cases, CEMA can negatively impact the functionality of a computer system or even destroy a technical component, data, or network. CEMA – regardless of scale, intensity, type or form – has a reprehensible objective or purpose from the end-user and cyber defender's perspective, and may or may not necessitate a response from the organization(s) impacted and/or the government where the CEMA incident was directed or originated (assuming the government is aware of the activity).

Hacktivism is any unauthorized access to a computer system for political purposes.[33] Examples of hacktivism include WikiLeaks and political protests using Web application vulnerabilities. They are meant to politically embarrass corporations, not necessarily steal from them. If the purpose of the CEMA is to gather or gain information of a corporate, military, or political nature which the competing organization or nation wishes to hold secret, then that CEMA is classified as *cyber-espionage*.

If the purpose is to interfere with the proper functioning of a computer system, with fraudulent or dishonest intent of procuring, without right, an economic benefit for oneself or for another person, then that should be labeled *cyber-crime*.[34]

The *Tallinn Manual* (produced in 2013) is an internationally accepted cyber manifesto is a nonbinding study produced by an "International Group of Experts" (IGOE) assembled in Tallinn, Estonia. The manual outlined terms for cyberspace in accordance to the international law of armed conflict (LOAC). According to the *Tallinn Manual*, if the CEMA is designed to penetrate another nation's cyberspace for the political purposes of causing strategically significant damage or disruption equivalent to a use of force or armed attack that causes damage or destruction to objects or injury or death to persons, then that should be referred to as *cyber-war* or simply *war*.[35]

Within the definition of CEMA is a notion of scale and intensity (e.g., from low to high, or short to long, or few to many) and includes many other often-used terms such as cyber incident, attack, operation and a new term, Cyber Incident of National Significance (CINS). Each term is more momentous than the previous one, and is explained below.

CEMA Life-Cycle

Cyber-enabled malicious activity follows a typical progression for the achievement of the nefarious actor's objectives. The CEMA life-cycle is one way to explain the process a hacker uses to target an organization.[36] The hypothetical life-cycle of a "*hack*" begins by conducting background research on the intended target – gathering intelligence – be that general searches on the Internet or detailed social profiling of the members of the organization. Second, the hacker will conduct an initial event to establish a foothold in the organization's network for the purpose of conducting initial exploiting. Tactics used to gain the initial foothold include: employing a "*zero-day*" (malware to exploit a previous unknown vulnerability), using *social engineering, spear phishing,* or *water holing*.[37] Third, the hacker establishes a covert enterprise-wide, persistent presence and conducts reconnaissance of the organization. Fourth, the hacker moves laterally to more lucrative sections of the organization's network and establishes an elevated level of privilege or access so that greater objectives may be achieved. Finally, with that elevated access, the hacker gathers valuable information, encrypts it, exfiltrates the data, and then works to maintain the undetected presence.

Cyber-Incident

A "cyber incident" or event is *a single case where CEMA is executed against a single end-user or organization (includes the broad categories of exploitation, theft, disruption, and destruction of data or information in cyberspace…also related to the CIA Triad).* A cyber incident would be a short-term CEMA event with a specific nefarious purpose, that when it achieved its objective, did not lead to some larger CEMA case. An example of a cyber incident is a limited email phishing (either singularly or as part of a larger short-term effort) sent to target end-users in order to gain access to their computer and more broadly an organization's network and data. CEMA that continues beyond a short-term timeframe with limited scope/objectives, would then rise to a *cyber-attack* or *cyber-enabled malicious operation*.

Cyber-Attack

The term "*cyber-attack*" is one of the most overused cyber terms, and yet the term is one that should be applied with deliberate purpose and not to sensationalizing the news. Besides oftentimes being used to dramatize a story in the press, the term is applied by lawyers and policy-makers to denote a level of significance in effect or action that may/should compel a nation to react – either in self-defense or in preemption and will be discussed in the "cyberwarfare" section. Cyber pundits often conflate cyber-attack and cyberwarfare, the latter being invoked within the international law of armed conflict and strictly a political decision or declaration.

A useful cyber-attack definition that characterizes the realities of the CEMA seen currently should describe a threshold for action inclusive of and yet also short of a "use of force" or "armed conflict." According to United States Navy Admiral (Ret) James Stavridis, cyberspace affords opportunities to affect nonviolent but impactful consequences. The Council of Europe's *Convention of Cybercrime,* which took place in Budapest Hungary in 2001, is a widely accepted treaty which has been ratified by dozens of countries to include the United States. The Budapest Convention, as it is commonly called, requires signatories to the convention to take law enforcement actions as a nation when intentional cyber-criminal offenses occur within their sovereign borders.[38] It is important to point out that for our purposes, cyber-attack is closely related to criminality in and through the virtual domain. Understanding how the international community views cyber-crime is critical to defining cyber-attack. Specifically, this international treaty describes the following cyber acts as crimes:

"the access to the whole or any part of a computer system without right;"[39]

"the interception without right, made by technical means, of non-public transmissions of computer data to, from or within a computer system, including electromagnetic emissions from a computer system carrying such computer data;"[40]

"the damaging, deletion, deterioration, alteration or suppression of computer data without right;"[41]

"the serious hindering without right of the functioning of a computer system by inputting, transmitting, damaging, deleting, deteriorating, altering or suppressing computer data;"[42]

"the production, sale, procurement for use, import, distribution or otherwise making available of," or the possession of: "a device, including a computer program, designed or adapted primarily for the purpose of committing any of the offences," or "a computer password, access code, or similar data by which the whole or any part of a computer system is capable of being accessed," where the action is taken "without right" and "with intent that it be used for the purpose of committing any of the offences;"[43]

"the input, alteration, deletion, or suppression of computer data, resulting in inauthentic data with the intent that it be considered or acted upon for legal purposes as if it were authentic," when done "without right;"[44]

"the causing of a loss of property to another person by . . . any input, alteration, deletion or suppression of computer data . . . [or] any interference with the functioning of a computer system, with fraudulent or dishonest intent of procuring, without right, an economic benefit for oneself or for another person," when done "without right."[45]

Beyond being extremely inclusive, the aspect of the Budapest Convention that makes this definition especially useful is the fact that it directs each ratifying state to "adopt such legislation and other measures as may be necessary to ensure that the criminal offenses...are punishable by effective proportionate and dissuasive sanctions, which include deprivation of liberty."[46] By defining cyber-crime this way, the Budapest Convention aptly and fully describes the activities that constitute malicious types of cyber-enabled activity. CEMA defined with this clarity and directed at a state's critical infrastructure or key resources would then constitute a "cyber-attack." By including the intended objective and defining the target based upon its significance to the vital functions of the state (Critical Infrastructure), cyber-attack is best defined. One could then tie legal sanctions or punishments to cyber-attacks perpetrated within the cyber domain that are below an act of war. Furthermore, the Budapest Convention proscribes a framework for internationally acceptable responses to cyber-attacks that can form the foundation to a national cybersecurity strategy.

I believe that the term "cyber-attack" should be more inclusive and representative of the realities and the ubiquity of the cyber-enabled assaults against the vital functions and activities upon which the nation is so dependent (e.g., water, energy, finance, commerce, transportation, defense, etc.). There are upper-end, significant possibilities where a cyber-attack would be equivalent to an "armed attack" or "use of force;" however, definitions that set an exceedingly high threshold restrict opportunities to influence situations that may affect national and economic security of the state. The DoD's *Law of War* Manual articulates their conundrum this way: "a bomb might break a dam and flood a civilian population, while insertion of a line of malicious code from a distant computer might just as easily achieve that same result...however; there are other types of cyber actions that do not have a clear kinetic parallel, which raise profound questions about exactly what we [DoD] mean by 'force.'"[47] Even the DoD's *Law of War Manual* writhes to accurately describe CEMA in a way that provides the United States' military with a proper conceptual paradigm in which to respond to the types of nefarious cyber activities for which many in private industry believe the government should be responsible (protect the nation). Attempting to shoehorn the conceptual physical notion of attack (equivalent to an "armed attack" or "use of force") into the virtual domain of cyberspace does not properly or adequately describe the realities of a great majority of CEMA or situations where government has not, but can and should be involved in the cyber defense of the nation.

For the United States government, a cyber-attack is a cyber activity that possesses effects in the real world beyond the cyber system itself and possesses "actions in cyberspace whose foreseeable results include damage or destruction of property, or death or injury to persons."[48] Mere degradation or denial of a system, for example, would not be a cyber-attack according to the government. In my research, the preponderance of CEMA effects did not have physical manifestations, and as for incidents that did have physical manifestations, they did not rise to the current understanding of a level of a "use of force" or equal to "an armed attack." Definitions that use physical manifestations as qualifiers to define the significance of CEMA miss the reality in which current cyber conflict occurs. Consequently, if the United States government uses such a high threshold for acting in the cyber domain, then it is unlikely they will ever respond to any of the current cyber incidents of national significance short of war, that are so economically costly to the state.

Additionally, my research shows that numerous definitions are based upon the rules or authorities possessed by each organization as part of the process of its directed mission or activity. Title 18 of the United States Code (USC T-18) is the criminal and penal code of the federal government that deals with federal crimes and criminal procedures. It includes several chapters and sections that define activities in cyberspace which are illegal. How Federal law enforcement agencies investigate, attribute, prosecute and disrupt CEMA in cyberspace is also spelled out in detail in USC T-18 and FBI operating procedures. Espionage is the collection of foreign intelligence for a state or other organization's own purpose or advantage. USC T-18 Chapter 37 defines espionage and the response to it for the United States government.[49] "According to the Economic Espionage Act (EEA), Title 18 U.S.C., Section 1831, economic espionage is (1) whoever knowingly performs targeting or acquisition of trade secrets to (2) knowingly benefit any foreign government, foreign instrumentality, or foreign agent; and Theft of Trade Secrets, Title 18 U.S.C., Section 1832, is (1) whoever knowingly misappropriates trade secrets to (2) benefit anyone other than the owner."[50] Private corporations consider any CEMA directed at them that steals corporate data or other insider information as a cyber-attack. When considering all of these definitions of cyber-attack, it is understandable then, why after more than 30 years of CEMA across all activities in cyberspace, there exists misunderstandings as to what an attack or CEMA is or who has responsibility for contending with the nefarious cyber activity. There continues to exist a high degree of confusion among U.S. policymakers regarding the nature of cyber aggression and how to contend with it.[51] If the United States government had a better understanding of CEMA along with more credible cyber response organizations and procedures, then it is possible the progressively worsening cyber threat activity could be slowed or reserved.

Cyber-Enabled Operation

When multiple CEMA incidents or attacks are grouped together for a broad goal beyond a single event, they are described as *cyber-enabled malicious operations* – CEMO. *CEMO is defined as multiple CEMA incidents with a specified duration, unified purpose, and which leads to greater malicious effect and number of end-users impacted.* An example of a

CEMO is the series of events directed at the United States Joint Chiefs of Staff (JCS) unclassified email network on July 25, 2015, which allegedly was conducted by the Russian government. In a socially engineered spear phishing campaign, hackers used secure social media accounts to track down key employees to target, devise the plan to achieve success with that target, and then deliver malware-infested emails. This malicious cyber operation directed at the JCS included several simultaneous and consecutive CEMA incidents executed for the purpose of penetrating the DoD servers and which took weeks to execute.

Cyber Incident of National Significance (CINS)

The next most severe type of CEMA in time, effect, and number of end-users affected (short of war) and which spans a substantial period of time is *Cyber Incidents of National Significance* (CINS). The proposed definition of CINS offered here encompasses the perspectives of all the organizations that deal with national cybersecurity (both government and private sectors) while remaining technology neutral and representative of the realities of the domain. The intent is not for this definition to be "all things to everyone" but rather to describe the threshold for national action in cases where CEMA meets this definition. CINS is used to better describe cyber conflict within the implementation of a national cybersecurity strategy and the coercion that supports that strategy. The term CINS was derived from the DHS' Federal Emergency Management Agency (FEMA) *Cyber Incident National Response Plan* term: Incident of National Significance, which is defined as "an organized cyber-attack, an uncontrolled exploit such as a virus or worm, a natural disaster with significant cyber consequences, or other incidents capable of causing extensive damage to critical infrastructure or key assets."[52] FEMA's term is adequate for a national "response" plan (after the fact) but is not satisfactory for a proactive national cybersecurity strategy and our discussion.

For our purposes, a *cyber incident of national significance – CINS – is defined to be any national or regional strategically momentous cyber-enabled malicious activity intended to impair substantially the vital function(s) of an organization's cyberspace for a political, economic, or national security purpose.*[53] This definition is preferred over DHS' definition because CINS specifies the effect (impair the vital functions) and motive (political or national security purposes) which allows for multiple United States governmental organizations to undertake cyber actions jointly in response to or in advance of CEMA intended for U.S. critical infrastructure. DHS' definition is designed for a response plan primarily under FEMA's framework and on which other governmental organizations cannot plan or base their action. Figure 2.1 summarizes CEMA, illustrating the notion of scale and intensity the scale, CINS as the most important event.

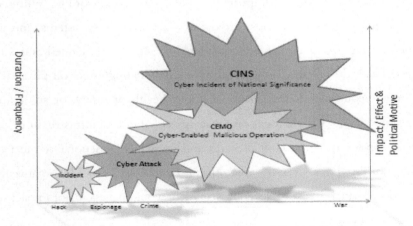

Figure 2.1 – CEMA Scale

Let us first examine each aspect of this definition to rationalize the language used and to illuminate the types of CEMA it includes.

National or regional strategically momentous cyber-enabled malicious activity (CEMA), includes events that possess some or all of the following characteristics: directed at a high-valued target, having a substantial impact on the intended target (both in time and magnitude), and executed by a sophisticated technical method of attack. This primarily objective-based definition focuses on the significance of the target attacked and the enormity of impact. For the United States, the types of momentous targets include national leadership and processes within the Executive, Legislative, and Judicial branches of government; the national or state military; the federal/national or state law enforcement organizations; and the national critical infrastructure and key resources. Sixteen critical infrastructure sectors define the functions that are crucially important to the American way of life. Within each one are portions that are the most important – whose assets, systems, and networks, whether physical or virtual, are considered so vital to the United States that their incapacitation or destruction would have a debilitating effect on physical security, national economic security, national public health or safety, or any combination thereof.[54] Here, we will focus on those aspects of critical infrastructure that are the most important to the United States and for which functionality must continue, even within times of war. Significant targets are typically organizations and functions, which if lost or severely degraded, would have a major impact regionally or nationally.

"Substantial impact" is meant to include a destructive or disruptive effect on operations beyond a mere nuisance[55] (such as a localized DDoS event lasting only a few hours) or beyond simply reducing the ability or capacity of the organization to deliver the prescribed service (such as the hijacking of a bank account to steal the funds within). Conversely, the lengthy DDoS attack levied against Estonia in 2007

40

would qualify as a CINS under this definition since it disrupted the banking and governmental services of the nation for several weeks. Inherent within the words "substantial impact" is an element of ambiguity for political leaders. Every situation will be unique and as such, defining what "substantial impact" is will be based upon the context of the event and factors associated with it. At times, political leadership may choose to take action and other times not. The overriding objective here is to imply that decision makers must decide if the significance, effect, and motive for the CINS warrant national action, which the other aspects of the definition help to quantify. The materiality of the event to nation's ability to properly protect its critical infrastructure should be kept in mind when determining "substantial impact."

Other examples of what constitutes "substantial impact" can be found United States National Security Council documents. Contained within the Presidential Executive Order on "Blocking the Property of Certain Persons Engaging in Significant Malicious Cyber-Enabled Activities" is a definition of a CINS actor who undertakes those activities "that are reasonably likely to result in, or have materially contributed to, a significant threat to the national security, foreign policy, or economic health or financial stability of the United States and that have the purpose or effect of: harming, or otherwise significantly compromising the provision of services by, a computer or network of computers that support one or more entities in a critical infrastructure sector; significantly compromising the provision of services by one or more entities in a critical infrastructure sector; causing a significant disruption to the availability of a computer or network of computers; or causing a significant misappropriation of funds or economic resources, trade secrets, personal identifiers, or financial information for commercial or competitive advantage or private financial gain."[56]

Also included in this definition is one mean-based criterion which would comprise cyber-enabled malicious operations executed by a *sophisticated technical method,* which connotes a capability most likely only possessed by the most capable of nefarious cyber actors – namely state or state-sponsored cyber organizations which are highly organized. By mean-based or method-based, this criterion emphasizes the "technique" rather than the "effect" that would explain why an event would raise the CEMA to the level of cyber-attack or CINS. Although the cost to enter cyber conflict is relatively low compared to the physical domain, there are still instances where only the most sophisticated cyber organizations with organized resources and highly capable cyber competencies can successfully attack highly fortified critical infrastructure, which places CINS in a different category from those of more rudimentary CEMA. Examples of *sophisticated technical means* of attack include Stuxnet in Iran in 2010 or the July 2015 CEMA against the United States military's Joint Chiefs of Staff (JCS) unclassified email system said to have "involved 'new and unseen approaches into the network' and was the 'most sophisticated' attack of its kind in military history" purportedly executed by Russia.[57] Although the scale of the JCS cyber-attack was lower on the scale of conflict, the CEMO was motivated by allegedly Russian cyber entities and targeted the leadership of the Department of Defense. The military is the organization responsible for defense of the nation and any event that reduces or eliminates that body's ability to command or control its mission is by definition, CINS. By attacking the leadership of military, the event warrants distinction and inclusion into the term CINS and for which national cyber response capabilities should be considered.

An example of a state-sponsored cyber organizations, China possesses numerous cyber units that conduct nefarious cyber operations (e.g., Units, 6137, 61398, 78020). One unit, 61398 in particular, was discovered by the cybersecurity firm Mandiant. According to Mandiant, this espionage unit possesses the considerable capabilities and capacity to hack "141 companies over a seven-year period, targeting any intellectual property it could find. During that time, Unit 61398 stole hundreds of terabytes of data, sometimes doing so over a period of years."[58]   Mandiant defined a profile of Unit 61398, which employs hundreds of staff that possess a wide-range of technical and linguistic skills. Usually only state or state-sponsored cyber units have the means to execute CEMO and CINS.   It is important to note however, that certain cybercriminals possess similar capabilities as state or state-sponsored cyber actors.   The most sophisticate cyber actors can undertake the types of CEMA associated with CINS and possess the robust organizations, command and control, and sophisticated capabilities necessary to carry out such a feat.   Cybercriminals benefit from the continued functioning of the organization that they are attacking so as to exploit (steal info or money). Cybercriminals' motives stem largely from financial gain.   That said, there can be overlap in the two categories in the situation where cybercriminals succeed on such a grand scale that the entire economy is affected by the CINS, which in turns negatively affects economic and national security.

"*Intended*" is meant to include CEMA successfully implemented by the attacker or adeptly denied by the network defender.   If a malicious cyber actor intends to cause harm by initiating the CEMA, then the act, whether successful or not, is included in the definition of CINS.   The focus in this definition is not on the achievement of the cyber-attack, but rather on the fact that the cyber-enabled malicious activity was deliberately planned and/or envisaged to cause harm once the "enter" button was pushed, thereby initiating the incident.   A note of caution is needed here: there may be times when intent is not known or knowable.   For example, if the malicious cyber actor poorly executes his attack or the outcome of the attack is different from what he actually intended, the defender may not comprehend that an attack was planned or know the actual target he desired to strike.   Intelligence plays a vital role in determining intent.

"*Substantially impair the vital function(s) of an organization's cyberspace*" means to intentionally disrupt, degrade, alter, steal or destroy data or processes that constitute the essential services, capabilities, or tasks within the organization.   The *2015 and*

2018 DoD Cyber Strategies also define "substantial impairment" in a similar way: "a disruptive, manipulative, or destructive cyberattack could present a significant risk to U.S. economic and national security if lives are lost, property destroyed, policy objectives harmed, or economic interests affected."[59] DoD's strategy goes onto state that leaders must mitigate the risks posed by the vulnerabilities present in their organizations. The vulnerabilities may be an open network or a fixed-function network; an organization's IT or OT. The central point here is the architecture that supports the vital functions, which if significantly damaged, would lead to an instance of CINS. For example, debilitating the ability of financial institutions to clear its daily global financial transactions or stopping the normal operation of the New York Stock Exchange (a fixed-function network) over an extended period of time, would have a detrimental impact on the United States and global economy, and therefore would constitute a CINS.[60] *"Cyberspace"* is included to emphasize that any portion or layer of cyberspace is susceptible to CEMA and should be considered. Conversely, mere cyber-espionage or cyber-exploitation would not constitute a CINS. To impair the vital functions of an organization's cyberspace substantially, the nefarious actor must accomplish more than unauthorized access along with passive or clandestine observation or copying of data. Such activities may be criminal and warrant a response, but they are not CINS.

"For a political, economic, or national security purpose" means to further distinguish from traditional cyber-crime in an objective-based fashion.[61] Cyber-crime may be included in the definition, but the emphasis or motivation of the attack should be beyond customary criminal activity and be primarily of a political or national security objective. Although an attack on the military's nuclear command and control network would be a crime, it would likely be undertaken by an adversary whose primarily focus would be political or national security reasons – and therefore meets this definition of CINS. An incident against Manhattan's power grid (a fixed-function network) would likely be undertaken for political reasons, possibly as a

prelude to war or as part of a terrorist attack. The North Korean CEMA directed at Sony Pictures in December of 2014 is an incident with confusing characteristics since it was instigated by a nation with fairly sophisticated means. The target, however, was a private corporation and not one of political significance other than the producer of a politically charged movie. Therefore, this would not qualify as a CINS by this definition, but would constitute a cyber-crime and a cyber-attack. Additionally, political or national security motives are not solely conducted by states – non-state organizations and individuals may initiate them as well.

The definition of CINS presented here deliberately ties the primarily objective-based attributes and one mean-based characteristic in an effort to define the magnitude and motive behind the types of CEMA, cyber-attack, or CEMO that rise to the level of cyber incident of national significance (CINS), while not excluding criminality. The 2007 Distributive Denial of Service (DDoS)[62] attack against Estonia in 2007 (conducted by Russia) that lasted three-plus weeks, or the 2013 cyber-attack by North Korea against the South Korean banking system meant as a political warning message, or the 2010 Stuxnet SCADA attack against Iran's Natanz nuclear facility to slow its uranium enrichment and nuclear weapons development capability are all examples of CINS.

Cyber Warfare

War is a political decision or declaration that has an extremely high threshold for action, not to mention implication for state-to-state interaction. The international legal framework by which cyber-enabled malicious activities are being examined is based upon customary international law,[63] statements in the United Nations' (U.N.) Charter, several U.N. General Assembly reports and resolutions, and the law of armed conflict.[64] Unfortunately, the two terms "use of force" and "armed attack" vis-a-vis cyberspace are not defined within the U.N. Charter, leaving individual states to debate what cyber warfare actually is. The cyber war threshold is defined by numerous states as any destructive cyber event within a sovereign state where an unlawful "use of force" will produce the effect of "an armed attack" likely to prompt the right of self-defense.[65] The loss of life or the meaningful destruction of strategically significant property is the test for defining war in cyberspace and would legitimize an armed response under a self-defense doctrine. According to the *Tallinn* Manual, the right of defense can be invoked if the attack was a cross-border event (that is was initiated by another state or state-sponsored entity) and "may be sufficiently grave to warrant classifying them as an 'armed attack' within the meaning of the [United Nations] Charter. This conclusion is in accord with the International Court of Justice's insistence in…that the choice of means of attack is immaterial to the issue of whether an operation qualifies as an armed attack."[66] In reality, very few cases of CEMA would actually meet this physical domain definition or threshold.

The *Tallinn Manual* goes to state that in "the view of the International Group of Experts, the term 'armed attack' is not to be equated with the term 'use of force' appearing in Rule II. An armed attack presupposes at least a use of force in the sense of [UN Charter] Article 2(4). However, as noted by the International Court of Justice, not every use of force rises to the level of an armed attack. The scale and effects required for an act to be characterized as an armed attack necessarily exceed those qualifying the act as a use of force. Only is the event that the use of force reaches the threshold of an armed attack is a State entitled to respond using force in self-defense."[67]

Michael Schmitt (the editor of the *Tallinn* Manual) argues in a separate paper that contemporary legal analysis of how states may respond to hostile cyber activities has generally ignored the option of countermeasures,[68] focusing instead on responses grounded in the law of self-defense. A customary law paradigm reflected in Article 51 of the U.N. Charter, the right of self-defense, permits states to respond forcefully to "armed attacks," including cyber operations qualifying as such. This self-defense centric analytical framework reflects state fears of a possible "cyber 9/11" in which another state or a transnational terrorist group mounts a cyber operation producing devastating human, physical, or economic consequences. Yet, preoccupation with cyber armed attacks is counter-experiential. Few, if any, cyber operations have crossed the armed attack threshold."[69] One of the major issues with using "armed attack" as a threshold for action in the cyber domain is that effects in cyberspace often have a temporary effect (can be reversed or undone) unlike effects in the physical world. In the cyber domain, even temporary effects (not equivalent to an armed attack) could lead to instances of CINS.

For example, in October of 2010, the FBI was alerted to malicious code designed to cause damage in the central servers of NASDAQ.[70] In the weeks and months that followed, the CIA and NSA were brought in to assist and investigate. Russian cyber entities were allegedly behind the CEMA which exploited vulnerabilities in NASDAQ's software code.[71] The fear was that even a temporary shutdown of the NASDAQ could cause a loss of confidence in the exchange which could then cause a corresponding run on the market and an economic recession – or worst yet, a depression. In this case, many international law experts might argue that the temporary nature of the CEMA would not be comparable to an armed attack, however the impact to the nation's economy warrants this example's inclusion into the category of CINS.

Most parties agree that cyber armed attack is a high-threshold, and there will be no question of whether or not a nuclear facility exploding as a result of CEMA is an armed attack. But the question vexing governments worldwide include how to respond to CEMA that does not reach this "armed attack" threshold and resides in a grey area between criminal activity and national security. Most cases of unauthorized access, network exploitation, espionage, and disruption do not meet the definition of an armed attack or use of force. However, when one examines the magnitude of nefarious cyber activity over the last decade alone, one is still struck by the sheer severity and alarming trend all modern nations face. Despite the considerable damages and cost to the United States as a result of recent degenerate cyber activities, the term cyber warfare as a definition is not useful and not the primary focus in this book. Revising the current "cyber-attack" vernacular is essential in order to better capture the realities of current day CEMA and the subsequent response options the government might take to protect the nation. As was shown above, the preponderance of current cyber-enabled malicious activity is below an act of war; consequently, with the proposed definitions provided above, now all of the nation's instruments of power (to include the military) could be applied to the cyber defense of the nation in case that rise to CINS.

Cyber Defense

Generally speaking, cyber defense is composed of those activities of security, including intelligence gathering, detection, and prevention of virtual intrusion or attack. Both domestic and international law are clear on the right of self-defense and the responsibility to hold perpetrators responsible. In fact, the International Court of Justice states that nations bear the responsibility for their internationally wrongful acts pursuant to the law of state responsibility.[72] Most cyber defense definitions acknowledge this international law within their language. *The United States National Military Strategy for Cyberspace Operations* defines cyber defense as those "[d]efensive cyberspace operations [which] direct and synchronize actions to detect, analyze, counter, and mitigate cyber threats and vulnerabilities; to outmaneuver adversaries taking or about to take offensive actions; and to otherwise protect critical missions that enable U.S. freedom of action in cyberspace."[73] This includes the right of self-defense.

The U.S. Cyber Command expanded the notion of defense by creating the term "*Defend Forward*" as way to enhance the military thought on engaging national threats as close to their technology as possible for defensive purposes. "Defending forward as close as possible to the origin of adversary activity extends our [U.S.] reach to expose adversaries' weaknesses, learn their intentions and capabilities, and counter attacks close to their origins."[74] *Defend Forward* aligns to the U.S. strategy of persistent engagement, which defines the requirement to engage to limit or prevent U.S. cyber foes. The *Defend Forward* explanation was extremely brief and missing of detail on how to accomplish the task, U.S. Cyber Command stated that it includes three general components: (1) positioning to degrade cyber operations; (2) warning to gather information about threats and inform defenses; and (3) influencing adversaries to discourage them from deploying cyber operations against the United States.[75]

According to an Austrian definition, the "term *'cyber defence'* refers to all measures to defend cyberspace with military and appropriate means for achieving military-strategic goals. Cyber defence is an integrated system, comprising the implementation of all measures relating to ICT [Information and Communication Technology] and information security, the capabilities of milCERT [Military Cyber Emergency Response Teams] and CNO (Computer Network Operations) as well as the support of the physical capabilities of the army."[76] The French military states that cyber defense is: "the set of all technical and non-technical measures allowing a State to defend cyberspace information systems that it considers to be critical."[77]

The *Tallinn Manual* discusses the passive nature of some cyber defenses. Passive cyber defense is defined as a "measure for detecting and mitigating cyber intrusions and the effects of cyber-attacks that does not involve launching a preventative, pre-emptive or countering operation against the source. Examples of passive cyber defense measures are firewalls, patches, anti-virus software, and digital forensic tools."[78] Cyber defender use passive cyber defenses as part of their network protection architecture and may use third party providers to augment existing in-house measures.

Cyber Response Options

The term *response option* is used to describe activities that may be conducted preemptively or reactively to protect against an ongoing or imminent threat.[79] According to Herbert Lin, response options may encompass a wide range of options outside the network which the government can take as a result of the cyber event.[80] Those options include law enforcement, diplomatic (demarche), economic and trade (sanction), cyber (retaliatory strike), and military threat of physical attack.[81] Based upon accepted international law, the response options (or countermeasures as they are labeled) must be necessary, immediate, and proportional to the attack suffered. The purpose of a response option is to return the situation to a condition of lawfulness without conducting illegal actions.

The *Tallinn Manual* further expounds upon this notion by discussing cyber defense in an active nature. Specifically, active cyber defense is a "proactive measure for detecting and obtaining information as to a cyber intrusion, cyber-attack, or impending cyber operation, or for determining the origin of an operation that involves launching a pre-emptive, preventative, or cyber counter-operation against the source."[82] It is important to point out that response options and active cyber defense are state activities that must be conducted in accord with international law and are not an option for private corporations since most states outlaw this activity. Active cyber defense and response options have limits to their use.

Cyber Resilience

Another term often used as a corollary to defense is *cyber resilience*. The Department of Homeland Security defines the term similarly to the White House as "the ability to prepare for and adapt to changing conditions and withstand and recover rapidly from disruptions. Resilience includes the ability to withstand and recover from deliberate attacks, accidents, or naturally occurring threats or incidents."[83] Cyber resilience is the strengthening of an organization's IT and OT so that CEMA would have only limited effect due to redundancy or rapid restoration capabilities. The *2015 DoD Cyber Strategy* enumerates resilience and redundancy this way. No organization can "necessarily guarantee that every cyberattack will be denied successfully, [therefore] the Defense Department must invest in resilient and redundant systems so that it may continue its operations in the face of disruptive or destructive cyberattacks."[84] Resilience is an organizational framework and ability to resist CEMA, react to and respond from potentially catastrophic cyber threats, while working towards secure and sustainable cyber operations.

Cyber Offense

The DoD defines cyber offense as "Cyberspace operations intended to project power by the application of force in or through cyberspace, also known as offensive cyber operations (OCO)."[85] OCO is intended to degrade, disrupt, or destroy access to, operation of, or availability of a target by a specified level for a specified time.[86] Cyber Offense or offensive security is a proactive and adversarial approach to protecting computer systems, networks and individuals from attacks. Conventional security -- sometimes referred to as "defensive security" -- focuses on reactive measures, such as patching software and finding and fixing system vulnerabilities. In contrast, offensive security measures are focused on seeking out the perpetrators and in some cases attempting to disable or at least disrupt their operations as a preemptive action.[87] Just like cyber defense, cyber offense can occur solely in the virtual domain for OCO objectives or cyber operations may be in support of offensive action predominantly in the physical domain (e.g., Counter Enemy Air Defense, Strategic Strike, or Power Projection). The United Kingdom's military views cyber offense as part of the broader tools of warfare. "Actions in cyberspace form part of the battlefield rather than being separate to it."[88] The *Tallinn Manual* defines cyber operations as the "employment of cyber capabilities with the primary purpose of achieving objectives in or by the use of cyberspace."[89] To more fully understand cyber conflict, we must first understand who is behind the CEMA.

Attribution

The character of the virtual domain makes attribution of CEMA difficult but not impossible. Every kind of CEMA—malicious or not—leaves a trail. Attributing the event to a specific individual, organization, or state is one of the first steps in determining what is actually occurring during a CEMA and who can be held accountable for the malevolent action. Oftentimes, cyber defenders may not know the exact identity of the attacker (actual computer used or the individual at the computer), as malicious cyber actors tend to hide their true origin. As a means to discover the evidence for attribution, it is critical to scrutinize the profile of the CEMA as it is not sufficient to rely on solitary evidence such as the source of an attack.[90] The process of identifying a malicious cyber actor involves building a "digital fingerprint" of the perpetrators and using that to identify one entity from all the others. "This process looks at the methods and tools the hackers use to get into systems, what information they choose to take and the care they exercise to disable alarms and remove any evidence."[91]

The art and science for analytic attribution has been refined over the past decade. The standards for attribution include "describing sources (including their reliability and access to the information they provide), clearly expressing uncertainty, distinguishing between underlying information and analysts' judgments and assumptions, exploring alternatives, demonstrating relevance to the customer, using strong and transparent logic, and explaining change or consistency in judgments

52

over time."[92]   Applying these standards assists analysts with the best and most accurate insight and context.   Cyber analysts integrate information from a wide range of sources, including "human sources, technical collection, and open source information, and apply specialized skills and structured analytic tools to draw inferences informed by the data available, relevant past activity, and logic and reasoning to provide insight into what is happening and the prospects for the future."[93]

The analyst's job is to explain uncertainties associated with major judgments based on the quantity and quality of the source material, gaps in knowledge, and the complexity of the event. When Intelligence Community analysts use words such as "we assess" or "we judge," they are conveying an analytic assessment or judgment. Much of the analysis is founded on assembled information, while the rest is based upon previous events and judgments. Analysts often include two important elements: "judgments of how *likely* it is that something has happened or will happen (using terms such as "likely" or "unlikely") and confidence levels in those judgments (low, moderate, and high) that refer to the evidentiary basis, logic and reasoning, and precedents that underpin the judgments."[94]

Analysts use the facts they gather, their constantly growing knowledge base of previous CEMA and known malicious actors, and their understanding of how cyber threats actors work and the tools that they use, to trace CEMA back to its origination. Analysts consider a "series of questions to assess how the information compares with existing knowledge and adjust their confidence in their judgments as appropriate to account for any alternative hypotheses and ambiguities. An assessment of attribution usually is not a simple statement of who conducted an operation, but rather a series of judgments that describe whether it was an isolated incident, who was the likely perpetrator, that perpetrator's possible motivations, and whether a foreign government had a role in ordering or leading the operation."[95]

Authors Rid and Buchanan further elaborate on the complexities of attribution and articulate that attribution is what each individual state makes of it for their specific purposes. Attributing an attacker to an event is an exercise in minimizing uncertainty on three levels: "tactically, attribution is an art as well as a science; operationally, attribution is a nuanced process not a black and white problem; and strategically, attribution is a function of what is at stake politically."[96] Successful attribution is based upon a vast array of skills, careful oversight, time, leadership, stress-testing, judicious communication, and recognizing constraints and limitations. Attribution is not a simple or quick process and requires multiple disciplines. There are three general features of attribution — it is usually overly extensive and complex for any single person to handle. Attribution proceeds incrementally on multiple levels, immediate technical collection of evidence, follow-up investigations and analysis, and then legal proceedings and building a case against competing evidence.[97]

The attribution process has a start and a finish, but does not always follow a sequential or chronological order, as "hypotheses are confronted with new details and new details give rise to new hypotheses in turn."[98] CEMA is complex, and uncovering its composition and designed intent requires a comprehensive set of experts. For example, a team of anti-virus researchers might devote an extensive time period reverse-engineering the malware, while computer engineers may concentrate on the design of the cyber payload. Additionally, a cyber analyst may be able to determine what language the source computer code's comments were written in or the filenames of the script modules (e.g., Chinese, Russian, etc.) as a way to narrow the field of likely culprits. Specifically identifying the malicious cyber actor(s) initiating the attack depends upon the ability to ascertain the distinguishing tradecraft and techniques of the CEMA for which governments and cybersecurity firms are improving daily. Criminal investigators are well acquainted with the detail and time required to investigate and attribute malicious conducted in the physical domain – cyberspace is no different. The amount of time and effort devoted to attribution is dependent upon the significance of the target and the nature of the CEMA.

The underlying goal is comprehending the CEMA primarily in its technical aspects, the *how*. The broader goal is understanding the CEMA's high-level architecture and the attacker's profile — the *what*. The end goal is determining to some level of certainty who is responsible for the CEMA, assessing the event's rationale, significance, appropriate response — the *who* and *why*.[99] More often than not at the technical level, cyber forensic analysts may be able to narrow the field of likely offenders (hackers) down to a small number with some level of certainty (e.g., high, medium, low) by analyzing the code, style, patterns, past cases, and methodology used.[100] As the attribution process flows from technical to operational to strategic, there are fewer questions to ask and those questions take on a broader focus. Consequently, the uncertainty of attributive tends to increase as the analysis transitions from technical to political. For example, the questions would transition from what was the method of gaining access to the network to what was the motive of the CEMA. The quality of the attribution improves at each level with an increase in the numbers and types of sources that can be used for answering the relevant questions. States with extensive intelligence and diplomatic sources and methods tend to fare better in the attribution development process. In cyberspace, it is difficult to produce evidence that links an intrusion to an individual within an organization; however, it has happened in the past. The ultimate goal is to identify the organization or nation behind the CEMA and not just the individual.

Within the attribution process, the operational layer is designed to piece together details from a variety of contrasting sources. These include analysis from the technical layer, non-technical analyses, and information on the geopolitical context.[101] Analysis from the operational layer aids in the development of alternative hypotheses that helps explain the intent behind the CEMA. Answers from the operational layer then contribute to asking the strategic questions. On a strategic level, leaders and analysts must aggregate the answers to operational questions and draw meaningful conclusions. The key element of the process is when cyber defenders and leaders question preliminary analyses, search for details, and alternative explanations. The evidence and preliminary conclusions need testing. Stress-testing the analysis can uncover weak assumptions. "Coaxing and probing for additional detail, or for alternative explanations, may require detailed knowledge of the process."[102] Finally, attribution for CEMA that rises to the level of attack, CEMO, or CINS, may be a law enforcement, military, and political process. Attribution is possible and has been occurring successfully for a long time. To better understand cyber conflict, let us explore the actors who engage in CEMA and the defenders who protect the cyber terrain.

Malicious Cyber Actors

There are numerous types of nefarious cyber actors whose intentions span the gambit of motivations and levels of technical sophistication. The following explanation is not exhaustive, but illustrates the variety and complexities of cyber actors currently operating in cyberspace. There are essentially three broad categories of cyber actors: the malicious actor (focused on nefarious intent), the defender (non-nefarious intent focused on cybersecurity of systems and functions), and the end-user (actors whose behavior and attitude are indifferent to cybersecurity and who are not intent on conducting nefarious activities).[103] The organizational structure of malicious cyber actors vary widely from a single individual (hacktivist) acting independently to a hierarchical organization of a state sponsored cyber unit such as the National Security Agency. Sophisticated malicious cyber actors operate with a high degree of organization and specialization.[104] All too often, cybersecurity experts focus on defense of their networks and systems, yet forget that the human element should also be factored into cybersecurity. End-users who fail to follow strict security protocols or who deliberately violate those protocols have had a monumentally negative impact on their organizations. For example, a well-intentioned end-user who unwittingly clicks on a hyperlink to malicious code can have the same effect as the nefarious insider who willfully gains access with the desire to steal, manipulate, or destroy the organization's cyber "crown jewels." One example of this occurrence was the previously mentioned 2015 cyber-incident against the Joint Chiefs of Staff (JCS) unclassified email network.[105] Properly training each end-user to avoid such situations is as important as state-of-the-art network defense and superb supply chain management.

Similarly, determining who the malicious actors are is vital to building options to counter those malcontents. Cybersecurity defenders who focus solely on cyber network and architecture security miss the underlying nature of cyber conflict by failing to comprehend the motivations and methods an adversary may have or use. By not fully understanding an adversary's motives, objectives, capabilities, and tactics, cyber defenders may not be able to develop strategies to protect one's organization sufficiently. Too often the human element of cyber conflict is not explored sufficiently because there is great deal of multi-disciplinary intelligence gathering and analysis required. To adequately understand the adversary in several dimensions (which in necessary to forecasting adversarial intentions and motive determination), one should combine aspects of criminology, sociology, engineering, economics, and political science. Many cybersecurity teams are made up of computer engineering experts, information technology specialists, and possibly intelligence analysts, none of whom possess the requisite education and experience in law, social science, economics, or strategy necessary for a multi-disciplinary cybersecurity solution. Even research and development of concepts necessary to address cybersecurity overly emphasize the technical aspects of the challenge while ignoring the social science. As Eric Bonabeau wrote, "it seems surreal that in an otherwise excellent document, the authors of a 2009 manifesto from Sandia National Laboratories entitled 'Complexity Science Challenges in Cybersecurity' have not dedicated a single line to human behavior."[106] Human behavior comprehension is an important component of cyberspace and should be factored into the education of the cyber domain similar to the way other disciplines study and define the human component.[107] Effective cybersecurity must weave the complexities of cyber conflict together with an understanding of the human element, the relevant aspects of cyberspace technology, the legalities of conflict in the domain, and the geopolitical environment in which we all live so as to better grasp what a holistic cybersecurity strategy might be. To help unravel some of the confusion surrounding CINS, let us examine those actors who might attempt CINS.

State or State-sponsored Cyber Organizations

The first set of malicious cyber actors who might commit CINS is the *state or state-sponsored cyber organization*. This group of actors is explicitly employed and/or directed by the government of a nation. State or state-sponsored entities (sometime called Advanced Persistent Threat – APTs) are extremely sophisticated in their craft and they practice operations security in order to remain unnoticed. APTs oftentimes act to extract secret or corporate proprietary information (espionage) or communications by means of gaining and maintain persistent access to an organization's cyberspace.[108] Two specific APTs warrant particular elaboration – China and Russia.

According to former U.S. Justice Department assistant attorney general for National Security John Carlin, "the scale of China's corporate espionage is so vast it constitutes a national security emergency, with China targeting virtually every sector of the U.S. economy, and costing American companies hundreds of billions of dollars in losses -- and more than two million jobs."[109] According to the 2018

Foreign Economic Espionage in Cyberspace report by National Counterintelligence and Security Center, "foreign economic and industrial espionage against the United States continues to represent a significant threat to America's prosperity, security, and competitive advantage" with China, Russia, and Iran being the most capable and persistent threats.[110] Intellectual property theft in and through the virtual domain remains a preferred method for a wide range of industrial espionage threat actors.

The 2018 report goes to state that there several threatening trends the United States must now focus on. Specifically, the area of most concern related to intellectual property theft within the United States' private sectors is software supply chain infiltration.[111] Foreign threat actors sell nefarious hardware in subcomponents, which U.S. companies buy as part of the products they build and sell to American customers. These nefarious subcomponents then "beacon back" to home (China, Russia, Iran) with the secrets accessed through the product. This theft of United States corporate secrets allows other nations to by-pass years of American research and development in a matter of minutes, thus saving hundreds of millions of dollars. According to the 2009 – 2011 Report to Congress on Foreign Economic Collection and Industrial Espionage, "Chinese leaders consider the first two decades of the 21st century to be a window of strategic opportunity for their country to focus on economic growth, independent innovation, scientific and technical advancement, and growth of the renewable energy sector."[112] China is driven by its longstanding policy of 'catching up fast and surpassing' Western powers. "An emblematic program in this drive is Project 863, which provides funding and guidance for efforts to clandestinely acquire U.S. technology and sensitive economic information."[113]

According to the 2015 U.S.-China Economic and Security Review Commission Report to Congress, "China causes increasing harm to the U.S. economy and security through China's coordinated, government-backed theft of information from a wide variety of U.S.-based commercial enterprises and widespread restrictions on content, standards, and commercial opportunities for U.S. businesses. Hackers working for the Chinese government—or with the government's support and encouragement—have infiltrated the computer networks of U.S. government agencies, contractors, and private companies, and stolen personal information and trade secrets."[114] The Chinese government provides stolen U.S. information to Chinese companies, Chinese state-owned businesses that compete with U.S. firms, and to portions of the Chinese economy that the government designated as "Strategic Emerging Industries," which China intends to nurture into global competitors.[115] The costs to the United States' economy and private corporations increase yearly as network intrusions become more sophisticated. The 2018 Intellectual Property Commission Report provided an estimate of the cost of intellectual property theft for the United States in three categories — counterfeit and pirated tangible goods, software piracy, and trade theft. That estimate is somewhere between $225 billion and $600 billion. The Office of the Director of National Intelligence estimates the cost as $400 billion.[116] The financial damage to the United States is in the form of lost trade secrets such as copyrights and patents, manufacturing processes, foregone royalties, the costs of cyber defense, lost business and jobs, and the expense of remediating and repairing the damage to computer networks.[117]

Despite the fact that many private corporations are global entities with business in China, they along with cybersecurity firms and the United States government are now more willing to release details on the attacks within their networks along with specifics on the malicious cyber perpetrators. The scale, intensity, and duration of the corporate espionage forced many U.S. based organizations to fight for their literal business survival, corporate advantages, brand or reputation, and/or proprietary corporate secrets. As stated above, at the heart of the Chinese cyber espionage capabilities is one organization – Unit 61398 that is believed to be part of the People's Liberation Army and is focused on spying on western corporations.

Another APT is Russia. The 2018 Foreign Economic Espionage in Cyberspace stated Russia uses CEMA as an instrument of intelligence collection to inform its political actions and benefit its economic interests. "Experts contend that Russia needs to enact structural reforms, including economic diversification into sectors such as technology, to achieve the higher rate of gross domestic product growth publicly called for by Russian President Putin."[118] Specifically, Russia's motivation is based upon its high dependence on natural resources, the need to diversify its economy, and the belief that the global economic system is tilted toward U.S. and other Western interests at the expense of Russia. Moscow used CEMO to collect intellectual property data from U.S. energy, healthcare, and technology companies. For example, Russian government hackers recently exploited dozens of U.S. energy firms, including their OT.[119] This activity is likely motivated by multiple objectives, including intelligence collection, gaining accesses for disruptive purposes, and providing sensitive intellectual property to Russian companies. Russia is noted as one of the world's preeminent cyber actors who continually targets the United States and will likely continue to do so for the foreseeable future with CEMA in order to achieve its political aims.

Like China, Russia engages in cyber espionage on a grand scale against United States government and corporate entities. According to a report by Recorded Future, "Russia poses a serious cyber threat to industrial control systems (ICS), pharmaceutical, defense, aviation, and petroleum companies. Russian government cyber operations aim to use malware to steal information on files, persist on ICS equipment, and commit espionage."[120] The report also states that there are primarily three families of Russian malware: Uroburos, Energetic Bear, and APT28, all of which have three goals: cyber intrusions to conduct espionage, pre-position Russian accesses for future cyber warfare, and to meddle and monitor geopolitical threat's in Russia's backyard.[121] These groups differ in their targets despite using similar delivery mechanisms and techniques. Furthermore, while all of their CEMA utilize user behavior in order to gain access to their victims, the varying objectives of the groups indicate a strategic level of planning and management. The lack of sharing of the different malware families across the darknet is notable. This suggests synchronization at all levels…tactical, operational, and strategic. This synchronization is symptomatic of Russia's reputation as a sophisticated cyber threat.[122] Several cybersecurity firms agree that the Russian government continues to lead the way in stealthy malware and cyber operations making their efforts hard to identify and analyze. Both Russia and China are state sponsors of cyber espionage for political reasons and direct their nefarious CEMA at the United States and other Western nations.

The current response by the United States government revolves around defensive actions and increasing law enforcement activities. Thanks to Chinese, Russian, and other state-sponsored CEMA, United States government cyber operations include initiatives to chip away at the high cyber threat activity. In July 2015, the FBI reported a substantial increase in the number of economic espionage investigations undertaken by the agency over the last 12 months, with a 53 percent increase in caseloads. A recent FBI survey of 165 U.S. companies found that China was the perpetrator in 95 percent of economic-espionage cases.[123] Unfortunately, despite the increase in cyber defense and law enforcement investigations, the malicious cyber trend continues to rise. The leaders in corporate America I talked to worry that the government is not adequately defending them or the country. Furthermore, the 2015 Congressional Report went so far as to state that the "United States is ill prepared to defend itself from cyber espionage when its adversary is determined, centrally coordinated, and technically sophisticated, as is the CCP [Chinese Communist Party] and China's government."[124]

A plethora of nations possess state or state sponsored cyber organizations, and examples include: China's 3 PLA, the United States' National Security Agency (NSA), the United Kingdom's Government Communications Headquarters (GCHQ), Israel's Unit 8200, and Canada's Communications Security Establishment (CSE), just to name a few. National and International law enforcement entities such as the Federal Bureau of Investigations (FBI), Interpol, and Germany's Bundesamt für Sicherheit in der Informationstechnik (German Federal Office for Information Security) fall into this category as well. Their motivations range from espionage and reconnaissance to influence operations directed at political and military leaders. When combined with physical conflict, their cyber motivations might include ensuring successful combat operations. One of the case studies in the next chapter will expound upon that motivation. State or state-sponsored organizations tend to be the most sophisticated in ability to conduct cyber operations since they have the greatest resources, organizational support structure, funding, and authorities of the state.

Non-state cyber actors

Non-state cyber actors include criminal organizations, cyber terrorists, hacktivists, individuals, as well as the technology sector. A criminal organization engages in illegal activity usually for profit (cyber-crime is generally not conducted by state or state-sponsored organizations). Organized cybercriminals primarily operate for financial gain, but also may target data assets that can be traded to others. High-end cybercriminals can even duplicate the sophisticated tactics of APTs due to their effectiveness and desire to target anything of value.[125] Criminal attacks may extort money from a victim or conduct corporate espionage. A recent report highlights the primary targets of cyber criminals are financial institutions, media and entertainment, and retail manufacturing.[126] INTERPOL states "[m]ore and more [cyber]criminals are exploiting the speed, convenience and anonymity of the Internet to commit a diverse range of criminal activities that know no borders, either physical or virtual, cause serious harm and pose very real threats to victims worldwide. Although there is no single universal definition of cybercrime, law enforcement generally makes a distinction between two main types of Internet-related crime: [1] Advanced cybercrime (or high-tech crime) – sophisticated attacks against computer hardware and software; and [2] Cyber-enabled crime – many 'traditional' crimes have taken a new turn with the advent of the Internet, such as crimes against children, financial crimes and even terrorism."[127]

A cyber terrorist—typically a dissident who is party to a known terrorist organization—devises attacks designed to cause terror or panic with an ideological or political goal. Terrorists such as the Islamic State in Iraq and Syria (ISIS) are organizations that are moving online. While ISIS has been recognized for its social media expertise, the growing cyber talent of its recruits has mostly been overlooked. "A number of individuals that have recently joined the movement of ISIS were folks that studied computer science in British schools and European universities," said Tom Kellermann, chief cybersecurity officer at security firm Trend Micro, who said ISIS's cyber capabilities are "advancing dramatically."[128] The Report of Congress discusses the growing role of non-state and non-corporate actors. "The migration of most business and technology development activities to cyberspace is making it easier for actors without the resources of a nation-state or a large corporation to become players in economic espionage [and CEMA]. Such new actors may act as surrogates or contractors for intelligence services or major companies, or they could conduct espionage against sensitive U.S. economic information and technology in pursuit of their own objectives."[129]

A *hacktivist* is an individual who conducts CEMA in order to draw attention to a cause such as free speech or human rights, or hinder the support of a cause. The hacktivist group Anonymous is one of the most notable in this category.[130]

Hacktivists can be quite "loud" in comparison to other threat actors, using social media to discuss activities and to recruit members to attack a target.[131] Hacktivists may focus on damaging reputations, disrupting operations, or making derogatory statements about an organization or individual they do not agree with. If the cause is political, and/or designed to inflict terror, they are instead considered a cyber terrorist.[132] This category of actors has a wide range of capabilities depending on the group's member.

Individuals, or *lone actors, are* not affiliated with any specific group or organization and who may conduct activities such as taking down a school network or hacking into a government email account just to show his/her cyber prowess. An example of an individual who caused substantial damage is "Mafiaboy." In 2000, Michael Calce, a Canadian high school student, decided to unleash a DDoS attack on a number of high-profile commercial websites including Amazon, CNN, eBay and Yahoo!. An industry expert estimated the attacks resulted in 1.2 billion dollars of damage.[133] This last category of actor typically does not possess great cyber capabilities, but on occasion (as Mafiaboy demonstrated) can inflict substantial harm and therefore cannot be ruled out.

Finally, the technology sector and/or cybersecurity firms are private, mostly for-profit entities that get involved in cyber defense. This non-governmental and non-law enforcement category of cyber actors contribute to the broader international cybersecurity community which seeks to secure the various layers of cyberspace (e.g., physical, logical, etc.) either for profit or on behalf of the Internet. These organizations include Microsoft's Defensive Crime Unit, Hewlett Packard's Cyber Hunter Team, Dell's SecureWorks, CrowdSource, FireEye, Kaspersky, Group IB, and McAfee just to name a few. These private entities help other corporations and governments prevent and investigate high-tech cyber-crimes and online fraud. Most of these cybersecurity firms have been active in the field of computer forensics and information security for years. Several of these organizations have tremendous cyber capabilities due to their control of and access to cyber information (Microsoft, Kaspersky, McAffee) and based upon the fact that they recruit from national or state-sponsored cyber organizations, such as the NSA.

Not all malicious cyber actors fit neatly into just one category. For example, an organization that predominantly conducts hacktivist activities by routinely advancing a cause, but on occasion also conducts political cyber activities unilaterally or based upon the direction of a government, crosses multiple categories and complicates how a victim state may choose to respond to that nefarious organization. Some states desire to have abstruse relationships with non-state cyber organizations in order to hide the state's true intent. These states generally do not conduct CEMA openly, but tend to hide their attacks through technical means and by perpetrating the attack through other organizations with ambiguous relationships.[134] One could look to Nashi, a pro-Kremlin youth movement stood up by Vladimir Putin which took responsibility for the 2007 Estonian distributed denial of service attack, as an example of this category with multiple relations. Nashi can be considered a pseudo state-sponsored organization since it is alleged that the business owners who fund Nashi "ingratiate themselves with the regime" and take direction from the Russian government, which wishes to obfuscate its involvement in any CEMA.[135] The cyber actors and their motivations, either malicious or peaceful, may not always fit neatly into just one category and therefore paint an extremely complicated and complex picture with which the government charged with defending the nation must contend.

Malicious Cyber Actor's Decision-Making Calculus

To understand cyber conflict more fully, one must comprehend the decision-making processes of the malicious cyber actors. When examining cyber conflict from the adversary's perspective, most malicious cyber actors have negligible consequences imposed upon them for their nefarious cyber actions – their benefits of executing CEMA outweigh any perceived costs and risks. The process of investigating, attributing, tracking, and prosecuting malicious cyber actors is extremely complicated, especially when compared to cases of physical crime. Many malicious cyber actors evade prosecution due to limitations in criminal laws that do not address technological means of offending. Determining the location of an incident and overcoming positive and negative conflict of laws can present difficulties for law enforcement officers when issuing warrants, drafting subpoenas, and committing a case for trial.[136] Compared to significant violations of human rights, many instances of cybercrime do not invoke the 'principle of universality' as justification for criminal jurisdiction. Doctrines in one nation's legal system may not apply in another nation's jurisdiction. The 'sovereign equality' existing between nation-states is a fundamental principle of international law, and demands respect for the lawmaking autonomy of other countries.[137] Even when law enforcement entities identify and track a cyber-criminal, bilateral agreements between nations must be in place before the criminal can be extradited. Since that process is lengthy and sometime absent, criminals can move from country to country and avoid the ramifications of the law. Imposing costs on malicious cyber actors is therefore problematic and inconsistent.

Furthermore, malicious cyber actors perceived only modest risk, especially given law enforcement's overwhelming task of finding and prosecuting the overabundance of cyber criminals. For example, in early 2015, it was alleged that Russian cyber criminals stole nearly one trillion dollars from various banks across globe while evading capture.[138] Cyber-crimes of a lesser scale are common and cyber criminals are able to remain either beyond the long arm of the law (e.g., hide in Russia) or constantly move faster than the law enforcement agencies can investigate and track, resulting in the paradigm where cyber criminals do not experience the punishment of the law while reaping benefits that far outweigh any costs of perpetrating the CEMA. In cases of state or state-sponsored cyber-attacks, there are even fewer options for imposing consequences on malicious cyber actors. For example, one may conclude that the Russian cyber perpetrators who instigated the attack on the Ukrainian electrical grid in December 2015 must have determined that the costs and risks associated with the cyber-attack did not compare to the benefit of undertaking the nefarious deed, especially in light of the dynamics of the conflict between Ukraine and Russia.

The situation is further exacerbated by the number of cyber-attacks below the level of cyber incidents of national significance, given that the majority of the CEMA is targeted at private corporations. In these cases, corporate cybersecurity teams must be effective 100 percent of the time while the malicious cyber actor only needs to be effective once in order to achieve his aims. Moreover, U.S. laws prevent private cybersecurity entities from entering another entity's computer (often called "hacking back"), which limits the private corporation's response options to those purely defensive in nature. "Loosely defined, 'hacking back' involves turning the tables on a cyberhacking assailant: thwarting or stopping the crime, or perhaps even trying to steal back what was taken – hacking back quickly runs afoul of the Computer Fraud and Abuse Act (CFAA).[139] The CFAA unfortunately only applies to U.S. corporations and civilians, and therefore international actors are not subject to the law. This law has undergone numerous revisions since it was first enacted in 1986, but Title 18, Sec. 1030 is clear on the point that using a computer to intrude upon or steal something from another computer is illegal."[140]

This reality is further aggravated when one examines how the state struggles in its role to defend the corporation from cyber-attack. The Westphalian notion of a state's role in national security was not envisioned to defend individual businesses or a virtual domain created five centuries later.[141] Combine that with the already stated disparity over attack definitions and roles to contend with the CEMA, and one can envisage why adequate strategies and consequences for CEMA and CINS are not sufficiently present. The stealthy nature of CEMA combined with the high pay-off for malicious cyber actors, make the benefits of CEMA attractive to many cyber actors. Even as greater government and private cyber capabilities are added to defend against CEMA, the current situation favors malicious cyber actors. Although greater defensive capabilities reduce benefits and raise costs, the costs will not outweigh benefits because real consequences are difficult to impose on malicious cyber actors under the current national cybersecurity paradigm.

Conclusions

The United States has led the world in technological innovation and cyberspace development for decades. The advancements in cyberspace that the United States provided the world improved global commerce, medical knowledge, and societal interactions, just to name a few. Other modern nations and financial alliances (i.e., European Union) also contributed significantly to the evolution of global technology. Now, more humans are better connected virtually than ever before. Unfortunately for every modern nation, they have become extremely dependent upon their technology which brings with it, tremendous vulnerabilities. As more people are connected to friends and businesses, cyber threats also are coupled to the targets they wish to exploit. Accordingly, the future of CEMA looks bleak. Hackers are persistent and oftentimes brute-force their way through obstacles or find ways to bypass them. Hackers will invest weeks and months devising new methods to achieve their aims. There's no Moore's Law[142] for hacking innovation, but hackers' techniques get bolder and more sophisticated each year.[143] The new trends include extortion hacks, attacks that change or manipulate data, chip-and-pin innovations, and more the discovery of more backdoors. Understanding the cyber domain and the actors involved are the necessary starting points to contending with the conflict within the domain.

69

Because the preponderance of past CEMA consequences do not have physical manifestations and do not rise to the level of a "use of force" or equal to "an armed attack," it is not surprising that there exists misperception as to what an attack is or who has responsibility for contending with the CEMA. The deliberately chosen definitions provided in this chapter characterize the realities of CEMA and describe a threshold for action inclusive of and yet less than an act of war. These definitions allow multiple organizations to act in parallel and jointly in an effort to integrate and synchronize a "whole of government" strategy. With the proper and complete understanding of cyberspace and its lexicon, one may discuss conflict within the cyber domain and the corresponding appropriate responses to defend, deter, and/or influence decision making towards national objectives. Only through comprehending the malicious cyber actors, their motivations, and values, will the modern nation be able to influence the behavior of state or state-sponsored malicious cyber actors in cases where they threaten national and economic security. Understanding the domain in which cyber-enabled malicious activity exists is critical for developing strategies to outpace the cyber threat – and is essential for the modern nation's continued vitality and prosperity.

---

[1] Barry Rosenberg

[2] United States Department of Defense Joint Publication 3-12 (R) *Cyberspace Operations*, 5 February 2013, found at: http://www.dtic.mil/doctrine/new_pubs/jp3_12R.pdf.

[3] Paul Martyn, "Risky Business: Cybersecurity And Supply Chain Management," *Forbes Online Magazine*, June 23, 2105, accessed online 31 Dec 2015, found at: http://www.forbes.com/sites/paulmartyn/2015/06/23/risky-business-cyber-security-and-supply-chain-management/.

[4] The Federal Reserve Bank Services online site accessed 31 Dec 2015, found at: https://www.frbservices.org/operations/fedwire/fedwire_funds_services_statistics.html. Fedwire is the Federal Reserve Bank Service mission-critical, same-day transaction service that includes the electronic payments and securities transfer services from banks, businesses and government agencies

to other financial entities. For more on Fedwire see Federal Reserve Bank Services at: https://frbservices.org/fedwire/index.html.

5 SCADA is a system that operates with coded signals over communication channels so as to provide control of remote equipment (using typically one communication channel per remote station). It is important to note the approximately 90 percent of all U.S. critical infrastructure is owned and operated by private entities. Keith Stouffer, Joe Falco, and Karen Kent, "Guide to Supervisory Control and Acquisition (SCADA) and Industrial Control Systems (ICS) (Draft)," (Department of Commerce, National Institute of Standards and Technology (NIST), Special Publication 800-82, Sept 2006), pg. 1.

6 For a complete discussion on vulnerabilities in technology hardware and software, see http://www.hq.nasa.gov/security/it_threats_vulnerabilities.htm.

7 "Software assurance" is defined as "a level of confidence that software is free from vulnerabilities, either intentionally designed into the software or accidentally inserted at any time during the lifecycle, and that the software functions in the intended manner." Nancy R. Mead, Julia H. Allen, W. Arthur Conklin, Antonio Dormmi, John Harrison, Jeff Ingalsbe, James Rainey, and Dan Shoemaker, "Making the Business Case of Software Assurance," (Carnegie Mellon, Software Engineering Institute, April 2009), pg. vii. Found at: http://www.sei.cmu.edu/reports/09sr001.pdf.

8 Paul Martyn.

9 Merriam-Webster Online Dictionary accessed online 24 Sept 2015, found at: http://www.merriam-webster.com/dictionary/cyberspace.

10 Obama, *International Strategy for Cyberspace: Prosperity, Security and Openness in a Networked World*, pg. 3.

11 Gartner IT Glossary of Terms, accessed online 31 Dec 2015, found at: http://www.gartner.com/it-glossary/it-information-technology.

12 Ibid.

13 *United States National Military Strategy for Cyber Operations* and described online on 18 Oct 2015, found at: http://fas.org/sgp/crs/natsec/R43848.pdf.

14 U.S. Congressional Research Report R43848, Catherine A. Theohary and Anne I. Harrington, "*Cyber Operations in DOD Policy and Plans: Issues for Congress*", 15 September, 2015, accessed online 18 Oct 2015, pg.2, found at: http://fas.org/sgp/crs/natsec/R43848.pdf.

15 As defined by: http://whatis.techtarget.com/definition/Confidentiality-integrity-and-availability-CIA.

[16] Adithya Chemudupati, et al, "The convergence of IT and Operational Technology," (ATOS Scientific Community, 2012), accessed online 5 Jan 2016, found at: https://atos.net/.../ascent-whitebook -the-convergence-of-it-and-operational-technology.pdf.

[17] As described by Microsoft's "The OSI Model's Seven Layers Defined and Functions Explained," found at: https://support.microsoft.com/en-us/kb/103884.

[18] Shawn Riley, "'Cyber Terrain': A Model for Increased Understanding of Cyber Activity," Oct 7, 2014, found at: https://www.linkedin.com/pulse/20141007190806-36149934--cyber-terrain-a-model-for-increased-understanding-of-cyber-activity.

[19] See https://en.wikipedia.org/wiki/OSI_model.

[20] "In the client-server architectural model, a system is decomposed into client and server processors or processes. Servers provide computational resources (or services), which clients consume." Craig, Borysowich, "Network Architecture Types," *Toolbox for IT Online*, Sep 17, 2010, accessed online 31 Dec 2015, found at: http://it.toolbox.com/blogs/enterprise-solutions/network-architecture-types-41375.

[21] "Peer-to-peer file sharing is the distribution and sharing of digital media using peer-to-peer (P2P) networking technology. P2P file sharing allows users to access media files such as books, music, movies, and games using a P2P software program that searches for other connected computers on a P2P network to locate the desired content." Carmack, Carman. "How Bit Torrent Works," *How Stuff Works Online,* accessed 2 Feb 2016, found at: http://computer.howstuffworks.com/bittorrent1.htm. See also, Clive Thompson, The Bittorrent Effect", *Wired Online,* Jan 1, 2005, found at: http://www.wired.com/2005/01/bittorrent-2/ and Bit Torrent.Com found at: http://www.bittorrent.com/.

[22] J.H. Saltzer, D.P. Reed, and D.D. Clark, *End-to-End Arguments in System Design*, (M.I.T. Laboratory of Computer Science, Nov 1984), found at: http://web.mit.edu/Saltzer/www/publications/endtoend/endtoend.pdf.

[23] Ernst and Young Cyber Advisory, "Cyber Threat Intelligence – How to get Ahead of Cybercrime," Nov 2014, pg. 2, found at: http://www.ey.com/Publication/vwLUAssets/EY-cyber-threat-intelligence-how-to-get-ahead-of-cybercrime/$FILE/EY-cyber-threat-intelligence-how-to-get-ahead-of-cybercrime.pdf.

[24] "Cyber: War in the Fifth Dimension," *The Economist,* Jul 1, 2010, accessed online 31 Dec 2015, found at: http://www.economist.com/node/16478792?story_id=16478792&fsrc=rss. For more on former Secretary of the Air Force Thomas C. Reed's memoirs, see *At the Abyss: An Insider's History of the Cold War*, (Presidio Press, New York, NY, 2005).

[25] Cliff Stoll, *The Cuckoo's Egg*, Bantam Doubleday Dell Publishing, New York, New York, 1986.

[26] Kim A. Taipale, *"Cyber Deterrence"*, Stilwell Center for Advanced Studies in Science and Technology Policy, World Policy Institute, USA, April 2010 (v2.1), pg. 3.

[27] Ibid.

[28] Ponemon Institute LLC., "2017 Cost of Cyber-Crime Study," Dec 2017, found at: https://www.accenture.com/t20170926T072837Z__w__/us-en/_acnmedia/PDF-61/Accenture-2017-CostCyberCrimeStudy.pdf.

[29] Ibid.

[30] This number is likely much higher since many companies do not report every breach. Ibid.

[31] Michael Daniel, "Our Latest Tool to Combat Cyber Attacks: What You Need to Know," The United States White House Executive Order on Sanctions, April 1, 2015, accessed online 31 Dec 2016, found at: https://www.whitehouse.gov/blog/2015/04/01/our-latest-tool-combat-cyber-attacks-what-you-need-know.

[32] Owen Tullos and Gary Brown, "On the Spectrum of Cyber Operations," *Small Wars Journal*, found on-line Nov 24, 2019 at: https://smallwarsjournal.com/jrnl/art/on-the-spectrum-of-cyberspace-operations.

[33] According to the Merriam-Webster dictionary, a hacker is a person who illegally gains access to and sometimes tampers with information in a computer system. Found at: http://www.merriam-webster.com/dictionary/hacker.

[34] Derived from the *"Proceeding from the Workshop on Cyber Crime,"* Council of European Convention on Cyber Crime, pg. 211, accessed online 18 Oct 2015 and found at: https://cs.brown.edu/courses/csci1950-p/sources/lec16/Vatis.pdf.

[35] See Cyber Warfare term in Michael N. Schmitt, ed., *The Tallinn Manual on the International Law Applicable to Cyber Warfare*, (Cambridge University Press, UK, 2013), pg. 141.

[36] The Life-Cycle explanation is derived from Ernst and Young's "Cyber Threat Intelligence – How to Get Ahead of Cybercrime," pg. 6. Other organizations such as Lockheed Martin and MITRE, prefers to describe the cycle as the "Cyber Kill Chain", see https://attack.mitre.org/resources/enterprise-introduction/.

[37] A zero-day vulnerability refers to a hole in software that is unknown to the vendor. This security hole is then exploited by hackers before the vendor becomes aware and hurries to fix it—this exploit is called a zero-day attack. Social engineering is an attack vector that relies heavily on human interaction and often involves tricking people into breaking normal security procedures. Spear phishing is an email that appears to be from an individual or business that you know. But it isn't. It's from the same criminal

hackers who want your credit card and bank account numbers, passwords, and the financial information on your PC. Watering Hole is a computer attack strategy identified in 2012 by RSA Security, in which the victim is a particular group (organization, industry, or region). In this attack, the attacker guesses or observes which websites the group often uses and infects one or more of them with malware.

[38] Council of Europe, Convention of Cybercrime, Sept 23, 2001, Budapest, Hungary, Article 11. Accessed online 31 Dec 2015, found at: http://www.europarl.europa.eu/meetdocs/2014_2019/documents/libe/dv/7_conv_budapest_/7_conv_budapest_en.pdf . Although the Budapest Convention is widely accepted and ratified my many states, notably absent from the list of signatories is Russia and China.

[39] Ibid, Article 2.

[40] Ibid, Article 3.

[41] Ibid, Article 4.

[42] Ibid, Article 5.

[43] Ibid, Article 6.

[44] Ibid, Article 7.

[45] Ibid, Article, 8.

[46] Council of Europe, pg. 8.

[47] U.S. Department of Defense, *Law of War Manual*, June 2015, FN 15 on pg. 998, found at: http://www.defense.gov/Portals/1/Documents/pubs/Law-of-War-Manual-June-2015.pdf.

[48] Brown and Tullos.

[49] Originally in U.S. Code Title 50, the law has been moved under T-18. See 18 United States Code, Chapter 37 "Espionage and Censorship."

[50] Federal Bureau of Investigation website found at: https://www.fbi.gov/about-us/investigate/counterintelligence/economic-espionage and USC T-18 Section 1831 and 1832.

[51] Committee on Offensive Information Warfare.

[52] Department of Homeland Security, Federal Emergency Management Agency National Response Plan, Cyber Incident Annex, December 2004, pg. CYB-2. Found at: https://www.fema.gov/media-library-data/20130726-1825-25045-8307/cyber_incident_annex_2004.pdf.

[53] Although moderately modified, this definition is based on the definition of cyber-attack as written in the *Yale Law Review*, posted Nov, 16, 2011, titled: "The Law of Cyber-Attack" by Oona A. Hathaway, Rebecca Crootof, Philip Levitz, Haley Nix, Aileen Nowlan, William Perdue, and Julia Spiegel, pg. 10.

[54] They include: Chemical Sector, Commercial Facilities Sector, Communications Sector, Critical Manufacturing Sector, Dams Sector, Defense Industrial Base Sector, Emergency Services Sector, Energy Sector, Financial Services Sector, Food and Agriculture Sector, Government Facilities Sector, Healthcare and Public Health Sector, Information Technology Sector, Nuclear Reactors, Materials, and Waste Sector, Transportation Systems Sector, and Water and Wastewater Systems Sector. Found at: http://www.dhs.gov/sector-specific-agencies.

[55] Nuisance is a relative term, but for the purposes of this book, it relates to the perspective of the state and continued functioning of the vital functions of the nation's critical infrastructure. It is realized that private corporations may not consider DDoS a nuisance; however, as long as their vital functions and operations continue without hindrance, then the effect is a nuisance.

[56] Barak Obama, "Executive Order -- "Blocking the Property of Certain Persons Engaging in Significant Malicious Cyber-Enabled Activities," April 1, 2015, found at: https://www.whitehouse.gov/the-press-office/2015/04/01/executive-order-blocking-property-certain-persons-engaging-significant-m.

[57] Morgan Chalfant, "Russia Behind 'Sophisticated Cyberattack' on Pentagon Computer *System*", *The Washington FreeBeacon*, 2015, accessed online 1 Nov 2015, found at: http://freebeacon.com/national-security/russia-behind-sophisticated-cyberattack-on-pentagon-computer-system/.

[58] The Conversation, "How hackers who commit cyber-attacks are traced," *MyBroadBand Online*, 5 Dec 2015, accessed online 5 Dec 2015, found at: http://mybroadband.co.za/news/security/148621-how-hackers-who-commit-cyber-attacks-are-traced.html .

[59] U.S. Department of Defense, *2015 DoD Cyber Strategy*, (Washington DC, 2015), pg. 2, found at: http://www.defense.gov/Portals/1/features/2015/0415_cyber-strategy/Final_2015_DoD_CYBER_STRATEGY_for_web.pdf.

[60] A note of caution – "detrimental" is a subjective descriptor and is meant to be based upon the perspective of the nation's ability to continue executing it vital daily functions (CI). There is no desire here to estimate exactly how long the effect would last or how quickly the state could reconstitute. The point is that a threshold was crossed and the government is responsible for the proper functioning of its national economic security apparatus. Each case of CINS would be unique and would necessitate

an evaluation as whether or not the CEMA crossed this threshold.

61 Hathaway, et al, pg. 15.

62 DDoS is a programmed flood of legitimate Internet traffic designed to overwhelm or crash the target networks for a specified period of time and usually originates from several "vectors" through the use of botnets.

63 Customary international law differs from the U.N. Charter in that it is not necessarily found in a signed treaty of compact. It is a product of "the general and consistent practice of states if the practice is followed out of a sense of legal obligation." In discussing the state of customary international law regarding CEMA below the use of force threshold, "cyberspace is a permissive regime" as long as "cyber activity remains below the level of use of force and does not otherwise interfere with the target nation's sovereignty, it would not be prohibited by international law." Colonel Gary Brown and Major Keira Poellet, "The Customary International Law of Cyberspace," *Strategic Studies Quarterly*, Fall 2012, (Air University Press, Maxwell AFB AL.), pg. 126, found at: http://www.au.af.mil/au/ssq/2012/fall/brown-poellet.pdf.

64 Michael N. Schmitt, "Below the Threshold Cyber Operations: the Countermeasures of Response Option and International Law," *Virginia Journal of International Law*, Vol 54:3, Nov 2013, pg. 698, accessed online 2 Nov 2015, found at: http://www.vjil.org/assets/pdfs/vol54/Schmitt-v7-JRN FINAL TO PUBLISH.pdf .

65 Antolin-Jenkins, pg. 168.

66 *Tallinn Manual*, pg. 54.

67 *Tallinn Manual*, pg. 54.

68 The notion of "countermeasures" will be explored fully in Chapter Four.

69 Michael N. Schmitt, pg. 698.

70 Michael Riley, "How Russian Hackers Stole the Nasdaq," *Bloomberg Business News*, July 17, 2014, found at: http://www.bloomberg.com/bw/articles/2014-07-17/how-russian-hackers-stole-the-nasdaq.

71 Ibid.

72 Michael N Schmitt, pg. 700.

73 *United States National Military Strategy for Cyberspace Operations*, Defense Cyber Operations as explained by IT WikiLaw, accessed online 8 Nov 2015, found at: http://itlaw.wikia.com/wiki/Defensive_cyberspace_operations.

74 U.S. CYBER COMMAND, ACHIEVE AND MAINTAIN SUPERIORITY IN CYBERSPACE: COMMAND VISION FOR U.S. CYBER COMMAND (March 2018), pg. 6, found at: https://www.cybercom.mil/Portals/56/Documents/USCYBERCOM%20Vision%20April%202018 .pdf?ver=2018-06-14-152556-010.

75 Ibid.

76 The Austrian Military, "The Austrian Cyber Strategy", March 2013, Vienna, Austria, accessed online on 3 Oct 2015, found at: https://www.bka.gv.at/DocView.axd?CobId=50999.

77 The French Ministry of Defence, "Information Systems Defence and Security – France's Strategy", Feb 2011, accessed online 3 Oct 2015, found at: http://www.ssi.gouv.fr/uploads/IMG/pdf/2011-02- 15_Information_system_defence_and_security_-_France_s_strategy.pdf.

78 The *Tallinn Manual*, pg. 261.

79 JP 3-12(R) defines response action (a similar term) as those deliberate, authorized defensive actions which are taken external to the DODIN to defeat ongoing or imminent threats to defend DOD cyberspace capabilities or other designated systems. See Joint Publication 3-12 (R), pg. II-3.

80 Schmitt, pg. 714.

81 Herbert Lin, "Responding to Sub-Threshold Cyber Intrusions: A Fertile Topic for Research and Discussion," *Georgetown Journal*, Georgetown University, 2015, pg. 6, accessed online 5 Dec 2015, found at: http://journal.georgetown.edu/wp-content/uploads/2015/07/127_gj124_Lin-CYBER-20111.pdf.

82 Most authors agree that "counter-cyber" or "counter operations" would appear offensive to the adversary. The perspective of recipient of the action would be different than the initiator of the action or response. See the *Tallinn Manual*, pg. 257.

83 Department of Homeland Security (and Presidential Policy Directive 21) terms accessed online 18 Oct 2015, found at: http://www.dhs.gov/what-security-and-resilience.

84 *2015 DoD Cyber Strategy*, pg. 11.

85 DOD Military Dictionary of Terms, accessed online 3 Oct 2015, found at: http://www.dtic.mil/doctrine/dod_dictionary/.

86 United States Military Joint Publication 3-12 (R), pg. II-14.

87 http://whatis.techtarget.com/definition/offensive-security.

[88] Alex Stevenson, "UK to develop offensive cyber capability," Politics.co.uk, 12 Nov 2010, accessed online 15 Nov 2015, found at: http://politics.co.uk/news/2010/11/12/uk-to-develop-offensive-cyber-capability.

[89] *The Tallinn Manual*, pg. 258.

[90] The Conversation.

[91] Ibid.

[92] The Office of the Director of National Intelligence (ODNI), "Background to "Assessing Russian Activities and Intentions in Recent US Elections": The Analytic Process and Cyber Incident Attribution," Jan 6, 2017, pg. 1, found on-line at: https://www.dni.gov/files/documents/ICA_2017_01.pdf.

[93] Ibid, pg.1.

[94] Ibid, pg. 2.

[95] Ibid, pg. 2.

[96] Thomas Rid and Ben Buchanan, "Attributing Cyber Attacks," *The Journal of Strategic Studies*, 2015 Vol. 38, Nos. 1–2, pg. 4, found at: http://dx.doi.org/10.1080/01402390.2014.977382.

[97] Ibid, pg. 5.

[98] Ibid, pg. 9.

[99] Ibid, pg. 10.

[100] For more details on what is involved in the technical attribution process see, Eric F. Mejia, Colonel, USAF, "Act and Actor Attribution in Cyberspace: A Proposed Analytic Framework," in *Strategic Studies Quarterly*, Spring 2014, found at: http://www.au.af.mil/au/ssq/digital/pdf/spring_2014/Mejia.pdf, and Greg Farnham, "Tools and Standards for Cyber Threat Intelligence Projects," SANS Institute, found at: http://www.sans.org/reading-room/whitebook_s/warfare/tools-standards-cyber-threat-intelligence-projects-34375.

[101] Rid and Buchanan, pg. 21.

[102] Ibid. pp. 24-26.

[103] Department of Homeland Security Report: "DHS Intelligence Assessment: Malicious Cyber Actors Target US Universities and Colleges," Jan 14, 2015, found at: https://publicintelligence.net/dhs-university-cyber-threats/.

[104] Roderic Broadhurst, Peter Grabosky, Mamoun Alazab and Steve Chon, "Organizations and Cyber Crime: An Analysis of the Nature of Groups engaged in Cyber Crime," (International Journal of Cyber Criminology, Vol 8 Issue 1 January - June 2014, ANU Cybercrime Observatory, Australian

National   University,   Australia),   pg.   2,   found   at: http://www.cybercrimejournal.com/broadhurstetalijcc2014vol8issue1.pdf.

[105] Gordon Lubold and Damian Paletta, "Pentagon Sizing Up Email Hack of Its Brass," *The Wall Street Journal*, April 7, 2015, found at: http://www.wsj.com/articles/pentagon-sizing-up-email-hack-of-its-brass-1438989404 .

[106] Eric Bonabeau, "Cyber-Security Can't Ignore Human Behavior" accessed online 14 Nov 2015, found   at: http://www.theatlantic.com/technology/archive/2011/03/cyber-security-cant-ignore-human-behavior/72826/ .

[107] For example, the financial profession requires a course in Human Behavior for many MBAs, and the New York Stock Exchange tracks a fear index (VIX) as an indicator or gauge for volatility of the market based upon human behavior. Menacham Brenner and Dan Galai, "New Financial Instruments For Hedging Changes in Volatility," *Financial Analysts Journal*, Jul/Aug 1989, 45, 4, ABI/INFORM Global, pg. 61.

[108] Ernst and Young, "Cyber Threat Intelligence," pg. 5.

[109] As quoted from the 2016 interview by Lesley Stahl titled "The Great Brain Robbery," for CNS News conducted on Jan 17, 2016, found at: http://www.cbsnews.com/news/60-minutes-great-brain-robbery-china-cyber-espionage/.

[110] "2018 Foreign Economic Espionage in Cyberspace," Report by National Counterintelligence and Security Center, pg. 1, found at https://www.dni.gov/files/NCSC/documents/news/20180724-economic-espionage-pub.pdf.

[111] Ibid, pg. 1.

[112] Ibid, pg. 5.

[113] ONCE, pg. 7.

[114] U.S.-China Economic and Security Review Commission, "2015 Report to Congress," (Washington DC, 2015) pg. 11.

[115] Ibid, pg. 12.

[116] Nicholas Eftimiades, "The Impact of Chinese Espionage on the United States," The Diplomat, Dec 4, 2018, found on-line at: https://thediplomat.com/2018/12/the-impact-of-chinese-espionage-on-the-united-states/.

[117] U.S.-China Economic and Security Review Commission, pg. 12.

[118] The 2018 Foreign Economic Espionage in Cyberspace Report, pg. 8.

[119] Ibid, pg. 8.

[120] Recorded Future, "Breaking the Code on Russian Malware," Nov 20, 2014, found at: https://www.recordedfuture.com/russian-malware-analysis/.

[121] Ibid.

[122] Ibid.

[123] As noted by the Federal Bureau of Investigation Report " Economic Espionage," July 23, 2015, found at: https://www.fbi.gov/news/stories/2015/july/economic-espionage/economic-espionage

[124] 2015 Report to Congress, pg. 12.

[125] Ernst and Young, "Cyber Threat Intelligence," pg. 5.

[126] The Intel Team at Mandiant, "Not Your Average Cybercriminal: A Look at the Diverse Threats to the Financial Services Industry," September 23, 2013, accessed online 8 Nov 2015, found at: https://www.fireeye.com/blog/threat-research/2013/09/average-cybercriminal-diverse-threats-financial-services.html.

[127] See INTERPOL's website at: http://www.interpol.int/Crime-areas/Cybercrime/Cybercrime.

[128] Cory Bennett and Elise Viebeck, "ISIS preps for cyber war," *The Hill Online*, May 17, 2015, accessed online 5 Jan 2016, found at: http://thehill.com/policy/cybersecurity/242280-isis-preps-for-cyber-war.

[129] ONCE, pg. 10.

[130] Anonymous (used as a mass noun) is a loosely associated international network of activist and hacktivist entities. A website nominally associated with the group describes it as "an Internet gathering" with "a very loose and decentralized command structure that operates on ideas rather than directives". The group became known for a series of well-publicized publicity stunts and DDoS attacks on government, religious, and corporate websites. https://en.wikipedia.org/wiki/Anonymous_(group)

[131] Ernst and Young, "Cyber Threat Intelligence," pg. 5.

[132] Surfwatch, "Cyber Intelligence" accessed on 25 Oct 15 at: https://www.surfwatchlabs.com/threat-categories.

[133] Matt Richtel, "Canada Arrests 15-Year-Old In Web Attack," *The New York Times*, April 20, 2000, accessed online 24 Nov 2015, found at: http://www.nytimes.com/2000/04/20/business/canada-arrests-15-year-old-in-web-attack.html.

[134] Oona A. Hathaway, Rebecca Crootof, Philip Levitz, Haley Nix, Aileen Nowlan, William Perdue, Julia Spiegel, "The Law of Cyber Attack", *California Law Review*, 2012, pg. 29.

[135] Hathaway, pg. 41.

[136] Cameron S. D. Brown, "Investigating and Prosecuting Cyber Crime: Forensic Dependencies and Barriers to Justice," *International Journal of Cyber Criminology*, Vol. 9, Issue 1 Jan – 1 Jun 2105, pg. 6, found at: http://www.cybercrimejournal.com/Brown2015vol9issue1.pdf.

[137] Ibid.

[138] Martin Evan, "Hackers steal £650 million in world's biggest bank raid," *The Telegraph*, London, UK, accessed online 3 Dec 2015, found at: http://www.telegraph.co.uk/news/uknews/crime/11414191/Hackers-steal-650-million-in-worlds-biggest-bank-raid.html.

[139] The CFAA prohibits anyone from accessing a computer "without authorization" or by "exceeding authorized access" for certain purposes, which includes attempts to "obtain information" from a "protected computer" if doing so includes "interstate or foreign … communication." For more on the Computer Fraud and Abuse Act (CFAA) see 18 U.S.C. Section 1030.

[140] Melissa Riofrio, "Hacking back: Digital revenge is sweet but risky," *PCWorld Magazine Online*, May 9, 2013, accessed online 9 Jan 2016, found at: http://www.pcworld.com/article/2038226/hacking-back-digital-revenge-is-sweet-but-risky.html.

[141] Westphalian sovereignty is the principle of international law that each nation state has sovereignty over its territory and domestic affairs, to the exclusion of all external powers, on the principle of non-interference in another country's domestic affairs, and that each state (no matter how large or small) is equal in international law. The doctrine is named after the Peace of Westphalia, signed in 1648.

[142] Moore's Law is a computing term which originated around 1970; the simplified version of this law states that processor speeds, or overall processing power for computers will double every two years. A quick check among technicians in different computer companies shows that the term is not very popular but the rule is still accepted. See "Moore's Law" at: http://www.mooreslaw.org/.

[143] Kim Zetter, "The Biggest Security Threats We'll Face in 2016," *Wired Magazine*, Jan 1, 2016, accessed online 2 Jan 2016, found at: http://www.wired.com/2016/01/the-biggest-security-threats-well-face-in-2016/.

CHAPTER THREE

ASSESSING THE THREAT: CYBER INCIDENTS OF NATIONAL SIGNIFICANCE

O ver the past decades, several cyber incidents of national significance (CINS) occurred, each with varying motives, scales, severity, and outcomes. Looking at cases that fall into the high end of CEMA (that lie beyond cyber-attack but short of the threshold of war on the spectrum of cyber conflict) is also informative for any modern, Internet-connected nation that is developing a coercive cyber strategy. The four cases presented below show examples where the United States may choose to posture itself for response options beyond relying on just corporate cyber defense, cyber information sharing, and law enforcement activities. At the level of CINS, a whole of government effort should focus on the touch-points or intersections where government support, collaboration, or coordination might better enable private sector response; or in other cases where the government should consider transitioning from 'industry-led mitigation with government support' to 'government-led mitigation with industry support.' With the CINS framework, the modern national government should possess a conceptual understanding of the types of CEMA for which they could take proactive action. These cases are presented so that all modern nations may understand and relate the observations to their respective countries and national cybersecurity policies.

This chapter's research uses Stephen Van Evera's definition of historical explanatory research within case studies which uses deduction to explain the causes, patterns, or consequences of historical cases. A case study is used for several reasons, but mini-case studies are used to illustrate cases that use cyber effects for intrinsic political or national security import. In this chapter, the mini-case studies will test how CEMA affected a target state and if it can be determined that such CEMA was selected as an instrument of state power of choice over or in conjunction with other instruments (e.g., economic, diplomatic, military) for the goal of a political or national security purpose. Specifically, this chapter aims to test the theory that asserts "states or state-sponsored organizations will use CEMA, even to the level of CINS, as a means to influence and pressure a target state while avoiding a full fledge war" by asking a series of questions such as "did the victim state generally act in an ad hoc manner when attacked, or did it develop effective strategies to integrate its national security resources?" And, "What were the elements of national power that the victim state used to respond to the CEMA?" The full list of questions is evaluated at the end of the chapter. By examining the cases in detail through the lens of investigating several questions, common factors can be determined and the reliability of the theory may be strengthened. The goal of this chapter is to discover the factors that explain why CEMA was selected as the desired instrument employed.

Given the relative infancy of cyber conflict and the over-classification that many states place on their incidents of CEMA, there are not many cases available for this investigation. Although four is not a large sample size, they do illustrate the relevant points necessary for an ample understanding of cyber conflict, and for which a cogent discussion may be had concerning coercion in the cyber domain in subsequent chapters. Those points include, but are not limited to: the vulnerability to the victim state to CEMA, the nature of the threat, the structure and capabilities (to include possessing a national cyber strategy) to defend against the CEMA, the nature and types of response(s) the victim initiated during the CINS, the reliance (or not) on private partners in that response, and the geopolitical context of the conflict. Optimally, a greater number of examples, both with similar and disparate characteristics would strengthen the examination.

The brief generalizations below of such complex cases may not capture all of the nuisances of each conflict, however, this chapter will isolate several of the relevant points mentioned above within each case to explain the political factors involved and the choice of state means used to achieve the effects. Consequently, the findings of the mini-case studies should be regarded as an illustration of the various motives, scale, severity, and outcomes the United States may encounter in the future. The observations and conclusions drawn from these studies set the foundation for policy making and the application of coercion within a national cybersecurity strategy.

Case selection was based upon several criteria. The first criterion was based upon cases where one state (the victim) experienced CINS as part of a larger conflict between another state or state-sponsored entity. The second criterion was based upon instances where a conflict was centered upon political or national security reasons. The third criterion was based upon cases where the actors were identical (Russia is used in two cases), but their use of CEMA was different. The fourth criterion for selection was cases where the situation was considerably different in type (method, sophistication, delivery means, etc.) of cyber-attack. In the Russian attacks against Georgia and Ukraine, CEMA was a component of a broader warfare strategy, whereas in Estonia, CEMA was executed in a purely non-kinetic fashion. The indictment of the five Chinese 3 PLA officers for corporate espionage case was selected because China was the protagonist and the objective and type (i.e., espionage) was distinctively different than the first two cases. Stuxnet was selected as the fourth case because it involved the United States and Israel allegedly along with the notably unusual method of CEMA delivery that presents rather alarming conclusions about the future of CINS and the use of cyber means in conflict.

Estonia, 2007 -*Denial of Service Attacks*

On April 26, 2007, the small Baltic state of Estonia experienced a sustained, three-week combination distributed denial of service (DDoS) attack, e-mail spam, website defacement, and domain name server attacks directed at the government, the Estonian news services, and major financial institutions.[1] This was the first large-scale CINS directed at a state and was a coercive instrument in a political conflict between a North Atlantic Treaty Organization (NATO) nation and Russia. Not only are the geopolitical implications significant, but this case also sheds light on the organizational aspects of national cybersecurity and the role of the global partnerships to reestablish Estonia's cyberspace functionality post-event.[2]

The overpowering 2007 cyber-enabled malicious operation was in response to growing tensions between the Estonian government and the ethnic Russian minority (approximately 25% of the Estonia's total population).[3] The multi-faceted CEMA event arose due to the Estonian government's removal of a bronze monument of a Soviet Union soldier in Tallinn, Estonia following months of tension between the government and the ethnic Russian citizens.[4] This event was part of a longer history of tension between Russia and Estonia that dated back to the Cold War. During the Cold War, the Soviet Union's leadership relocated thousands of ethnic Russians to Estonia to "Russify" the Baltic state and to build cohesion throughout the Soviet Union.[5] Following the fall of the Berlin Wall in 1989, Estonia was quick to separate itself from Russia and joined NATO in 2004.

Estonia's move into NATO and away from its previous Soviet alliance, now represented by Russia, caused Russia to be alarmed since it relied on neighboring states to "buffer" it from potential Western aggression. Estonia's move away from Russia was a source of increasing tension between the two nations, further enflamed by the events of April 2007. The Soviet soldier monument represented the "Suppressor of Independence" to the Estonians while the diaspora of ethnic Russians viewed the statue as a symbol of the Red Army's role in World War II.[6] The Parliament's decision to remove the monument sparked rioting in the streets of Tallinn and the beginning of the DDoS shortly thereafter. The rioting and DDoS gave rise to escalating hostilities (physical and virtual), which were festering as a result of the underlying tension between the Russian minority and the rest of the Estonian people.[7]

Fortunately, Estonian's decision to invest heavily in cyberspace, including innovations that embraced the creation of Skype, paid dividends for the nation from a societal perspective, but also created significant vulnerabilities to cyber-attack.[8] Estonia is a small nation that significantly incorporates cyberspace into its normal daily functions, which include a large number of government services (the first nation in the world to go strictly to on-line voting[9]), news services, communications, banking, and education.[10] In fact, more than 355 government services are solely on line.[11] According to Mihkel Tammet, the IT Director of the Estonian Defense Ministry, the country is so reliant upon the Internet for services that the government is referred to as a "bookless government."[12] Further, 97 percent of all bank transactions occurred online in 2007, with 60 percent of Estonians claiming they used the Internet on a daily basis.[13] Additionally, over 40 percent of Estonians access online news sources daily.[14] Consequently, Estonia is a nation quite reliant on cyberspace for normal government and private services. Estonia's dependency on technology and cyberspace however was also a vulnerability. The 2007 DDoS attacks targeted hundreds of government, banking, newsbook (Estonia's on-line news sources), and university websites for slightly longer than three weeks.[15] The extensive reliance on cyberspace for Estonian daily government and private services provided Russian hackers with the opportunity to send a message to the leadership of Estonia – namely, Russians can apply pressure in the form of CEMA upon the Estonian government.

Disruptive denial of service attacks have been used by hackers since the mid-1980s, but the 2007 Estonian attack was unusual in its scale (number of government and private entities targeted simultaneously), duration (three weeks[16]), and effect (loss of functionality in several strictly online services due to high cyberspace dependency). DDoS attacks principally target specific websites and networks to block the access of legitimate users, rendering the site or network unavailable. DDoS attacks can be initiated through any number of methods, "including the relentless transmission of irrelevant information to tie up [or overwhelm] a server so that legitimate requests for information remain unanswered."[17] Malicious cyber actors also use CEMA to block the transmission of routing information, which prevents legitimate requests from reaching their destination. Alternatively, hackers also use CEMA to impede communication between servers or networks so that information cannot be transmitted or received.

The DDoS did not come as a surprise to the Estonian government or the Internet security community who were watching events deteriorate in Tallinn. Oftentimes in Estonia, when there were riots in the streets, the conflict would "go cyber."[18] In the days leading up to the DDoS attacks, several cybersecurity entities were monitoring the hackers' call to cyber-arms in an attempt to find comrades willing to participate in the DDoS attack. Four hours after the DDoS attack began, at 2:00 AM on Friday 27 April, the governmental cyber teams responsible for the national networks and servers realized they had to move services to "well-defended" web servers in the hopes of handling the excessive traffic. What began as a nuisance, in a matter of hours escalated into a national security issue and exceeded what the Estonian government could handle by themselves.[19] Political institutions were the first to be targeted and the Estonian Parliamentary email servers had to be shut down. "The main causes for concern were the DDoS attacks on the Estonian infrastructure, as they endangered the availability and functionality of services crucial to the functioning of Estonian society."[20] Within the first hours of the DDoS attacks, the news outlet *Postimes Online* was also shut down.[21] By the end of the first day of CEMA, the main targets were the websites of: the Estonian presidency and its parliament, almost all of the country's government ministries which operate solely online, the political parties, three of the country's six big news organizations, two of the largest banks, and several firms specializing in communications.[22]

Financial organizations, universities, Internet Service Providers, and other government institutions were overwhelmed with CEMA in the following days. The attacks came in three waves: from April 27, when the Bronze Soldier riots erupted, climaxing around May 3; then on May 8 and 9, a couple of the most celebrated dates in the Russian calendar (when Russia marks Victory Day over Nazi Germany and when President Vladimir Putin delivered another hostile speech attacking Estonia and indirectly likening the Bush administration to the Hitler regime); and finally during the week of May 14th.[23] Cyber defenders attempted to restore functionality while blocking attacks from IP addresses originating from Vietnam, Egypt, Peru, the United States, and Russia.[24] On May 10, the CEMA had forced Hansabank, Estonia's largest bank and a pioneer of many of Estonia's IT developments in the 1990s, to shut down its Internet-based operations. This was significant on three counts: first, it forced the cessation of the online banking capabilities for Estonians in a country so dependent on online banking; second, it severed the connection between Hansabank and its ATMs throughout Estonia (thus disallowing customer access to their money); and third, the CEMA broke the connection between

Hansabank and the rest of the world, thus preventing Estonian debit cards from working outside of the country.[25] Other Estonian banks were also hit, but they did not publish the impact to their operations for fear of loss of confidence in their firms. Many researchers concluded the impacts felt by each of the financial institutions were similar to Hansabank.

Beyond the above noted sectors cyber incidents, national leaders worried that the cyber-attacks could also impact other key services such emergency response communications, hospital services, power distribution, etc. There was no knowing in the opening salvos of the CEMA where the adversary would stop and it was alarming to leaders in Estonia and around the world, just how vulnerable a technological advanced nation could be to cyber-attacks.

Estonia activated its Computer Emergency Response Team (CERT) early in the series of CEMA in order to resolve the malicious cyber activity. However, over the course of the three week CINS, targeted websites grew to number in the hundreds as government services, banking systems, media outlets, and Estonian universities were systematically attacked and shut down.[26] Because of the combination of DDoS attacks, e-mail spam, website defacement, and domain name server attacks directed at the government and private corporations, the Estonian government elected to sever the nation's connection to the Internet – a singularly catastrophic event for such a hyperconnected government and society. This allowed Estonia, along with the assistance from several other government and private cybersecurity partners to contend with the remaining CEMA in a manageable way. If it were not for the help of Finland's, Germany's, Israel's, and Slovenia's CERTs, Estonia would not have been able to restore government and private services. The services were eventually restored by increasing Estonia's Internet services, by adding filtering mechanisms to drop malicious data before they reach the intended targets, and by blocking access and dropping traffic from outside the country.[27] The 2007 Estonian DDoS attacks were not just a single attack, but a series of attacks (CEMO) of varying scale, sophistication, and effect that forced government leaders to take extraordinary measures to overcome the political pressures as a result of escalating tensions between Estonia and Russia.

Although at least one arrest was made (Dmitri Galushkevich, an ethnic Russian student residing in Estonia), most assume the perpetrators were hacktivists of Russian ethnicity – the definitive role of the Russian government in the attacks against Estonia is still being debated. As mentioned earlier, Nashi (the Russian youth organization started by Vladimir Putin) took responsibility. Several cyber experts and researchers studied the events in Estonia and assessed with high probability that the Russian government was behind the CEMA in 2007.[28] Researchers opined that despite clear proof of Russian leadership direction, the systemic coordination and synchronization of the three week CINS was possible only by a sophisticated state actor with the vast means, command and control, capability, and capacity that Russia possessed. Hackers orchestrated the CEMA through the use of weblogs, web journals, and Russian-language chat rooms and would post the times and dates of scheduled attacks, lists of vulnerable Estonian sites, and even provide instructions on how to execute the DDoS against the Estonian infrastructure.[29] Additionally, many of the hackers used botnets from all over the globe – the "zombie computers commandeered in the attacks on Estonia alone resided in over fifty countries."[30] To further the claim of Russian coordination, researchers point to the fact that the tactic of using "third parties" or non-state affiliated organizations to implement Russian direction is common place. In several examples (prior and since the Estonia DDoS case), Russian leadership is known to "apply pressure" to countries that chose to disregard or move away from the former Soviet Republic's sphere of influence.[31] On occasion, former Soviet partners (e.g., Latvia, Georgia, Ukraine) sought to join Western Europe, namely NATO or the European Union (EU), and then incurred substantial costs (in the form of cessation of delivery of vital good/resources, withdrawal of funding or military support, or the use of insurgents to foment violence in the neighboring state) for leaving Russia's sphere of influence. It was not uncommon for Russia to cut off natural gas supplies to neighboring countries that did not do as the Russian leadership demanded.[32] Russia often asserted political pressure upon its allies who left Russia's political control and the Estonian DDoS cyber-attacks were typical of Russian political intimidation.

When weighing the factors of attribution, most international cyber experts cite these aspects as an indicators of Russian direction or complicit agreement in the execution of the 2007 Estonia CINS: Kremlin and other Russian IP addresses were used; online and offline protests were systematically coordinated in Russian chat rooms (as explained earlier); the scale (the great number of public and private sites attacked and the three week duration) and sophistication (size of CEMO and coordination involved) of the DDoS was beyond what typical hacktivists can usually orchestrate; the CEMA required lengthy (weeks) preparations and planning (more indicative of state or state-sponsored cyber organization); Nashi claimed responsibility; Russian political tactics were used; and Russian law enforcement refused to cooperate with Estonian counterparts.[33] Whatever the role Russia had in the attack, they played a key role in mobilizing the activists and ensuring the tension remained elevated.

Consequences of the Attacks

This was a prominent event that generated interest around the world. Although not a cyber war, cyber-enabled malicious operations can take on an element of coercive diplomacy when directed at critical infrastructure and government services. A few conclusions can be drawn.

No one died as a result of the Estonian cyber-attack, but the malicious effect was felt across government and private industry for months. Although no comprehensive study was conducted to determine the economic effect of the DDoS attacks on Estonia's economy, one of Estonia's sixteen banks reported a direct loss of $1 million during one 90-minute outage (remember that the DDoS lasted three weeks and occurred in three waves).[34] Other banks experienced similar outages, however none reported their losses. It was also recounted that credit cards and automatic tellers were non-functioning for an extended period during the CINS, which is significant when several of those institutions operate solely online.[35] For the customers of those financial institutions, three weeks of denied access to one's money is not a trivial affair. The losses were likely covered by the financial institutions' profit margins and the customers adapted to the hardships (else there would have been much more reported about the hardships in the press). The point to be made is not the financial impact, although that was an issue, but rather the political pressure applied to Estonia from an external source that forced privations on both government and private services in such a way that Estonia's leadership had to take Draconian actions (disconnected the country from the Internet, severing all virtual ties to the rest of the world[36]) in order to restore normal state functionality. Due to Estonia's reliance upon cyberspace, the effect of the forced isolation from the Internet and the resultant loss of online services and business was the resultant condition that another state or state-sponsored entity can impose costs upon a victim nation in the form of CEMA.

Had Estonia possessed the means and/or the strategy to defend itself effectively, then the CINS would have been easier to shield against and Estonia could have mitigated the malicious effects more certainly. Thanks to the other nations' CERTs, Estonia was able to respond to the CEMA (albeit after three weeks). Possessing the inherent cybersecurity capabilities is desired; however, possessing robust cybersecurity partnerships adds to a state's capabilities and capacities. As noted above, as the days and weeks progressed in 2007, Estonia developed a strategy to contend with the CEMA. It is advisable that other nations learn from Estonia's lessons prior experiencing a similar event and develop the means and strategy to defend critical their infrastructure – or else endure a comparable fate. Furthermore, had the event been more destructive (an elevated attack beyond DDoS), Estonia's ability to deliver daily services for its critical infrastructure (e.g., power, water, communication, financial, medical and lifesaving, etc.) would also been at risk. Moreover, in a more destructive CEMA, the effect incurred by Estonia may be similar to an armed attack – and an act of war. Although short of war, this case demonstrates how CEMA is not far removed from a level similar to kinetic military actions, and therefore should not be considered lightly.

In this case, the government did not comprehend what its key cyber terrain was and build in redundancy and resiliency in order to prevent devastating disruptions to normal daily life. Had the key cyber terrain (critical infrastructure) been identified prior, Estonia could have then expended the effort necessary to protect it and mitigate the effect of any cyber-attacks.

Regardless of whether or not Russia actually conducted or aided the attack, this style of cyber-attack fits well within the Russia's tactic of pressuring its neighbors that do not acquiesce to Russian supremacy/ideology and does not fit well with widely accepted norms of international state behavior. It was demonstrated in this case that a state can be pressured through the execution of CEMA directed at its vital centers of gravity (critical infrastructure). The sovereign responsibility of the state is to ensure the protection of its citizens and the good governance of the society; consequently, any external interference with that state's obligation is in violation of customary international law.[37] By directing, or at least tacitly condoning Nashi's CEMA, Russia was not acting as a responsible state. This political conflict points to the need to ensure international norms of behavior are enforced in cyberspace (legal aspects of cyber conflict will be covered in detail in Chapter Four). State action and responsibility in cyberspace is a topic of much discussion lately.[38]

This event highlights the need for international support and assistance both in the mitigation response but also in political solidarity and reaction for neighboring hostile states. This is especially relevant to small and developing states that do have the means to defend themselves in cyberspace. Furthermore, the assistance provided to Estonia during this conflict was not just from nation-states, but also from private cybersecurity industry firms and experts. Estonia had several well-established relationships with private Estonian cyber organizations and other nations' government and private cybersecurity firms which aided Estonia immensely during the conflict. Before conflict erupts, each nation should determine how and when it will seek the assistance of private industry in its national cyber defense, as well as when the state should take the lead in directing government and private actions.

Finally, the 2007 DDoS attacks against Estonia qualify as a cyber incident of national significance due to the scale, duration, and severity of the CEMO as well as the fact the attack was clearly the result of political tensions between Estonia and Russia. Most likely, Russia (through Nashi) used CEMA (which rose to the level of CINS) as a means to intimidate Estonian leadership while avoiding a full fledge war through triggering a NATO Article 5 response. Although the tensions were high between Estonia and Russia for decades, the events of 2007 further escalated those tensions by targeting CEMA at critical Estonian government and private online services. It is my assessment that the CINS was most likely perpetrated in lieu of more physical instruments of power such as a military strike or an insurgency, and was intended to send a message to Estonian leadership. CEMA provides protagonists with other less violent means of political intimidation and may be an instrument of national power of choice when war or physical conflict is not desired. The political motivation of the CINS was most likely meant to posit substantial pressure on Estonia for its continued move away from Russia's sphere of influence.

Russia's Invasion of Georgia in 2008 and Ukraine in 2014 - CEMO and Hybrid Warfare

The 2007 cyber-attacks against Estonia showed how a political disagreement, which included nations (Russia, Estonia) and hacktivists, led to the exertion of pressure on a sovereign nation, but not how CEMO might be used in coordination with physical forces to create even more powerful effects. The cyber-attacks in combination with physical attacks on Georgia in 2008 and Ukraine in 2014 demonstrate the highest level of a state's use of cyberspace for political ends. Although not declared wars, these two conflicts witnessed armed attacks and the use of force. The combined effects across the virtual and physical domains for political ends is called *hybrid warfare*. According to Russian General Valery Gerasimov, Chief of the General Staff of the Russian Federation, "[i]n the 21st century, a tendency toward the elimination of the differences between the states of war and peace is becoming discernible. Wars are now not even declared, but having begun, are not going according to a pattern we are accustomed to."[39] He went on to say, "[t]he very 'rules of war' have changed. The role of non-military means of achieving political and strategic goals have grown, and, in many cases, they have exceeded the power of force of weapons in their effectiveness."[40] These statements were in response to the Georgia conflict in 2008, but apply equally well in Ukraine in 2014-2016. In both conflicts, CEMO preluded and accompanied the initiation of physical combat within neighboring territories surrounding Russia. Hybrid warfare as General Gerasimov describes is the preferable method of conflict as currently envisioned by Russia. Technology has paved the way for new uses for cyberspace operations that allow for the execution of hybrid warfare – a significant evolution from guerilla warfare.

As with Estonia, both conflicts in Georgia and Ukraine demonstrate that ethnic differences abound all along Russia's periphery, which drove Russia's attempt to maintain influence in those two states' political circles. Given the centuries of Russian influence in Georgia and Ukraine (as well as in its other proximate neighbors), it was no surprise to leaders of both countries and to the international community when tensions spiraled out of control and Russia turned to intimidation and conflict. However, what was not anticipated was how Russia chose to use CEMO and hybrid warfare as a means to gain control of the conflict, invade those two sovereign nations, pressure leaders, maintain the strategic global narrative, and achieve its political goals.

Prior to and throughout both conflicts, Russian cyber-attacks increased the pressure on Georgia and Ukraine leaders. Both Georgia and Ukraine relied on technology and cyberspace for several vital national daily life functions. Consequently, during the conflicts, the victim states were largely blinded as to what was occurring while losing their ability to direct a national response. When the Russian cyber-attacks commenced, the victim states experienced an escalation of CEMA against governmental and private organizations and online infrastructure.[41] Both conflicts began with the denial and degradation of communication capabilities that left each country with substantially less ability, not only to communicate with their populace and military, but also the inability to tell their side of the struggle to the world.[42] Russia dominated the international narrative. Then cyber-attacks began with CEMO directed at military forces, Parliament, the Foreign Ministry, the Ministry of the Interior, law enforcement entities, news agencies, and banks.[43] The Russian hackers used sophisticated DDoS techniques, cross-site scripting, and SQL injection techniques[44] to overwhelm Georgian and Ukrainian cyber defenses.[45] Russian hackers made several attempts to sway international public opinion while simultaneously attacking banking. Although international opinion was not totally swayed, the international account of the conflict was largely controlled by Russia.

In December 2015, Russian cyber forces stepped up its CEMO to achieve even greater destructive cyber effects against Ukrainian electrical substations. This was the first time in history in which a nation struck another nation's power distribution system, leaving people without power. Highly destructive malware infected at least three regional power authorities in Ukraine that led to a power failure which left 225,000 people without electricity.[46] Researchers from antivirus provider ESET established that several Ukrainian power authorities were infected by 'BlackEnergy,' (malicious code discovered in 2007 included a host of new functions, including the ability to render infected computers unbootable and a component dubbed KillDisk, which destroys critical parts of a computer hard drive to sabotage industrial control systems.)[47] The latest BlackEnergy version also included a backdoored utility that gave attackers access to infected computers. A report by SANS and the Electricity Information Sharing and Analysis Center (EISAC) stated to the contrary that the CEMA were mislabeled as solely linked to BlackEnergy 3 and KillDisk. "BlackEnergy 3 was simply a tool used in Stage 1 of the attacks and KillDisk was an amplifying tool used in Stage 2 of the attacks."[48] In actuality, BlackEnergy 3 malware was used to gain a foothold into a multitude of organizations within Ukraine and not just the three impacted power distribution systems. This CEMA was enabled by a variety of approaches to gain access and use existing assets within Ukraine.

Confirming Russian attribution in the Ukrainian cyber-attack is still on-going.[49] However in 2014, the group behind BlackEnergy, which cybersecurity firm iSIGHT dubbed the Sandworm gang, "targeted the North Atlantic Treaty Organization, Ukrainian and Polish government agencies, and a variety of sensitive European industries. iSIGHT researchers say the Sandworm gang has ties to Russia, although readers are cautioned on attributing hacking attacks to specific groups or governments."[50] Conversely, researchers are clear to point out that definitive proof of Russian direction or responsibility is not possible since the perpetrators of the CEMA skillfully concealed their attack origins.[51] As with much of the sophisticated CEMA witnessed recently, it is difficult to definitively attribute the CEMA.

Consequently, policymakers rely on degrees of certainty when concluding who conducted the CEMA. Despite definitive attribution, accusations that the Russian military, Russia's intelligence service (the FSB), Russian nationalists, and Russian organized criminal organizations were behind the cyber-enabled malicious operations persist. The sheer scope, scale, sophisticated means and methods used, and the synchronization and integration of CEMA with Russian military operations places the attribution with high certainty (this author's opinion) on Russia. Regardless of who conducted the attacks, cybersecurity analysts from around the world concluded the bulk of the attacks originated from Russian IP addresses and only Russia gained from the CEMA during each conflict.[52] Ultimately, only Russia had the motive for and gained from the CINS perpetrated against Ukraine.

Ukrainian forces were clearly unprepared to defend their critical infrastructure against CEMA. Moreover, the use of CEMA directed at a nation's power supply system crosses a new threshold of CEMA although it fits within Russia's past use of conflict to intimidate its neighbors. If Russia is confirmed to have executed the electrical grid cyber-attack, then that act counters Article 2(4) of the U.N. Charter that stipulates member states "shall refrain in their international relations for the threat of use of force against the territorial integrity or political independence of any state, or in any other manner inconsistent with the Purposes of the United Nations."[53] The question remains however, what will the international community do about the attack on Ukraine's power system?

Both conflicts also had a hefty economic impact. The banks in each country had to cease their electronic services, which paralyzed Georgian and Ukrainian payments systems, leaving many citizens with no financial means for several weeks.[54] Although the conflict in Georgia was relatively short, its economy (measured by gross domestic product) fell 3.8% in 2009.[55] Ukraine's conflict is still ongoing and consequently its economy was hit much harder. In 2014, the Ukrainian economy fell 6.8% and for 2015 the economy dropped another 9% in 2016, while its inflation rate soared by 46%.[56] The conflicts in both countries resulted in a downturn in goods and services exchanged, an increase in unemployment, lack of investing, and a severe decrease in spending from both domestic and international sources. For the Ukrainian economy, the national economic depression continues today.[57]

Most of the CEMA directed at Georgia and Ukraine were in coordination with Russian ground combat advances. The ground combat was the primary source of costs imposed during these two conflicts; however, CEMA contributed in notable ways to the well-executed attacks on Georgia and Ukraine. Cyberspace presents a synergistic method for escalating the intensity of physical conflict. When combined with physical force (i.e., military combat), CEMA can be a force multiplier for the coercer. More importantly, through properly timed operations, the aggressor may use specific cyber-attacks to improve the success of military attacks by virtually blinding the enemy's ability to perceive what is occurring while denying him the ability to direct responses. Furthermore, the aggressor may deliberately initiate cyber-attack outside military attacks in an effort to cause pain and coerce the victim to alter his strategy or acquiesce completely.

A New Paradigm

CEMO will likely precede and/or accompany future physical conflict between states that possess cyber forces. Modern nation should take a lesson from these Russian cyber-attacks as a warning of what to expect in hybrid warfare. CEMO in conjunction with war or physical hostilities will likely target military forces, communications, political command and control, financial institutions, and other vital infrastructure functions given the nefarious actors' ability to inflict considerable economic, political, and physical damage with little cost to the attacker. Nations must be prepared to operate in that paradigm.

The structure of future conflict will likely witness an amalgamation of forces and capabilities that will attempt to keep the conflict below the threshold of a 'declared' war, so as to keep the international community on the sidelines. Furthermore, if future conflict is to remain below the threshold of declared war, then the methods of attack will also likely remain below the threshold that would necessitate the involvement of allies and international partners. If that is the case, the United States should include a threshold for action (even preemptively) less than an act of war and include the characterization of cyber-attack. Doing so will provide decision-makers with greater options and triggers for action in the defense of the nation.

The cyber-attack directed at Ukraine's electrical grid demonstrated what a sophisticated cyber actor can do to an adversary's critical infrastructure. This attack demonstrated how quickly a vital component of a nation's power supply can be debilitated through CEMA, which can affect hundreds of thousands, if not millions, of citizens and can result in the loss of life. Every modern nation relies of continuously flowing power for daily life. The cyber-attack on Ukraine's electric grid represents another example of an external entities ability to interfere with the state's sovereign responsibility to properly support good governance and the protection of its citizens. This act crosses the threshold for a state's obligation to defend against (even if the critical infrastructure is privately owned and operated) since the potential degradation or destruction could lead to widespread damage and possible loss of life. Consequently, modern nations should have a cyber strategy and the cyber forces prepared ahead of time to defend against such an attack that targets critical infrastructure.

Lastly, the malicious cyber activities directed at Georgia in 2008 and Ukraine in 2014-2016 clearly rose to the level of cyber incident of national significance given their scale (number, types, and magnitude of targets struck), severity (impact to government and private industry services debilitated), duration (beyond just one attack – lasted weeks to months), and political motives (used by Russia in conjunction with the application of military force during a conflict). For Russia, the political stakes were obviously higher in Georgia/Ukraine than in Estonia; and consequently, Russian leaders elected to implement the concept of hybrid warfare and employ cyber capabilities as a prelude to and in conjunction with other instruments of national power – most notably its military. Russia clearly showed the world its hybrid strategy and capability to execute CEMA in conflict. For Georgia and Ukraine, their ad hoc responses, lack of national strategy, and nascent cyber capabilities combined to make both states ripe for CINS directed at their key cyber terrain. The United States should anticipate that any future conflict in the physical domain will likely be accompanied by conflict in the virtual domain, and therefore should plan on fighting both simultaneously.

Chinese Corporate Espionage in the US - Titan Rain to Byzantine Hades

The world of international espionage usually does not capture the attention of the general public; however recent espionage events have rattled American corporations and government unlike any past cases. Espionage has been around since biblical times when Moses sent spies to Canaan, and is generally expected from foreign governments (even tolerated, but not wanted). Past cases have been relatively isolated to government spying on other governments to gain political, economic, or military information. The case of Titan Rain to Byzantine Hades however is quite significant because of its immense scale and the fact that it targeted the United States' most sensitive military and proprietary corporate secrets, processes, and technologies.

Over the last three decades China used cyber-espionage to become more economically and militarily competitive with the United States through the theft of key technology and advanced manufacturing techniques.[58] During the 1990s, various Chinese cyber-enabled activities were directed at the United States. In 1999, as a result of an inadvertent bombing of the Chinese embassy in Serbia, and in 2001 when a United States Air Force spy plane was forced by Chinese fighters to land in China, China began exploring CEMA as a tool of political influence. During these two highly charged political incidents, Chinese hackers forced United States websites (and NATO websites in the Serbian incident) to shut down for a short period of time, signaling China's displeasure. Although Chinese hackers had little impact on the West's online sites, China realized they had much to learn in cyberspace operations. Following these events, China continued to build up and improve its cyber capabilities appreciably. In 2000, Chinese strategists wrote that China must send a message to its enemies through computer network attack, forcing the enemy to give up without fighting.[59] China wanted to be considered a respected world power and would use cyberspace as a domain in which to achieve its aims.

To understand China's motives for cyber-espionage, one must comprehend China's decades-old policy of returning to dominance on the global economic stage. China's policy stems from a legacy of the "four modernizations" policy, launched by Deng Xiaoping in 1978. "The targets of Deng's remarkably successful development policy were the core economic sectors of society, and foreign intellectual property was seen as crucial for each."[60] Over the decades, the policy to obtain and develop technology existed under different titles. China's indigenous innovation policy included a direction to consolidate companies within industry so that one or a few Chinese companies would dominate key sectors. "After decades of reforms, state-owned enterprises today produce an estimated half of China's total manufacturing and services output, and they dominate such sectors as energy, telecommunications, and transportation."[61] In China's 12th five-year plan (2011–15), developing technological capabilities across industries remained a top priority. Added to the plan in July 2012 were "national strategic emerging industries" of special interest, including new energy, auto industry, energy saving and environmental protection, information technology, biotechnology, high-end manufacturing, new energies, and new material industry.

China's previous broader motives from the 2005 to 2010 time period continued – namely to conduct corporate espionage with the aim of improving the Chinese economy and military. The prolonged series of theft of research and development data throughout the first decade of the twenty-first century allowed China to improve its economic posture rapidly in relation to the global economic leaders. Mandiant, along with other private and government cybersecurity agencies, tracked the exfiltration of data through Taiwan to China and publicly attributed the series of CEMA to China.[62] In 2009 it was reported the Chinese hackers stole data related to U.S. Air Force's newest stealth fighter aircraft, the F-22 and F-35.[63] The stolen data from the stealth fighters allowed China to bypass decades of research and development to build their versions of fifth-generation fighters, rapidly closing the gap with the United States.[64] The cyber-espionage of military secrets fit equally well with China's policy of economic espionage.

In 2011, Chinese hackers infiltrated the cybersecurity firm RSA (the letters taken from initials of its co-founders, Ron Rivest, Adi Shamir and Leonard Adleman). At that time RSA helped defend the networks (they operated key network systems administrator positions and issued security tokens) of the White House, the National Security Agency (NSA), the Pentagon, the Department of Homeland Security, and most of the top defense contractors.[65] With this new founded and unauthorized access in RSA, China then moved laterally across several other government organizations to gain access to other networks to steal sensitive data. Chinese hackers initiated a sophisticated penetration of RSA to compromise 760 other organizations, including four major defense contractors and the Massachusetts Institute of Technology.[66] China had effectively exploited the United States government and the private network defenders employed by the government. This approach to the United States government was a stepping-stone to gain access to some of the most sensitive political, military, and intelligence data of the United States.

Other U.S. military losses to Chinese cyber spies included the air refueling schedules of the U.S. Pacific Command, the military command that would be engaged in any future conflict with China. Furthermore, it was "revealed that the Air Force's networks were infiltrated by Chinese hackers, an attack that resulted in the loss of 33,000 records for general and field grade officers. Navy losses to Chinese hackers included data on missile navigation and tracking system, nuclear submarine and anti-aircraft missile design and over 300,000 user identification and passwords."[67] The Chinese also acquired sensitive science and technology data related to U.S. networks, International Traffic and Arms Restrictions secrets, and contractor research and development details. Over the first decade of this century it was revealed that the cyber-espionage of classified military data was a significant impact to the United States military. Much of U.S. state-of-the-art military weapons data was now in Chinese hands while the advantage that the United States endeavored to maintain gradually eroded.

In the first decade of the new century, China pursued the programming code on several key computer operating systems and technologies through which China could find and exploit economic vulnerabilities. In 2001, China pressured Microsoft Chief Executive Officer, Bill Gates to provide China with the operating system code (which Microsoft refused to do for its largest American customers) or be banished from Chinese government procurement possibilities. Under substantial business pressure, Gates acquiesced and provided China with the operating system.[68] With the operating system code from Windows, China could examine the program in detail and discover the weaknesses of the software. Vulnerabilities in the code allowed China to gain access to networks and technologies it did not currently possess. From 2000 to 2003, Microsoft's Windows increasingly became the target of CEMA and the scrutiny of cybersecurity analysts. In 2005, in response to the outcry of vulnerabilities and cyber intrusions, Bill Gates announced a new and significantly more secure version of Microsoft Internet Explorer for Windows XP, expanding anti-spyware protection by including the Windows AntiSpyware technology.[69] This programming improvement did not stop China however.

During the early 2000s, China began inserting counterfeit hardware in the United States military and cyberspace supply chains. These counterfeit technologies provided China another avenue of access to confidential industry networks which then provided China with the opportunity to steal sensitive data while establishing a continual presence in those networks.[70] In 2008, "the FBI seized $76 million of counterfeit Cisco (CSCO) routers that the Bureau said could have provided Chinese hackers a backdoor into U.S. government networks. A number of government agencies bought the routers from an authorized Cisco vendor, but that legitimate vendor purchased the routers from a high-risk Chinese supplier."[71] Chinese hardware was being illegally inserted into the United States' cyberspace supply chain. In 2011, "9,539 banned businesses were found to have sold technology to the United States government. Roughly 10% of those incidents involved counterfeit parts or equipment."[72] China used this capability to gain unauthorized access to various government organizations (mostly military) and private industry networks and then steal terabytes of data.[73]

In 2003, China announced the creation of cyber warfare units as part of the Third Technical Department of the People's Liberations Army (3 PLA), which had cyber capabilities that included: "planting information mines, conducting information reconnaissance, changing network data, releasing information bombs, dumping information garbage, disseminating propaganda, applying information deception, releasing clone (sic) information, organizing information defense, and establishing network spy stations."[74] Recently China announced that it established several units focused on cyberspace. According to Mark Stokes, executive director at Virginia think tank Project 2049 Institute, one of 3 PLA's cyber units, Unit 78020, a technical reconnaissance bureau based in the southwestern Chinese city of Kunming, "is one of more than two dozen such bureaus within the PLA tasked with intelligence gathering, analysis and computer network defense and exploitation."[75]   Another 3 PLA unit, Unit 61398, is known to have conducted an overwhelming percentage of the attacks on American corporations, organizations and government agencies.[76] While Unit 61398 exfiltrated terabytes of data from companies such as Coca-Cola, increasingly its preferred targets were the U.S. critical infrastructure sectors. "According to the security researchers, one target was a company with remote access to more than 60 percent of oil and gas pipelines in North America."[77]   China had obviously embraced cyberspace as the domain with numerous opportunities for exploitation, which allowed them to meet their national objectives.

Through the use of spear-phishing and other more sophisticated tactics, Chinese 3 PLA hackers were able to implant remote access tools (rat) by which they could establish a launching point to explore their victim's networks and databases and exfiltrate terabytes of information.[78]   The tool proved extremely lucrative and was also used on American defense contractors and the DoD to extract the newest military capabilities and sensitive information.   By 2005, the publicly released information (codename Titan Rain) exposed the fact China had gained unauthorized access to Lockheed Martin, Northrup Grumman, and BAE Systems plus DoD's Army Information Systems Engineering Command, the Defense Information Systems Agency, the Naval Ocean Systems Center, the Army Space and Strategic Defense Installation, NASA, Redstone Arsenal, and the British Foreign Office.[79] "In September 2010, the Missile Defense Agency found that the memory in a high-altitude missile's mission computer was counterfeit. Fixing the problem cost $2.7 million. Had the missile launched, it most likely would have failed..."[80]   Upon the compromise of the classified codename Titan Rain, a new codename was established by the United States Intelligence Community to categorize Chinese espionage –

Byzantine Hades. China continues to use the cyber domain to achieve it political and security interests.

The FBI Indictments

The FBI's May 2014 indictment of five 3 PLA officers for corporate espionage helps explain the significance of this CINS. This was the first time the FBI publicly named and indicted military officers from another state who were conducting CEMA against the United States. According to the FBI, "Wang Dong, Sun Kailiang, Wen Xinyu, Huang Zhenyu, and Gu Chunhui, who were officers in Unit 61398 of the Third Department of the Chinese People's Liberation Army (PLA). The indictment alleged that Wang, Sun, and Wen, among others known and unknown to the grand jury, hacked or attempted to hack into U.S. entities named in the indictment, while Huang and Gu supported their conspiracy by, among other things, managing infrastructure (e.g., domain accounts) used for hacking."[81] The American organizations attacked were listed as: Westinghouse Electric Co. (Westinghouse); U.S. subsidiaries of SolarWorld AG (SolarWorld); United States Steel Corp. (U.S. Steel); Allegheny Technologies Inc. (ATI); the United Steel, Book and Forestry, Rubber, Manufacturing, Energy, Allied Industrial and Service Workers International Union (USW); and Alcoa Inc.[82] Then United States Attorney General, Eric Holder stated, "[t]his is a case alleging economic espionage by members of the Chinese military and represents the first-ever charges against a state actor for this type of hacking."[83]

Summary of Defendants' Conduct Alleged in the Indictment		
Defendant	Victim	Criminal Conduct

Sun	Westinghouse	In 2010, while Westinghouse was building four AP1000 power plants in China and negotiating other terms of the construction with a Chinese SOE (SOE-1), including technology transfers, Sun stole confidential and proprietary technical and design specifications for pipes, pipe supports, and pipe routing within the AP1000 plant buildings. Additionally, in 2010 and 2011, while Westinghouse was exploring other business ventures with SOE-1, Sun stole sensitive, non-public, and deliberative e-mails belonging to senior decision-makers responsible for Westinghouse's business relationship with SOE-1.
Wen	SolarWorld	In 2012, at about the same time the Commerce Department found that Chinese solar product manufacturers had "dumped" products into U.S. markets at prices below fair value, Wen and at least one other, unidentified co-conspirator stole thousands of files including information about SolarWorld's cash flow, manufacturing metrics, production line information, costs, and privileged attorney-client communications relating to ongoing trade litigation, among other things. Such information would have enabled a Chinese competitor to target SolarWorld's business operations aggressively from a variety of angles.

Wang and Sun	U.S. Steel	In 2010, U.S. Steel was participating in trade cases with Chinese steel companies, including one particular state-owned enterprise (SOE-2). Shortly before the scheduled release of a preliminary determination in one such litigation, Sun sent spear phishing e-mails to U.S. Steel employees, some of whom were in a division associated with the litigation. Some of these e-mails resulted in the installation of malware on U.S. Steel computers. Three days later, Wang stole hostnames and descriptions of U.S. Steel computers (including those that controlled physical access to company facilities and mobile device access to company networks). Wang thereafter took steps to identify and exploit vulnerable servers on that list.
Wen	ATI	In 2012, ATI was engaged in a joint venture with SOE-2, competed with SOE-2, and was involved in a trade dispute with SOE-2. In April of that year, Wen gained access to ATI's network and stole network credentials for virtually every ATI employee.
Wen	USW	In 2012, USW was involved in public disputes over Chinese trade practices in at least two industries. At or about the time USW issued public statements regarding those trade disputes and related legislative proposals, Wen stole e-mails from senior USW employees containing sensitive, non-public, and deliberative information about USW strategies, including strategies related to pending trade disputes.

		USW's computers continued to beacon to the conspiracy's infrastructure until at least early 2013.
Sun	Alcoa	About three weeks after Alcoa announced a partnership with a Chinese state-owned enterprise (SOE-3) in February 2008, Sun sent a spear phishing e-mail to Alcoa. Thereafter, in or about June 2008, unidentified individuals stole thousands of e-mail messages and attachments from Alcoa's computers, including internal discussions concerning that transaction.
Huang		Huang facilitated hacking activities by registering and managing domain accounts that his co-conspirators used to hack into U.S. entities. Additionally, between 2006 and at least 2009, Unit 61398 assigned Huang to perform programming work for SOE-2, including the creation of a "secret" database designed to hold corporate "intelligence" about the iron and steel industries, including information about American companies.
Gu		Gu managed domain accounts used to facilitate hacking activities against American entities and also tested spear phishing e-mails in furtherance of the conspiracy.

Table 3.1 – Summary of Charges against 3 PLA Officers

The indictment alleged that the 3 PLA officers conspired to hack into American organizations to maintain unauthorized access to their networks and to steal information from those entities that would be useful to their competitors in China, including state-owned enterprises. In some cases, the FBI alleged, the conspirators stole trade secrets that would have been particularly beneficial to Chinese companies at the time they were stolen. In other cases, the FBI alleged, the hackers "stole sensitive, internal communications that would provide a competitor, or an adversary in litigation, with insight into the strategy and vulnerabilities of the American entity."[84]

According to the FBI's indictment, it is out of bounds to use state-run intelligence assets to seek commercial advantage. Attorney General Holder said "[w]hen a foreign nation uses military or intelligence resources and tools against an American executive or corporation to obtain trade secrets or sensitive business information for the benefit of its state-owned companies, we must say, 'enough is enough.'"[85] *The New York Times* report went on to state, "[i]t was significant that the indictment dealt almost exclusively with Unit 61398 — also known as Comment Crew — but did not detail the case against another roughly 20 Chinese hacking groups, some associated with the military, that the United States regularly tracks."[86]

The FBI's investigation took years to complete. A major challenge in bringing the case forward was convincing the targeted corporations to publicly acknowledge the attacks since many feared losses of revenues from their operations in China or retaliation by the Chinese state.[87] The FBI gathered compelling evidence and then convinced the American companies to go public, despite fear of retaliation. The indictment "is not about what the United States will do with these hackers, but what China will do with them. The indictment is meant to send a clear public message to China that they need to take action."[88] Unfortunately, the FBI's indictment did not address Chinese CEMA aimed at the Defense Department or major defense contractors.[89]

111

Despite the FBI's indictment and without any real consequences for their malicious cyber actions, China once again increased their CEMA on American government and corporate entities. Even non-governmental and non-economic corporations were targeted. In 2010, Google announced it had been compromised by China and was a victim of highly sophisticated and targeted CEMA on its corporate infrastructure, originating in China and resulting in the theft of intellectual property.[90] According to Google, "Chinese spies had penetrated its networks, stolen source code, and used Google both to spy on its users and to worm their way into many other companies."[91] Over a period of five years, the world gradually began to grasp the magnitude of what China was accomplishing. Fourteen U.S. intelligence agencies co-authored a report describing a far-reaching cyber-espionage campaign by Chinese. The report detailed the magnitude of CINS, which had been in the works for years and was focused across a large number of industries: biotechnology, military, telecommunications, and nanotechnology, as well as clean energy. The report noted that Chinese hackers were able to steal sensitive technology from one American metallurgical company that cost $1 billion and 20 years to develop.[92]

Beyond the advantage China gained by stealing America secrets and technologies, the impact to the United States was felt through the loss of revenue and jobs. According to the *2013 Report of the Commission on the Theft of American Intellectual Property*, the annual losses of American IP theft to China (the leading bad actor) is comparable to the current annual level of U.S. exports to Asia—over $300 billion.[93] The Commission went on to state:

"The scale of international theft of American intellectual property (IP) is unprecedented—hundreds of billions of dollars per year, on the order of the size of U.S. exports to Asia. The effects of this theft are twofold. The first is the tremendous loss of revenue and reward for those who made the inventions or who have purchased licenses to provide goods and services based on them, as well as of the jobs associated with those losses. American companies of all sizes are

112

victimized. The second and even more pernicious effect is that illegal theft of intellectual property is undermining both the means and the incentive for entrepreneurs to innovate, which will slow the development of new inventions and industries that can further expand the world economy and continue to raise the prosperity and quality of life for everyone. Unless current trends are reversed, there is a risk of stifling innovation, with adverse consequences for both developed and still developing countries. The American response to date of hectoring governments and prosecuting individuals has been utterly inadequate to deal with the problem."[94]

According to *US News*, the "price tag for intellectual property (IP) theft from U.S. companies is at least $250 billion a year. That's far more than what businesses pay in federal corporate income taxes."[95] The theft of American IP and cyber-espionage is quite significant – the effects of which notably impacts the United States' economy, American jobs growth, and wealth that the United States depends on for its innovation and continued growth. "By 2010, IP-intensive businesses accounted for more than a third of U.S. GDP and, directly or indirectly, for nearly 28 percent of all U.S. jobs."[96] Corporate America relies upon its IP for commercial advantages over its competitors. Companies spend their hard-earned money to innovate, develop, and then sell their products. As the IP Commission Report describes, China's corporate espionage is systematically and negatively affecting the United States' corporate and military dominance while eroding America's potential to remain an economic global leader.

In 2013, Mandiant disclosed that "hundreds of terabytes of data from 141 companies in 20 different industries had been stolen remotely by China, and traced the theft back to a specific office in the People's Liberation Army known as unit 61398."[97] The U.S. government could have made similar disclosures years earlier but chose silence. Based upon my research, the silence may have been the result of an uncertainty of to what to disclose and how to proceed (e.g., through law enforcement channels or by a cyber response/retaliation). Given the secrecy surrounding the nature of investigating China's corporate espionage, the U.S. government was concerned about revealing its sources and methods involved with gaining the vital intelligence. It was not until private cybersecurity firms (such as Mandiant) began investigating and revealing the IP theft, that the U.S. government publicly acknowledge the problem and the origins of the theft. Furthermore, there is an understandable reluctance of private companies to publicize successful or even attempted breeches. After the 2013 Mandiant report, however, the larceny had become too blatant and pervasive to ignore. As mentioned above, in May of 2014, a Federal grand jury indicted five Chinese military personnel associated with unit 61398 for economic espionage and related crimes against U.S. companies and a U.S. labor union. Unfortunately, that conviction was just one of a plethora of required cyber-criminal prosecutions needed to impose real costs on China. To date, China has not experienced any real degradation or impact to their cyber-espionage capabilities.

The United States' response to Chinese cyber-espionage throughout this time period was limited. In addition to the FBI indicting five Chinese cyber actors, the United States' policy in this area was largely in the form of talking to foreign leaders and trying to convince them to develop more effective intellectual property rights programs. Furthermore, "the U.S. Department of Justice prosecuted individual employees of American companies who have been caught attempting to carry trade secrets with them to foreign companies and entities. This policy of jawboning and jailing a few individuals has produced no measurable effect on the problem."[98] The United States continued to have sensitive corporate and military data stolen by Chinese cyber actors. In 2016, the United States Director of National Intelligence published a *National Counterintelligence Strategy for the United States of America 2016*. In this monograph, five mission objectives are laid out:

"(1) deepen our understanding of foreign intelligence entities' plans, intentions, capabilities, tradecraft, and operations targeting U.S. national interests and sensitive information and assets; (2) disrupt foreign intelligence entities' capabilities, plans, and operations that threaten U.S. nationals interests and sensitive information and assets; (3) detect, deter, and mitigate threats from insiders with access to sensitive information and assets; (4) safeguard sensitive information and assets from foreign intelligence entities' theft, manipulation, or exploitation; and (5) identify and counter foreign intelligence entities' cyber activities that attempt to disrupt, exploit, or steal sensitive information, to include personally identifiable information, from U.S. networks."[99]

This counterintelligence strategy is not actually a strategy, but rather only a guidance document that establishes the aim or purpose of United States counterintelligence agencies. Furthermore, the "strategy" does not specify how, with what means, or against what threats the U.S. intelligence community is to accomplish its objectives. Moreover, because the document is primarily focused on counterintelligence, the rest of the United States' instruments of power for which the Chinese cyber-espionage case should be employed, are conspicuously absent. Furthermore, the United States does not possess a cyber strategy to counter the Chinese cyber detailed above. Consequently, American private corporations are left to work with Federal law enforcement agencies and private cybersecurity firms to defend themselves. Similarly, the U.S. government organizations struggle to defend their own networks from Chinese exploitation. Collaboration between government and private entities is driven by the Department of Homeland Security (DHS), but in limited ways, and is not effective at countering the Chinese cyber threat.

According to the DHS, as the lead Federal agency for national cybersecurity, it "works with other federal agencies to conduct high-impact criminal investigations to disrupt and defeat cyber criminals, prioritize the recruitment and training of technical experts, develop standardized methods, and broadly share cyber response best practices and tools."[100] DHS is charged with coordinating the sharing of cyber threat information and advocating for cybersecurity standards. DHS designated the National Protection and Programs Directorate to lead the national effort to strengthen the security and resilience of the nation's physical and cyber critical infrastructure, including supporting federal agencies in securing their information systems and information.[101] In the Jan 2016 General Accounting Office (GAO) Report to Congress titled: "Information Security: DHS Needs to Enhance Capabilities, Improve Planning, and Support Greater Adoption of Its National Cybersecurity Protection System, " the GAO stated that DHS is only partially achieving its Federal cybersecurity objectives.[102] Governmental and corporate cybersecurity efforts occur in isolated areas and sectors. Unfortunately, there is not unity of effort to integrate and synchronize cyber actions across the United States government. The continuing theft of American data demonstrates that the United States has yet to develop or field a strategy or plan that adequately contends with Chinese cyber-espionage. I submit in this book that a coercive strategy is key to contending with such espionage.

In October of 2018, the cybersecurity firm Crowdstrike, published a new study that stated China has resumed its widespread cyber operations targeting U.S. private corporate intellectual property after a three-year hiatus.[103] Earlier, in 2015, then President Obama confronted Chinese President Xi Jinping for the corporate espionage witnessed over the last decade. Through political talks and China's perceived desire to be taken seriously as a global leader, China agreed to cease its CINS corporate espionage directed at the United States. However, as the result of significant U.S. tariffs imposed on Chinese goods imported to the America in 2018, China evidently reversed course to once again take up significant corporate espionage. Crowdstrike reported in 2018 (?) that Beijing has resumed stealing intellectual property from U.S. companies on a "massive scale" in sectors including biotechnological, defense, mining, pharmaceutical, professional services, and transportation.[104]   Once again, the United States faces a substantial cyber threat (CINS), but does not have a policy or strategy to adequately contend with Chinese aggression.

The Importance of Government to Private Partnerships

The Titan Rain - Byzantine Hades series of CEMA constitutes a major theft of intellectual property and sensitive data from the United States' industry and governmental organizations.   As the IP Commission Report states, IP theft is not new, but with the advent of cyberspace, cyber-espionage has taken on a new significance.

"Compared with prior eras, today's economic world is far more interconnected and operates at a far higher speed, with product cycles measured in months rather than years. Companies in the developing world that steal intellectual property from those in the developed world become instant international competitors without becoming innovators themselves. Bypassing the difficult work of developing over decades the human talent, the business processes, and the incentive systems to become innovators, these companies simply drive more inventive companies in the developed world out of markets or out of business entirely."[105]

Through its cyber-espionage campaign, China was able to skip decades of private and military research and development to rapidly advance to the status of an "instant international competitor" to the United States economically and militarily. Previous NSA and Cyber Command commander, General Keith Alexander, called these attacks the "greatest transfer of wealth in history."[106] Cyber-espionage is clandestine and often occurs unnoticed; however, for this level of espionage to go unchecked or uncontested places the United States' economic future at risk. China avoided the costs of evolutionary improvements and saved as much as three trillion dollars in research and development costs that, in the span of a decade, placed China in a position to challenge the current world order dominated by the United States and its allies. History provides numerous examples where economic challenges accompanied by geopolitical tension were a recipe for international confrontation, conflict, and war. Furthermore, by not imposing real consequences on China (such as greater judicial indictments and prosecutions, exposing the clandestine Chinese cyber units, imposing economic sanctions of the individuals and Chinese governments, and imposing tariffs on those goods where the U.S. can prove China's cyber- espionage gained an unfair advantage) for their gross violation of intellectual property theft, one can argue the United States is largely ignoring the negative effects of cyber-espionage while risking its competitive edge as the world technological and economic leader. While there are ill consequences to overreacting to such malicious activities, there are ill consequences to underreacting as well!

Political espionage is conducted and tolerated by all nations, but the scale and impact of Chinese cyber theft combined with the political policy of skipping decades of governmental and corporate research and development qualifies as a cyber incident of national significance for which defensive and proactive U.S. responses could/should apply. China's motives were politically, economically, and national security driven – and cyberspace provided the domain by which China could achieve its aims without employing other instruments of national power. One can say that cyberspace is the means China uses to bolster its other instruments of national power. Without the United States' cyberspace dependency and vulnerability to theft, China could not have succeeded to the magnitude witnessed during first decade of the twenty-first century. For the United States to succeed, it must have a national cyber strategy.

Since the United States does not possess a national cyber defense strategy, it will continue to struggle against this cyber threat. According to the United States

Intelligence Community in their Report of Congress on Foreign Economic Collection and Industrial Espionage, 2009 – 2011, "[b]ecause the United States is a leader in the development of new technologies and a central player in global finance and trade networks, foreign attempts to collect U.S. technological and economic information will continue at a high level and will represent a growing and persistent threat to U.S. economic security. The nature of the cyber threat will evolve with continuing technological advances in the global information environment…We judge that the governments of China and Russia will remain aggressive and capable collectors of sensitive economic information and technologies, particularly in cyberspace."[107] If the United States' Intelligence Community is correct, then the United States should develop the strategy and cyber capabilities to defend itself in order to not fall to this espionage, which qualifies as CINS.

Additionally, this case further highlights the importance of government to private partnerships in the defense of and response to CINS. Private corporate entities could not contend with several of the techniques and capabilities that the government of China amassed. It was only through a partnership with the FBI that investigations and indictments were possible in the case of the five 3 PLA officers. That partnership however struggled to develop due to the fear private industry has in the face of state threats and in the ability of the United States government to protect American corporations from retribution. Furthermore, the United States government still struggles to understand what other instruments of national power (e.g., military, information, economic) can be employed against state or state-sponsored cyber threats when private corporations experience significant CEMA. Partnerships are vital to cybersecurity; consequently, the United States must determine how to develop even more robust and productive relationships to contend with the present cyber storm.

Stuxnet 2010 - Malware Attack

During the 1990s, Iran endeavored to develop and build nuclear power plants to generate clean power and to be considered a "player" on the international geopolitical stage. In 1995 Iran enlisted help from the Russian government, which sent nuclear experts to assist in the building of its first nuclear plant in Bushehr. Shortly thereafter, Iran began working on an underground nuclear material enrichment facility at Natanz,[108] which started operating in 2002.[109] Iran's nuclear program worried numerous nations throughout the West along with Saudi Arabia and Israel, which sought to ensure Iran's nuclear power capability would not be applied to nuclear weapons development – a process that would require enriching its uranium to a weapons-grade quality. Tensions grew in 2009 when President Ahmadinejad stated Iran's goal to enrich its uranium to weapons grade had been reached. Despite previous problems, Iran had crossed a technical milestone and had succeeded in producing 839 kilograms of low-enriched uranium—enough to achieve nuclear-weapons breakout capability."[110] The concern across western nations rose and President George W. Bush pressed his Western counterparts to impose strong sanctions as a consequence.[111] In addition, the United States, along with the United Nations, entered into discussions with Iran to discover a way to contain Iran and its nuclear program, which included sending the International Atomic Energy Agency (IAEA) to Bushehr and Natanz to inspect the nuclear centrifuges and to confirm the actual intentions and capabilities of Iran's nuclear program.

In January 2010, the United States, along with other international partners, convinced Iran to let IAEA inspectors visit the Natanz plant. During the IAEA's visit, the inspectors noticed Iran's centrifuges were failing at an unprecedented rate. The cause was unknown to both the inspectors and the Iranian technicians swapping out the centrifuges. Months later, an apparently unrelated Iranian episode ensued for which a Belarus computer security firm (VirusBlokAda) was hired to troubleshoot a series of components that were constantly crashing and rebooting.[112] The source of the problem was unknown, until the firm's technicians discovered malicious files on one of the systems. Stuxnet, as it came to be known, was unlike any other previous known malware. The VirusBlokAda technicians discovered a potential Microsoft Windows operating system *zero-day exploit* (previously unpatched and unpublished vulnerability) within WinCC.[113] WinCC was used by Siemens in its industrial control systems (ICS) and was installed as a key component of Iran's centrifuges. Rather than simply controlling the computers and stealing data, Stuxnet was designed to manipulate the ICS that controlled the centrifuges' rate of oscillation (components that are extremely sensitive to the slightest variance or vibration), thereby destroying the centrifuges.[114] Stuxnet's code was sent to Microsoft for analysis and soon several cybersecurity firms were analyzing the malware in an effort to evaluate the code and discover how it was delivered to a closed network (one not connected to the Internet).[115]

Cyber experts studied the new malware and traced the path of Stuxnet from an Iranian company, Neda, to Natanz.[116] Neda had engineered and installed ICS and other components for several of Iran's industries, including energy and mining sectors. Evidentially, Neda installed Siemens S7 programmable logic controllers (PLC) in several gas pipeline operations in Iran and at the Esfahan Steel Complex. "Neda had been identified on a proliferation watch list for its alleged involvement in illicit procurement activity and was named in a U.S. indictment for receiving smuggled microcontrollers and other components."[117] The designer of the Stuxnet attack had figured out that Neda was likely also involved with Natanz's nuclear program and used Neda to target Natanz. It is uncertain how long Stuxnet took to "migrate" to Natanz after infecting machines at Neda, but according to cyber experts, between June and August 2010 the number of centrifuges at Natanz began to drop.[118] Only 4,592 centrifuges were enriching at the plant, a decrease of 328 centrifuges since June. By November, that number had dropped to 3,936, a difference of 984 in five months. Additionally, although more centrifuges were being installed, none of them were being used.[119]

Stuxnet was extremely effective as a destructive cyber-attack. Stuxnet did not operate independently, but rather was controlled by two servers located in Malaysia and Denmark.[120] The malware was sent data to the servers, which could then direct updates and the deployment of malicious activities to the infected machines. The servers also directed updates to Stuxnet if configurations were changed in the infected targets due to malware updates. Furthermore, Stuxnet could update older versions of the malware when it came in contact with them on other computers.[121]

While Stuxnet had a debilitating effect at Natanz, it spread worldwide to over 100,000 hosts in 155 countries without any significant effect.[122] Stuxnet was a highly precise cyber weapon and one that very few cyber actors could design or deliver. Two years later, Stuxnet ceased to exist, either as a result of a designed feature or due to malware disinfecting features of cybersecurity software, which were updated with the signature of Stuxnet. In June 2012, the *New York Times* reported that the Obama administration had extended a Bush administration cyber operation known as OLYMPIC GAMES, which according to the *Times'* sources, targeted Iran's nuclear program.[123] It is alleged that the United States and Israel developed Stuxnet to slow Iran's nuclear progress. If correct, the United States may have had an ulterior motive in working with Israel to create and launch this cyber-weapon that was designed to slow Iran's nuclear program. One could argue that to prevent Israel from launching a pre-emptive air strike on Natanz unilaterally (and potentially starting a Middle-East war), some alternative, non-kinetic or virtual solution might appease the Israeli leadership.[124] Iran had earlier stated a desire to wipe Israel from the face of the earth and nuclear weapons would be a sure-fire method of achieving those aims. In 2010, the United States had to convince Israel that a different line of attack would prevent Iran from obtaining nuclear weapons and therefore closely collaborated with Israel in the Stuxnet attack.[125] Although there was no irrefutable evidence that the United States and Israel launched Stuxnet, it is widely believed to be accurate.

The Iranian response to Stuxnet occurred in two ways – politically and technically. Early responses revolved around identifying, mitigating, and removing the malware. Due to the closed nature of the Iranian government and its nuclear program, it is unknown exactly how long Iran took to figure out and correct Stuxnet's effects. After Stuxnet became public knowledge, Iran emphatically blamed Israel and the United States. In March 2011, Iranian national news reported the establishment and commencement of cyber operations of a cyber unit in Basij.[126] Shortly thereafter, cybersecurity firms accused Iran of attempting to gain website certificates from Google, Microsoft, Yahoo, Mozilla, and Skype.[127] Had Iran's CEMA been successful, "Internet users in Iran could log onto Gmail or Yahoo Mail, for instance, and been automatically re-directed to a fake website, which could have been used to steal usernames and passwords, or to install malware that could have been used to track online activity."[128] Iran had entered the CEMA playing field. Although Stuxnet slowed Iran's nuclear enrichment processes, it did not result in program termination.[129] Currently, the United States, along with the members of the United Nations, continues to engage with Iran concerning its nuclear program in an effort to ensure Iran does not develop nuclear weapons.

A Cyber-to-Physical Effect

From a cyber conflict perspective, Stuxnet clearly rises to the status of a cyber incident of national significance (CINS) due to the political nature (constrain Iran's nuclear program), the technical sophistication of the delivery of the CEMA, military implications of the target (centrifuges designed to enrich uranium to weapons grade), and the magnitude of the CEMO (all of Natanz's centrifuges while not impacting other targets worldwide). In hacker jargon, Stuxnet is an example of a "cyber-to-physical effect." Regardless of whether or not the United States and Israel perpetrated the attack, Stuxnet demonstrated what a sophisticated state-sponsored cyber-attack could achieve. More specifically, a determined cyber actor, who possesses the innovative tools to work around arduous cyber problems, can penetrate closed networks. The United States should evaluate its vitally important cyberspace infrastructure (open and closed) and assess its current cyber defenses in order to truly understand the risks to its economic and national security. No matter how secure cyberspace may be designed, determined adversaries can discover a way to breach the defenses and exploit the vulnerabilities.

In the case of Stuxnet, political and national security motives drove the attackers to use sophisticated cyber delivery tactics and CEMA to achieve their goals without resorting to the use of other instruments of national power. Once again, government to private cybersecurity partnerships were vital to discover, analyze, and mitigate CEMA of a sophisticated fashion. Without private cybersecurity assistance, Iran would not have determined the cause of their centrifuge failure. The final lesson from Stuxnet is not to rely solely on defense, but also to devise redundant and resilient systems that may gracefully degrade when attacked, while simultaneously pursuing the means and the strategy to deter malicious cyber actors from ever considering such an attack.

Cyber Conflict Analysis

Following are several questions that were raised at the beginning of the chapter and are grouped together for the reader's comparison.

Case Study Question 1	How dependent on cyberspace and vulnerable to attack was the victim state?

Estonia	Extremely dependent (most wired nation in Europe); Extremely vulnerable to attack without a national cyber defense strategy or processes to prevent, mitigate or respond to the CEMA.
Georgia/Ukraine	Both were fairly dependent on cyberspace for national command and communications; Both were vulnerable to cyber-attacks without a competent defending cyber force or national cyber strategy.
Indictment of Five 3PLA Officers in Titan Rain - Byzantine Hades	The American business sectors were extremely dependent upon cyberspace for the global operations; extremely vulnerable to CEMA against sophisticated cyber espionage. Private entities cannot compete with the robust cyber organization China possesses.
Stuxnet	Iran was very dependent upon cyberspace, but operated a closed network in an attempt to mitigate vulnerabilities. Iran employed good security to prevent intrusions.
Case Study Question 2	Were the cyber-attacks alleged to have had a state structure behind them (were they allegedly perpetrated or supported by a state or state-sponsored entity)?
Estonia	Yes - Allegedly Nashi is supported by Russia; Complexity of CEMA operation pointed to sophisticated state sponsorship beyond what youth hacking entity could achieve.

Georgia/Ukraine	Yes - both nations were engaged in combat with Russia and consequently it was alleged that Russia conducted the CEMA to support physical military operations. Further, the complexity and synchronization with physical operations points to Russian involvement.
Indictment of Five 3PLA Officers in Titan Rain - Byzantine Hades	FBI indicted five 3 PLA officers for several cases of cyber espionage (just one case to highlight China's vast CEMA enterprise). The sophisticated and complexity of the various CEMA directed at corporate entities points to state involvement.
Stuxnet	Yes - allegedly the U.S. and Israel. Given the significant sophistication of the CEMA employed pointed to state involvement.
Case Study Question 3	Did the victim state generally act in an ad hoc manner when attacked, or did it develop effective strategies to integrate its national security resources?
Estonia	Ad hoc - Estonia reacted to the events with progressively more effectiveness although not until after the damage was done; Estonia learned how to defend against DDoS.
Georgia/Ukraine	Ad hoc - both Georgie and Ukraine responded in a piecemeal fashion and struggled to restore cyber capabilities attacked. Both states worked to better integrate cyber defenses with other national security resources.

Indictment of Five 3PLA Officers in Titan Rain - Byzantine Hades	Ad hoc - individual private entities had little chance to compete with state cyber capabilities. U.S. struggled to aid, prevent, and mitigate the CEMA directed at private organizations. U.S. had no national strategy to defend corporations
Stuxnet	Ad hoc - Iran did not realize the centrifuges were failing due to CEMA; sought the assistance of outside help to determine cause. Worked to clean networks and replace centrifuges.
Case Study Question 4	What were the elements of national power that the victim state used to respond to the CEMA?
Estonia	Diplomacy - directed at Russia, called for help from NATO allies; Information - a media campaign; did not have a credible military national cyber force nor economic instruments to use in this incident to any great degree.
Georgia/Ukraine	Both states relied on government cyber capabilities to respond to the CEMA encountered; both nations struggled to use information as a weapon to counter Russian control of the media; neither country possessed a capable national cyber force.
Indictment of Five 3PLA Officers in Titan Rain - Byzantine Hades	Law enforcement primarily. Resorted to diplomacy and information to pressure China. No military or economic actions were reportedly taken.
Stuxnet	Only used information as a tool of national power; no other power used.

Case Study Question 5	Were private entities part of the response? How critical were partnerships between private cyber entities and the victim state in that response?
Estonia	Eventually yes - several private firms called in to assist in defense; corporate firms struggled to defend themselves; Partnerships grew in importance as the events progressed; No whole of nation strategy emerged.
Georgia/Ukraine	Eventually yes - both states sought the assistance from outside private entities to host services and aid in restoration of cyber capabilities; both states grew to value their relationships with private cyber entities to compensate for their lack of national capabilities.
Indictment of Five 3PLA Officers in Titan Rain - Byzantine Hades	Yes - private entities were involved from the beginning (victim businesses and private cyber security firms). Corporations relied on partnerships with government and other private firms to assist in defense, mitigation, and recovery, albeit well after the damage was done.
Stuxnet	Yes - due to inadequate national cyber forensics and analytical capabilities, Iran relied solely on private assistance. No national strategy for cyber defense existed.
Case Study Question 6	Why was this case considered a CINS?

Estonia	Yes - due to the scale, political motivations, duration, and organizations attacked. Also, in the absence of any strategy or defending force, Estonia was ripe for CEMA.
Georgia/Ukraine	Yes - both states witnessed CINS due to scale, types of targets hit, political motivation to tie cyber to kinetic military operations, and duration of the CEMA. Also, in the absence of any strategy or defending force, both nations were ripe for CEMA.
Indictment of Five 3PLA Officers in Titan Rain - Byzantine Hades	Yes - due to the scale, nature of the targets, duration of the CEMA, political and economic motives, and the fact that China was attacking United States.
Stuxnet	Yes - due to the significance of the targets, the mode of delivery to a closed network, and the actors involved.

Table 3.6 – Case Study Findings

Several findings may be drawn from the four cases of CINS presented above. CEMA directed at a target state could pressure and/or manipulate that state's leadership's decision making and actions either as the primary instrument of national power or in conjunction with other instruments (e.g., military) for the goal of a political or national security purpose. The contrary question can then be asked: could the aggressor have achieved the same results without using CEMA? If so, why did it not? In the Estonia case, Russia likely could not have pressured Estonia so rapidly with just ethnic riots and was not likely to escalate the tensions by resorting to military force for fear of NATO invoking Article Five of the NATO treaty (escalation to war). Consequently, CEMA was used to pressure Estonia leadership without external physical force. In the Georgia and Ukraine case, Russia could have achieved its objectives without CEMA given its overwhelming military might compared to Georgia or Ukraine. However, by using CEMA in conjunction with military force (and sometimes unilaterally), Russia achieved improved effects (by synchronizing and integrating virtual and physical effects) on its adversaries while ensuring attainment of its objectives, which included controlling the international narrative to downplay its aggression in those two countries. CEMA was not always necessary, but proved synergistic. In the Chinese cyber-espionage case, it would have been exponentially more difficult to rely solely on human intelligence (physically gaining access to American facilities and stealing the documents) to achieve its policy goals as quickly as China did. CEMA proved (and continues) to be an invaluable method for extracting terabytes of data with ease and over a prolonged period of time. One could say that CEMA was sufficient. Finally, in the Stuxnet case, the perpetrators could have used a military air strike to achieve a delaying effect on Iran's nuclear enrichment operation; however, that likely would have escalated tensions in the region to the point of military hostilities and war. Using CEMA provided an alternative method of achieving the perpetrator's goal in a less aggressive fashion and mostly unattributable way.

States or state-sponsored organizations will use CEMA, even to the level of CINS, as a means to influence a victim state while avoiding a full fledge war. Responses to CINS are more likely to contend with the CEMA if the state has a well thought out strategy and possesses credible cybersecurity capabilities. Preparatory thought, planning, capabilities development, and partnerships established before a CINS ensures the state will have greater likelihood of success during the cyber event.

Cyber-enabled malicious activities and operations may be designed to steer politics, propel agendas, and gain competitive advantage/economic power by targeting the nation's key cyber terrain and/or the critical infrastructure, such as banking, communications, power, and government services. If an adversary is able to gain access to a state's critical infrastructure, that foe may influence how the victim state acts or responds in an international situation. This is especially true when an aggressor state has an advantage of possessing sophisticated cyber capabilities or there are disparate vulnerabilities within each protagonist's critical infrastructure. For example, if State A and State B were experiencing political discord over state boundaries, and State A could cyber-attack State B's natural gas pipes from State C without State B having the ability to prevent that, then State B may be less likely to escalate or challenge State A for fear of loss of the natural gas.

Cyber conflict may be a prelude to conflict in the physical domain as was the case in Georgia and Ukraine. CEMO may be executed prior to and during a physical conflict in which an opponent possesses the modern, technologically sophisticated weapons and infrastructure that are vulnerable to cyber-attack. Future cyber conflicts will likely be executed in a manner that does not cross the threshold of an act of war (equal to an armed attack or use of force). Hybrid warfare will likely be the preferred method of conflict in the future and the cyber domain will be used simultaneously with or in advance of operations in the physical domain. The cases presented above may represent a new norm for state conflict in which one adversary coerces another nation through cyber means. Stuxnet is a clear example and message to the world demonstrating what a powerful nation or group is capable of, as a warning to all who might challenge them.[130]

State-on-state conflict does not often include private corporations; however, conflicts in cyberspace, as demonstrated in the cases above, show just how critical partnerships with private cyber entities can be. Even the sophisticated cyber nations must rely on the corporations under attack as well as private cyber firms for understanding what is occurring in cyberspace and how to contend with the CEMA. Conflict in cyberspace, unlike the physical domain, relies upon the government-private partnership to achieve national success. It behooves the United States to embrace this fact now and create the habitual relationships with private industry necessary to succeed in future cyber conflicts.

Finally, less advanced states and organizations can erode the economic vitality of the victim state, as was the case with the Titan Rain to Byzantine Hades case. If a malicious cyber actor is allowed to repeatedly and continually steal corporate and government data for the objective of the attacker's economic and military advancement, then the long-term effect on the victim nation will be the rise of 'instant international competitors' to challenge the status quo. Furthermore, the victim state may not recoup the revenue spent on research and development (now the competitor has that R&D and did not spend his R&D money to get the data), corporations may dissolve (or no longer compete), corporations may lose significant market share (not to mention profit losses), and nations and corporations may lose reputation and/or their brand. Additionally, America's current cyberspace vulnerabilities present in several corporate and government organizations will remain a lucrative target for future cyber-espionage and must be secured if the United States is to protect its future economic standing. Cyber conflict for financial advancement will continue to erode the United States' economic vitality if left unchecked. The United States must recognize that repeated espionage that grows in scale and scope can be considered CINS and threatens national and economic security not to mention its global political clout. Furthermore, the United States must be ever watchful for other challenging nations that seek to emulate Chain's performance through cyber-espionage.

Conclusions

Cyber-enabled malicious activity has grown in sophistication, frequency, and malicious impact over the last two-plus decades. CEMA has evolved from espionage and exploitation to disruption and destruction. More noteworthy is the fact cyber-criminals are no longer the lone actors on the stage – state or state-sponsored cyber actors have taken center stage in the role of cyber conflict. Furthermore, private cyber entities have grown in import as vital members of the national cyber defense team. Through hybrid warfare, as the new norm of state conflict, less physically powerful states and actors have struck powerful states with little fear of retribution as cyber conflict continues to remain below the established threshold of war. Consequently, new and evolved definitions of attack, as presented in this book, must be adopted to allow for greater cybersecurity options. These definitions should include of a wider set of responders and responses beyond what a state currently employs.

The four cases above elucidate situations where the duration of the CEMA was lengthy enough to be labeled CEMO and then rose to the classification of CINS. They illustrate that when the cyber operation impacts vital targets and populations, the effect on the nation was severe. In cases of CINS, there exists a threshold of mandatory action for the federal government…and beyond what private owner/operators of critical infrastructure can or should be forced to contend. In instances of CINS, the federal government must act to secure its critical infrastructure from cyber-attacks. All four cases should be a wake-up call for every modern nation that is dependent on cyberspace for the functionality of its critical infrastructure and government organizations. Even closed networks and infrastructure may be susceptible to sophisticated cyber adversaries. Furthermore, the global community must agree upon international norms and standards of behavior if the world is going to respond to the growing cyber chaos and anarchy present today. The reality of the current cyber paradigm necessitates a change in perspective, lexicon, and strategies for cyber conflict. Therefore, innovative strategies and organizations must be developed to thwart the malicious cyber actors' strategies and means of attacking key cyber terrain while simultaneously influencing adversary decision making in such a way as to induce a change in their behavior. That influencing of behavior is an aspect of coercion. Understanding what coercion is and its role in a national cybersecurity strategy is vital to the United States' national defense.

---

1 Jason Richards, "Denial-of-Service: The Estonian Cyberwar and Its Implications for U.S. National Security," in *International Affairs Review*, (The Elliott School of International Affairs, George Washington University, Washington DC), accessed online 1 Nov 2015, found at: http://www.iar-gwu.org/node/65.

2 Andreas Schmidt, *"Estonian Cyberattacks"*, in *A Fierce Domain: Conflict in Cyberspace, 1986 to 2012*, The Atlantic Council, Ed. Jason Healey, 2013, pg. 174.

3 See Central Intelligence Agency's *The World Factbook* at: https://www.cia.gov/library/publications/the-world-factbook/geos/en.html .

4 "Although the Estonian Parliament's decision to remove the Bronze Soldier memorial from Tallinn's main square served as the main precipitating event, other factors contributed to the vulnerability of Estonia's sociopolitical landscape. The first involved the scores of disaffected, disillusioned ethnic Russians who had been living within Estonia's borders since the end of the World War II. During the 1944-1991 Soviet occupation of Estonia, large groups of ethnic Russians moved into Estonian territory in search of a better life. By the time the Soviet Union collapsed, ethnic minorities comprised approximately 40 percent of the Estonian population." Jason Richards.

5 Stephen Herzog, *"Revisiting the Estonian Cyber Attacks: Digital Threats and Multinational Responses"*, Journal of Strategic Security, Volume 4, Number 2, Summer 2011, pg. 50, found at: http://scholarcommons.usf.edu/cgi/viewcontent.cgi?article=1105&context=jss

6 Andreas Schmidt, pg. 174.

7 Ibid, pg. 175.

8 Ibid, pg. 175.

9 Mike Collier, "Estonia: Cyber Superpower," in *Bloomberg News*, Dec 17, 2007, accessed online 1 Nov 2015, found at: http://www.bloomberg.com/news/articles/2007-12-17/estonia-cyber-superpowerbusinessweek-business-news-stock-market-and-financial-advice.

10 Jason Richards.

11 Mike Collier.

[12] BBC News, "*The Cyber Raiders Hitting Estonia*", May 17, 2007, accessed online 8 Nov 2015, found at: http://news.bbc.co.uk/2/hi/europe/6665195.stm

[13] Although some financial institutions continued to have "off-line" banking services, many banks were strictly on—line institutions. For those strictly online institutions, the 2007 DDoS was a crippling event. See Mike Collier.

[14] Joshua Davis, ""Hackers Take Down the Most Wired Nation in Europe," in *Wired.Com*, Aug 21, 2007, accessed 1 Nov 2015, found at: http://www.wired.com/2007/08/ff-estonia/.

[15] Jason Richards.

[16] According to an Incapsula study, their survey of 270 North American companies reported that 86% of companies experiencing DDoS lasted an average of 24 hours. The study states there is no predictable pattern for duration of DDoS, but 37% reported six hours or less, 31% reported 6-12 hours, and 18% stated 13-24 hours. The point here is that very few DDoS attacks last longer than a week and the sustained DDoS Estonia experienced is rare and significant. See Tim Matthews, "Incapsula Survey: What DDoS Really Cost Businesses," found at: http://lp.incapsula.com/rs/incapsulainc/images/eBook%20-%20DDoS%20Impact%20Survey.pdf. In another report from SANS, they claim the average duration of DDoS experienced by private corporations in 8.7 hours.

[17] "Cyberattacks can also include the use of malware, a program whose name is derived from the combination of the words "malicious" and "software;" such programs can destroy the victim's system software or hardware, or turn the victim's computer into a "zombie" system to be utilized in future attacks. These methods of attack manifest themselves in a number of ways through dozens of distinct denial-of-service attacks. The most common attacks known today are flood attacks, logic/software attacks, mailbombing, permanent denial-of-service (PDoS) attacks, accidental denial-of-service attacks, and distributed denial-of-service (DDoS) attacks." Herzog, pg.48.

[18] Mike Collier.

[19] Andreas Schmidt, pg. 178.

[20] Ibid, pg. 176

[21] Joshua Davis.

[22] Ian Traynor, "Russia accused of unleashing cyberwar to disable Estonia," in *The Guardian.Com*, May 16, 2007, accessed 2 Nov 2015, found at: http://www.theguardian.com/world/2007/may/17/topstories3.russia.

[23] Ibid.

[24] It was thought that these IP addresses were not the original source of the attacks, but were "bots" directed by the source. Joshua Davis.

[25] Jason Richards.

[26] Ibid.

[27] Herzog, pg. 54.

[28] Andreas Schmidt, pg. 188.

[29] Jason Richards.

[30] Ibid.

[31] Andreas Schmidt, pg. 190.

[32] Gas lines have been cut off several times in the last decade as a coercive political tool. See BBC's "Russia halts gas supplies to Ukraine after talks breakdown," 1 July 2015, found at: http://www.bbc.com/news/world-europe-33341322 and The Associate Press' "Russia's Gazprom Cuts Off Gas Supplies to Ukraine," Nov, 25, 2015, found at: http://www.nbcnews.com/news/world/russias-gazprom-cuts-gas-supplies-ukraine-n469351 .

[33] Andreas Schmidt, pgs. 189-190.

[34] Herzog, pg. 51.

[35] Ibid, pg. 51.

[36] The Economist, *"Estonia and Russia: A cyber-riot,"* May 10th, 2010, accessed online 8 Nov 2015, found at: http://www.economist.com/node/9163598

[37] The Friendly Relations Declaration (UN General Assembly, 1970), which included under the principle of non-intervention the following paragraph: No State or group of States has the right to intervene, directly or indirectly, for any reason whatever, in the internal or external affairs of any other State. Consequently, armed intervention and all other forms of interference or attempted threats against the personality of the State or against its political, economic and cultural elements are in violation of international law. See United Nations General Assembly Declaration.

[38] Admiral Michael Rogers, the head of Cyber Command and Director of the National Security Agency has argued, "norms create a basic structure for international political relations." Henry Farrell, "Why it's so hard to create norms in cyberspace," *The Washington Post,* April 6, 2015, accessed online 8 Jan 2016, found at: https://www.washingtonpost.com/blogs/monkey-cage/wp/2015/04/06/why-its-so-hard-to-create-norms-in-cyberspace/

[39] Valery Gerasimov, Lecture to the Voroshilov general Staff Academy titled, "*the Value of Science in Foresight: New Challenges Require Rethinking in the Forms and Methods of Warfare,*" reprinted in the Military-Industrial   Kurier,   27   Feb   2013,   found   at: http://fmso.leavenworth.army.mil/OEWatch/201412/Russia_03.html

[40] Ibid.

[41] *The Russo-Georgian War (2008): The Role of the cyber-attacks in the conflict*, May 24, 2012, pg. 5.

[42] Andreas Hagen, "The Russo-Georgian War (2008)", in "*A Fierce Domain: Conflict in Cyberspace, 1986 to 2012,*" Ed. Jason Healey, The Atlantic Council, Ed. Jason Healey, 2013, pg. 196.

[43] Robert Hackett, "Russian cyberwar advances military interests in Ukraine, report says," in *Fortune Online*,   (April   29,   2015),   accessed   online   1   Dec   2015,   found   at: http://fortune.com/2015/04/29/russian-cyberwar-ukraine/ .

[44] Cross-site scripting (XSS) is a type of computer security vulnerability typically found in web applications. XSS enables attackers to inject client-side script into web pages viewed by other users. A cross-site scripting vulnerability may be used by attackers to bypass access controls such as the same-origin policy. SQL injection is a code injection technique, used to attack data-driven applications, in which malicious SQL statements are inserted into an entry field for execution (e.g. to dump the database contents to the attacker).

[45] Andreas Hagen, pg. 197.

[46] Dan Goodin, "First known hacker-cased power outage signals troubling escalation," *Arstechnica Online,* Jan 4, 2016, accessed 7 Jan 2016, found at: http://arstechnica.com/security/2016/01/first-known-hacker-caused-power-outage-signals-troubling-escalation/

[47] See Robert M. Lee, Michael J. Assante, and Tim Conway, SANS Institute and Electricity Information Sharing and Analysis Center (EISAC) Report: "Analysis of the Cyber Attack on the Ukrainian Power Grid, Defense Use Case 5," March 18, 2016, found at: https://ics.sans.org/media/E-ISAC_SANS_Ukraine_DUC_5.pdf.

[48] Ibid.

[49] SANS Institute's Blogger, Robert M. Lee discussed the lost opportunity to make a more significant statement by the U.S. government leadership to attribute this CEMA to Russia in the ICS SANS Blog. Lee stated, where I believe there was a missed opportunity was for more senior levels of the [US] government to confirm the attack much earlier on with the high level styled assessment the ICS-CERT made, to have the ICS-CERT provide more deep technical analysis, and to have private sector companies such as SANS, ESET, iSight, Mandiant, TrendMicro, and others that were involved to further complement that technical assessment with interpretations and analysis. When dealing with

international incidents that set dangerous precedents, such as a clearly coordinated and intentional cyber-attack against civilian infrastructure, there must be a more coordinated effort with messaging to a variety of audiences. See "Thoughts on the ICS-CERT Ukraine Cyber Attack Report," 25 Feb 2016, found at: https://ics.sans.org/blog/2016/02/25/thoughts-on-the-ics-cert-ukraine-cyber-attack-report.

[50] Dan Goodin.

[51] David E. Sanger, "Utilities Cautioned About Potential for a Cyberattack After Ukraine's," *The New York Times,* Feb 29, 2016, accessed online 29 Mar 2016, found at: http://www.nytimes.com/2016/03/01/us/politics/utilities-cautioned-about-potential-for-a-cyberattack-after-ukraines.html?_r=0.

[52] Andreas Hagen, pg. 200.

[53] Hathaway, et al, pg. 27.

[54] The effects directly attributable to cyber is not possible to break out from the total. However, CEMA contributed considerably to the total. Andreas Hagan, pg. 198; and see The Economist's article "Ukraine in Crisis," (Jun 4, 2015), accessed online 1 Dec 2015, found at: http://www.economist.com/blogs/graphicdetail/2015/06/ukraine-graphics

[55] National Statistics Office of Georgia, GeoStat Website, accessed online 1 Dec 2015, found at: http://geostat.ge/index.php?action=page&p_id=119&lang=eng .

[56] BBC Online, "*Ukraine conflict taking heavy toll on economy says IMF*," 1 June 2015, accessed online 2 Nov 2015, found at: http://www.bbc.com/news/business-32954874.

[57] Andreas Hagen, pg. 198.

[58] Cybersecurity firms have also reported the China stole the negotiation strategies and financial information of energy, banking, law, and other industries to aid China's quest for economic and technical parity with the United States. Adam Segal, "*From Titan Rain to Byzantine Hades: Chinese Cyber Espionage*", in "A Fierce Domain: Conflict in Cyberspace, 1986 to 2012", The Atlantic Council, Ed. Jason Healey, 2013, pg. 166.

[59] Houqing, Wang and Zhang Zingye. "The Science of Military Campaigns," Beijing, China: NDU Press (2000).

[60] "The Report of the Commission on the Theft of American Intellectual Property," (The National Bureau of Asian Research, May 2013), pg. 16, found at: http://www.ipcommission.org/report/ip_commission_report_052213.pdf.

[61] Andrew Szamosszegi and Cole Kyle, "An Analysis of State-owned Enterprise and State Capitalism in China," prepared for the U.S.-China Economic and Security Review Commission, Oct

26, 2011, pg. 1, found at: http://origin.www.uscc.gov/sites/default/files/Research/10_26_11_CapitalTradeSOEStudy.pdf.

[62] James A. Lewis, "*Computer Espionage, Titan Rain and China,*" Center for Strategic and International Studies, (CSIS), Technology and Public Policy Program, December 2005, accessed online 12 Nov 2105, found at: http://csis.org/files/media/csis/pubs/051214_china_titan_rain.pdf .

[63] Ibid.

[64] A cyber-espionage operation by China several years ago produced sensitive technology and aircraft secrets that were incorporated into the latest version of China's new J-20 stealth fighter jet, according to U.S. officials and private defense analysts. Bill Gertz, "Top Gun takeover: Stolen F-35 secrets showing up in China's stealth fighter,", *The Washington Times,* March 13, 2014, accessed online 8 Jan 2015, found at: http://www.washingtontimes.com/news/2014/mar/13/f-35-secrets-now-showing-chinas-stealth-fighter/?page=all

[65] Michael Joseph Gross, "*Enter the Cyber-Dragon*", Vanity Fair, September 2011, accessed online 8 Nov 2015, found at: http://www.vanityfair.com/news/2011/09/chinese-hacking-201109.

[66] Joel Brenner, "The New Industrial Espionage," *The American Interest,* Dec 10, 2014, accessed online 8 Jan 2016, found at: http://www.the-american-interest.com/2014/12/10/the-new-industrial-espionage/.

[67] Bill Gertz, "NSA Details Chinese Cyber Theft of F-35, Military Secrets," *The FreeBeacon Online*, Jan 22, 2015, found at: http://freebeacon.com/national-security/nsa-details-chinese-cyber-theft-of-f-35-military-secrets/.

[68] Clarke, pg. 55.

[69] Microsoft Website, "Gates Highlights Progress on Security, Outlines Next Steps for Continued Innovation," Microsoft News Center, Feb 15, 2005, accessed online 8 Jan 2016, found at: https://news.microsoft.com/2005/02/15/gates-highlights-progress-on-security-outlines-next-steps-for-continued-innovation/

[70] David Goldman, "Fake tech has infiltrated the U.S. government," CNN News Online, November 8th, 2012, accessed online 5 Dec 2105, found at: http://money.cnn.com/2012/11/08/technology/security/counterfeit-tech/index.html

[71] Ibid.

[72] Ibid.

[73] Clarke, pg. 57.

[74] Ibid, pp. 57-58.

139

[75] Josh Chin, "Cyber Sleuths Track Hacker to China's Military," *The Wall Street Journal*, Sept 23, 2015, accessed online 31 Mar 2016, found at: http://www.wsj.com/articles/cyber-sleuths-track-hacker-to-chinas-military-1443042030.

[76] A growing body of digital forensic evidence — confirmed by American intelligence officials who say Unit 61398 has been an active cyber army unit for years. David E. Sanger, David Barboza, and Nicole Perlroth, "Chinese Army Unit Is Seen as Tied to Hacking Against U.S., *The New York Times*, Feb 18, 2013, accessed online 31 Mar 2016, found at: http://www.nytimes.com/2013/02/19/technology/chinas-army-is-seen-as-tied-to-hacking-against-us.html?emc=na&_r=1&.

[77] Ibid.

[78] Adam Segal, pg. 165.

[79] Ibid, pg. 166.

[80] Goldman.

[81] Federal Bureau of Investigations website, "U.S. Charges Five Chinese Military Hackers with Cyber Espionage Against U.S. Corporations and a Labor Organization for Commercial Advantage," May 19, 2014, found at: https://www.fbi.gov/pittsburgh/press-releases/2014/u.s.-charges-five-chinese-military-hackers-with-cyber-espionage-against-u.s.-corporations-and-a-labor-organization-for-commercial-advantage.

[82] Ibid.

[83] Ibid.

[84] Federal Bureau of Investigation Indictment "U.S. Charges Five Chinese Military Hackers with Cyber Espionage Against U.S. Corporations and a Labor Organization for Commercial Advantage," found at: https://www.fbi.gov/pittsburgh/press-releases/2014/u.s.-charges-five-chinese-military-hackers-with-cyber-espionage-against-u.s.-corporations-and-a-labor-organization-for-commercial-advantage.

[85] Michael S. Schmidt and David E Sanger, "5 in China Army Face U.S. Charges of Cyberattacks," *The New York Times*, MAY 19, 2014, found at: http://www.nytimes.com/2014/05/20/us/us-to-charge-chinese-workers-with-cyberspying.html?_r=0.

[86] Ibid. See also FBI Indictment "U.S. Charges Five Chinese Military Hackers with Cyber Espionage Against U.S. Corporations and a Labor Organization for Commercial Advantage."

[87] FBI Indictment "U.S. Charges Five Chinese Military Hackers with Cyber Espionage Against U.S. Corporations and a Labor Organization for Commercial Advantage."

[88] Ibid.

[89] FBI Indictment.

[90] David Drummond, *"A New Approach to China"*, Google Blog, March, 22, 2010, accessed online 8 Nov 2015, found at: https://googleblog.blogspot.com/2010/03/new-approach-to-china-update.html

[91] Brenner.

[92] Michael A. Riley and Ashlee Vance, "China Corporate Espionage Boom Knocks Wind Out of U.S. Companies," *Bloomberg Business News*, March 15, 2012, accessed online 8 Jan 2015, found at: http://www.bloomberg.com/news/articles/2012-03-15/china-corporate-espionage-boom-knocks-wind-out-of-u-s-companies

[93] "The Report of the Commission on the Theft of American Intellectual Property," pg. 2.

[94] Ibid, pg. 1.

[95] Carrie Lukas, "It's Time for the U.S. to Deal with Cyber-Espionage," *US News*, June 4, 2013, accessed online 8 Jan 2016, found at: http://www.usnews.com/opinion/articles/2013/06/04/chinas-industrial-cyberespionage-harms-the-us-economy .

[96] Brenner.

[97] Mandiant Report, "APT 1 Exposing One of China's Cyber Espionage Units," found at: http://intelreport.mandiant.com/Mandiant_APT1_Report.pdf .

[98] "The Report of the Commission on the Theft of American Intellectual Property," pg. 10.

[99] Office of the Director of National Intelligence, *National Counterintelligence Strategy for the United States of America 2016*, (Washington DC, 2016), pp. 3-, found at: https://www.ncsc.gov/publications/strategy/docs/National_CI_Strategy_2016.pdf.

[100] Department of Homeland Security website, "Combating Cyber Crime," found at: https://www.dhs.gov/topic/combating-cyber-crime.

[101] See General Accounting Office (GAO) Report to Congress: "INFORMATION SECURITY: DHS Needs to Enhance Capabilities, Improve Planning, and Support Greater Adoption of Its National Cybersecurity Protection System," Jan 2016, pg. 15, found at: http://www.gao.gov/assets/680/674829.pdf.

[102] Ibid, pg. 1.

[103] Crowdstrike Report, "Observations From the Front Lines of Threat Hunting", found at: https://www.crowdstrike.com/resources/reports/observations-from-the-front-lines-of-threat-hunting/.

[104] Ibid.

[105] "The Report of the Commission on the Theft of American Intellectual Property," pg. 10.

[106] Josh Rogin, "NSA Chief: Cybercrime constitutes the "greatest transfer of wealth in history", Foreign Policy, July 9, 2012, accessed online 8 Nov 2015, found at: http://foreignpolicy.com/2012/07/09/nsa-chief-cybercrime-constitutes-the-greatest-transfer-of-wealth-in-history/

[107] ONCE, pp. i-ii.

[108] In 2002, the dissident group "National Council of Resistance of Iran" revealed the existence of the underground facility at Natanz, sending panic across the West. Greg Bruno, "Iran's Nuclear Program", *Council of Foreign Relations*, March 10, 2010, accessed online 15 Nov 2015, found at: http://www.cfr.org/iran/irans-nuclear-program/.

[109] Adam Tarock, "Iran's Nuclear Programme and the West," *Third World Quarterly* 27, No. 4 (2006), pp. 645-664.

[110] Kim Zetter, "*An Unprecedented Look at Stuxnet, The World's First Digital Weapon,*" Wired, 3 Nov 2015, accessed online 15 Nov 2015, found at: http://www.wired.com/2014/11/countdown-to-zero-day-stuxnet/

[111] George W. Bush, "*Address to the American Legion National Convention*", The White House, August 2006, accessed online, 15 Nov 2015, found at: http://georgewbush-whitehouse.archives.gov/news/releases/2006/08/20060831-1.html

[112] Michael J. Gross, "*A Declaration of Cyber-War,*" Vanity Fair, April 2011, accessed online 15 Nov 2105, found at: http://www.vanityfair.com/culture/features/2011/04/stuxnet-201104 .

[113] Ibid.

[114] Ibid.

[115] Chris Morton, "*Stuxnet, Flame, Duqu – the OLYMIPIC GAMES,*" in "A Fierce Domain: Conflict in Cyberspace, 1986 to 2012," Jason Healey editor, Cyber Conflict Studies Association and the Atlantic Council's Brent Scowcroft Center on International Security, 2013, pp. 220-22.

[116] Ibid, pg. 222.

[117] Kim Zetter.

[118] Chris Morton, pg. 223.

[119] Kim Zetter.

[120] Michael J. Gross, "*A Declaration of Cyber-War,*" in Vanity Fair News online magazine, February 28, 2011, accessed online 28 Nov, 201, found at: http://www.vanityfair.com/news/2011/03/stuxnet-201104.

[121] Ibid.

[122] Chris Morton, pp. 217-18.

[123] David E. Sanger, *"Obama Order Sped Up Wave of Cyberattacks Against Iran,"* The New York Times, June 1, 2012, accessed online 28 Nov 2105, found at: http://www.nytimes.com/2012/06/01/world/middleeast/obama-ordered-wave-of-cyberattacks-against-iran.html?_r=0.

[124] Ibid

[125] Ibid.

[126] Morton, pg. 229.

[127] Andrew Couts, *"Iran accused of attempted cyber-attack on Google, Yahoo, Skype,"* Digital Trends, March 25, 2011, accessed online 28 Nov 2015, found at: http://www.digitaltrends.com/computing/iran-accused-of-cyber-attack-on-google-yahoo-skype/ .

[128] Ibid.

[129] According to *The New York Times*, an internal Obama administration document estimates the Iranian effort was set back by 18 months to two years, but some experts inside and outside the government are more skeptical, noting that Iran's enrichment levels have steadily recovered. David E. Sanger.

[130] Unfortunately, since the cyber-attack on Iran, Stuxnet has been reverse engineered and now many cyber actors possess the tools to attack the critical infrastructure of a nation with debilitating effect.

CHAPTER FOUR

EVALUATING THE EFFECTIVENESS OF THE CURRENT U.S. CYBERSECURITY STRATEGY

T he private U.S. critical infrastructure owners/operators invest in people, processes, and technology in an effort to defend against the growing cyber threats. "Nonetheless, the cyber risk environment may soon present national and economic security challenges that test the industry's capability to respond alone, requiring the Nation to evolve, strengthen and clarify roles in the essential partnership between the private sector and Government."[1] Above the level of CEMA that private industry can adequately contend, I believe that the United States is obligated to utilize all national instruments of power/statecraft to protect the nation and its critical infrastructure. Several questions arise then. Is the United States' cybersecurity strategy adequate for the task? Does the United States use coercion as an additional tool to influence the malicious cyber actors that threaten the nation's economic and national security? Conversely, can one assert that there is no need for a coercive strategy? Is the lack of past coercive actions intentional or simply the result of not wanting to deal with the complexity of putting together a coercive strategy? This chapter will examine several case studies to explore possible answers to these questions and to determine the effectiveness of America to contend with the current cyber storm.

The Approach of the Analysis

A central reason for designing a national coercive cybersecurity strategy is to influence the adversary's behavior in ways that are beneficial to the coercer. Cyber coercion involves a psychological and cognitive component, along with the capacity to influence the motives, cost-benefit calculations, and risk-taking propensities of adversaries, in order to convince that adversary that launching a cyber-attack would not serve their interests and objectives and that the costs and risks would outweigh any sensible calculation of benefits.[2] Crafting the proper blend of influential cyber tools and psychological capabilities to achieve one's aims is the foundation of a successful coercive strategy.

In cases of CINS, the United States government has a central role alongside private industry to protect the nation from major cyber-attacks that would negatively impact U.S. national and economic security (as the government does in cases of physical attacks). From that premise, we can explore whether or not coercion should be an essential element of an effective national cybersecurity strategy. Through several case studies, we will examine when and if pressuring the United States' cyber adversaries was accomplished as a result of CINS directed at U.S. critical infrastructure. In cases where the United States did not pressure the cyber foe, at the end of the chapter we will look at possible reasons why no pressure was applied by looking at three different perspectives: systemically across the Federal government (what national policy would direct possible action), organizationally across the government cyber entities with authority to act (what standard operating procedures would direct possible action), and individually across key national leaders who would or should influence United States cyber efforts to initiate actions to pressure the threat in coercive ways.

The selected case studies are used to answer these questions. The cases were selected because they met one or more of the following criteria:

The United States was the victim;

The CEMA witnessed by the critical infrastructure operator or company was of a level of sophistication, impact, and/or magnitude that was beyond that which the sector could contend solely;

The malicious cyber actor was a state or state-sponsored entity for which the critical infrastructure operator should not respond fully (i.e., it is the responsibility of the United States to respond); and

In some cases, although the nature of the CEMA witnessed did not reach the level of CINS, the incident was dangerously close and had the nefarious actor chose to escalate the incident, the event potentially would have reached the level of CINS.

The following questions assist in determining if and to what extent the United States' used coercion to influence the decision making of the malicious cyber actors that threaten United States critical infrastructure.

Did the United States possess an adequate cybersecurity policy or strategy to address the CINS? If not, was an ad hoc plan implemented in response to the incident?

Did the United States know who perpetrated the CINS? Was there an understanding of the malicious cyber actor's intent or objective within the larger geopolitical landscape?

Did the United States comprehend nature of the interests at stake or the risks involved prior to the event?

Was there a clearly established threshold for which the United States would take action? If so, did the United States take coercive action(s) that influenced decision making?

Was there political will exhibited by government leaders to take coercive action beyond just defense? Or was there evidence that showed the United States deliberately chose not to use coercion?

Did the United States use credible capabilities to contend with the CINS and the malicious cyber actor in a fashion to influence decision making? To what extent were the capabilities used across the spectrum of national cybersecurity activities?

Did the government partner with private industry to combat the threat?

Did the United States know and apply pressure to the adversary's centers of gravity in order to influence decision making?

Did the United States use inducements in order to influence decision making?

Did the United States use entanglements in order to influence decision making?

The following are the cases that this chapter will examine: Operation Ababil to Operation Cleaver; the Office of Personnel Management Theft of 21.5 million personnel security files; the Series of Russian CEMA targeting the United States Commercial Retail sector and United States Government; and the Series of CEMA Targeting U.S Healthcare Institutions. In order to properly examine these cases, we must first understand the cyber policies and capabilities within the United States that were available to contend with CEMA witnessed. A note of caution, although a chronological examination of U.S. cyber policy follows, not all of the policies were in place at the time of each case below. Regardless, each case will be assessed based upon the relevant policy and strategies present at the time of the CINS.

United States National Security Strategy

Before assessing the United States' cyber strategy, we first should understand the overall national security strategy of the United States and properly place cybersecurity within it. The United States' 2017 National Security Strategy (NSS) is the President's security policy directive that specifies how the United States government departments and agencies should work to protect America. The genesis of the NSS can be found in the 1947 National Security Act and the Goldwater-Nichols Act of 1986. These guidance documents make it clear that the purpose of the President to issue declarations of national security strategy and not use the NSS for politics or propaganda, but to ensure the safety of the United States.[3] In the 2017 NSS, the United States must safeguard the national interests through strong and sustainable leadership. Furthermore, the NSS "lays out a strategic vision for protecting the American people and preserving our way of life, promoting our prosperity, preserving peace through strength, and advancing American influence in the world."[4] The 2017 National Security Strategy provides the White House's perspective as to the broad strategic goals and interests that are important to America, but does not articulate the means and ways the nation should achieve these goals. The NSS is "a strategy of principled realism that is guided by outcomes, not ideology. It is based upon the view that peace, security, and prosperity depend on strong, sovereign nations that respect their citizens at home and cooperate to advance peace abroad. And it is grounded in the realization that American principles are a lasting force for good in the world."[5] These idealistic interests are the foundation for the United States government's lower level strategies and plans.

The NSS further stipulates that nation must pursue a comprehensive national security agenda in a collaborative way, allocate resources accordingly, and make difficult choices and policy tradeoffs if the nation is to be successful at protecting American interests globally. In order to succeed, the President described his four top priorities for the United States as: "First, our fundamental responsibility is to protect the American people, the homeland, and the American way of life… Second, we will promote American prosperity…Third, we will preserve peace through strength by rebuilding our military so that it remains preeminent, deters our adversaries, and if necessary, is able to fight and win…and Fourth, we will advance American influence because a world that supports American interests and reflects our values makes America more secure and prosperous."[6]   The NSS also clearly indicates that the whole of government efforts and operations required to address these strategic risks must be coordinated with and integrated across the government agencies and departments in order to maximize the finite resources the nation possesses.

Despite the fact that every administration publishes a National Security Strategy, national security experts both within and outside the United States government continue to opine over the years that these NSSs are simply policy pronouncements rather than "strategy" in the classical sense of the term. The Congressional Research Service was asked to assess the 2015 NSS for Congress. In their document the "2015 National Security Strategy: Authorities, Changes, Issues for Congress," the national security researchers lamented that the President's 2015 NSS lacked the strategic guidance required in a national security strategy – and the 2017 and 2019 NSSs are no different. Furthermore, researchers suggested that these monographs lacked clarity in the following areas: the National Security Strategies past and present did not accurately identify and properly emphasize key features and trends in the international security environment; do not adequately address the possibility that, since late 2013, a fundamental shift in the international security environment occurred which suggests a shift from the familiar post-Cold War era to a new and different strategic situation (e.g., the advancement of CEMA directed at United States critical infrastructure); do not qualify as a true strategy in terms of linking ends (objectives), means (resources), ways (activities), and in terms of establishing priorities among the goals; do not properly balance objectives against available resources, particularly in the context of the limits on defense spending established in the Budget Control Act of 2011; and were not aligned with the Administration's actual policies and budgets.[7] Moreover, the researchers were concerned that each

NSS did not provide details as to how the United States was to achieve the "strong and sustained leadership" which both Presidents Obama and Trump directed in their NSS. Without some level of detail in an NSS, then the United States government departments and agencies are left wondering how to define and execute their respective missions.

Outside the government, national security pundits also expressed concerns that past and present NSSs were incomplete and insufficient as a strategy. Some opined that the NSS objectives were too vague to be beneficial and that those objectives were "backed up only by various lists of tactical attempts... [which] fundamentally asks more questions than it answers."[8] Others articulate that the frequency and certainty with which the United States' strategy avows the centrality of national leadership betrays a growing insecurity among Americans about their country's prospects for exercising influence in the world. Some observers interpret President Obama's and Trump's call as their desire to withdraw the United States from global affairs and evade difficult policy choices. "The United States must prepare its foreign policy for a world where its economy will no longer be the largest in absolute terms; where disorder may well be an enduring feature of the strategic environment, not a passing aberration; where a dizzying, growing array of non-state actors exercises ever-growing influence; and where its [the United States'] signature postwar achievement, liberal world order, erodes indefinitely."[9] Experts both within and outside the government agree that both of the 2015 NSS and 2017 NSS are lacking as a national strategy.

Regarding cybersecurity in the 2017 NSS, President Trump admits that: "Cyberattacks offer adversaries low cost and deniable opportunities to seriously damage or disrupt critical infrastructure, cripple American businesses, weaken our Federal networks, and attack the tools and devices that Americans use every day to communicate and conduct business."[10] The 2017 NSS goes on to articulate that given the United States faces a substantial cyber threat, the nation with a secure cyber domain is a nation with a defensible cyber ecosystem that promotes economic growth, protects American liberties, and advances our national security.[11] The 2017 NSS further lays the Administration's five priorities for the cybersecurity for the nation: Identify and Prioritize Risk, Build Defensible Government Networks, Deter and Disrupt Malicious Cyber Actors, Improve Information Sharing, and Deploy Layered Defenses.[12] The 2017 NSS goes on to define three actions specifically related to "Preserve Peace through Strength." The first is: Improve Attribution and Response – "We will invest in capabilities to support and improve our ability to attribute cyberattacks, to allow for rapid response."[13] The second is: Enhance Cyber Tools and Expertise – "We will improve our cyber tools across the spectrum of conflict to protect United States Government assets and United States critical infrastructure, and to protect the integrity of data and information. United States departments and agencies will recruit, train, and retain a workforce capable of operating across this spectrum of activity."[14] The third is: Improve Integration and Agility – "We will improve the integration of authorities and procedures across the United States Government so that cyber operations against adversaries can be conducted as required. We will work with the Congress to address the challenges that continue to hinder timely intelligence and information sharing, planning and operations, and the development of necessary cyber tools."[15] Although laudable as specified actions, they are also incomplete in defining the overall goal for a national coercive cyber strategy. One must then look further back in time to President Obama's 2011 International Strategy for Cyberspace and the 2013 Executive Order 13636: "Executive Order -- Improving Critical Infrastructure Cybersecurity" for additional clarity in the creation of a national cyber strategy.

The goal of the 2011 International Strategy for Cybersecurity stated that the "United States will work internationally to promote an open, interoperable, secure, and reliable information and communications infrastructure that supports international trade and commerce, strengthens international security, and fosters free expression and innovation. To achieve that goal, we will build and sustain an environment in which norms of responsible behavior guide states' actions, sustain partnerships, and support the rule of law in cyberspace."[16] Although this is not a satisfying goal for this dissertation's purposes of defining a national coercive cybersecurity strategy, there is a subordinate objective of that goal that provides a foundation for clarity - "The Basis for Norms." Specifically, the objective declared:

"Rules that promote order and peace, advance basic human dignity, and promote freedom in economic competition are essential to any international environment. These principles provide a basic roadmap for how states can meet their traditional international obligations in cyberspace and, in many cases, reflect duties of states that apply regardless of context. The existing principles that should support cyberspace norms include: Upholding Fundamental Freedoms - states must respect fundamental freedoms of expression and association, online as well as off; Respect for Property - states should in their undertakings and through domestic laws respect intellectual property rights, including patents, trade secrets, trademarks, and copyrights; Valuing Privacy - individuals should be protected from arbitrary or unlawful state interference with their privacy when they use the Internet; Protection from Crime - states must identify and prosecute cybercriminals, to ensure laws and practices deny criminals safe havens, and cooperate with international criminal investigations in a timely manner; and Right of Self-Defense - consistent with the United Nations Charter, states have an inherent right to self-defense that may be triggered by certain aggressive acts in cyberspace."[17]

The three key statements that one should draw from the quote above are: the expectation of all states to respect another state's sovereign freedom; a state's responsibility to its citizens, interests, and property; an obligation to uphold law (both customary and international law) and the assistance in legal investigations; and the inherent right of state self-defense against grave imminent threats that threaten its ability to execute the above statements. These three strategic statements articulate the obligation of responsible international action by all states (in both cyberspace and the physical domain).

According to Executive Order 13636, the repeated cyber intrusions into critical infrastructure show the requirement for improved cybersecurity. The cyber threat continues to grow and represents one of the most serious national security challenges we must confront. The national and economic security of every modern nation depend on the reliable functioning of its critical infrastructure in the face of such threats. It is the policy of the United States to enhance the security and resilience of America's critical infrastructure and to maintain a cyber ecosystem that promotes efficiency, innovation, and economic prosperity while advocating safety, security, business confidentiality, privacy, and civil liberties.[18] This statement helps ties the 'obligation of international action' with the nation's critical pressure points (United States critical infrastructure) to define 'what must be protected.' Referencing back to the 2017 NSS above which stated the risks to United States interests as: an attack on the United States homeland or critical infrastructure, threats or attacks against United States citizens abroad and our allies, global economic crisis or widespread economic slowdown. These risks would include malicious cyber actors that chose to implement CEMA for those nefarious effects. One then could express a clear national cybersecurity goal, which is the first step in a strategy. From the above compilation of United States NSSs and policy documents, we may then survey the United States' national cybersecurity policies and structure.

United States' Cybersecurity Policy and Structure

First, it is important to comprehend the overall structure of the U.S. government as it pertains to presenting the cybersecurity policies and capabilities to defend America. When one examines current United States government cybersecurity polices, the overall observation is that the national framework is designed to accomplish four broad initiatives: protect the government's cyberspace; advocate for private cybersecurity efforts (civil defense); where possible, share government cyber threat information with private industry; and use Federal law enforcement to investigate and prosecute where possible.[19] For nearly three decades, several Administrations and Congresses have directed the creation and evolution of national policy and strategy related to cybersecurity. Several of the Presidents' policy documents and directives and Congressional legislations, along with the DHS and DoD cyber strategies, are discussed briefly below. Our examination begins with the cyber directives from the 1990s when the cyber threat started to attack critical infrastructure in earnest.

Former President Clinton launched the first substantial United States effort to contend with cyber defense and resilience issues with his Presidential Decision Directive (PDD)-63 in May 1998.[20] The PDD highlighted some of the vulnerabilities inherent in U.S. critical infrastructure and set forth a process for the development of an infrastructure assurance plan to protect the critical infrastructure assets. PDD-63 called for each sector to assess more fully their vulnerabilities and propose remedies for them while establishing response plans to mitigate attacks and restore capabilities.[21] PDD-63 also defined the still existent coordinating structure in which each sector was issued a "lead agency" that has primary responsibility for coordinating cybersecurity activities within the sector.[22] For example, Treasury was assigned to the financial sector, Energy to the electrical sector, and Health and Human Services to public health. The National Infrastructure Assurance Council (a group of non-Federal leaders from the critical infrastructure sectors and private industry) provided advice to the cybersecurity effort regarding the Federal government activities.[23]

From PDD-63, came the creation of sector specific Information Sharing and Analysis Centers (ISACs), which were designed (as the name specifies) to share cybersecurity information within the sector while providing analysis of that information.[24] Currently, each critical infrastructure sector has at least one ISAC with some sectors, such as Energy, possessing multiple ones. Also, there are several ISACs that now support other industries beyond critical infrastructure such as retailers, maritime, research and education networks, and others.[25] These ISACs interface with the lead agency and other governmental organizations as necessary to gain and share information and best practices. Private industry in turn works with their respective ISAC in defending their networks while sending cybersecurity information back to the ISAC.

In 2003, former President George W. Bush directed the National Strategy to Secure Cyberspace and its companion document, National Security Presidential Directive (NSPD)-38 the following year.[26] The National Strategy to Secure Cyberspace is a component of the larger National Strategy for Homeland Security and was drafted by the Department of Homeland Security in reaction to the September 11, 2001 terrorist attacks. Released on February 14, 2003, the "national strategy" offered suggestions, not mandates, to business, academic, and individual users of cyberspace to secure computer systems and networks. "It was prepared after a year of research by businesses, universities, and government, and after five months of public comment. The plan advises a number of security practices as well as promotion of cyber security education…The National Strategy to Secure Cyberspace identifies three strategic objectives: (1) Prevent cyber-attacks against America's critical infrastructures; (2) Reduce national vulnerability to cyber-attacks; and (3) Minimize damage and recovery time from cyber-attacks that do occur."[27] The National Strategy to Secure Cyberspace is more of a policy directive than a strategy since it does not articulate what means will be used, how they will implemented, and against which threats.

Former President Obama continued the national effort to emphasize cybersecurity in a growing threat landscape. In the name of economic and national security, the Obama administration prioritized cybersecurity upon taking office. After an in-depth review of the communications and information infrastructure, the Comprehensive National Cybersecurity Initiative was partially declassified and expanded to include "key elements of a broader, updated national U.S. cybersecurity strategy."[28] President Obama went on to issue several Executive Orders further clarifying Federal government initiatives in cybersecurity. Two noteworthy Executive Orders were the order on "Improving Critical Infrastructure Cybersecurity" and the "Blocking the Property of Certain Persons Engaging in Significant Malicious Cyber-Enabled Activities."

Obama issued Executive Order 13636 Improving Critical Infrastructure Cybersecurity in February 2013 to "increase the volume, timeliness, and quality of cyber threat information shared with U.S. private sector entities so that these entities may better protect and defend themselves against cyber threats."[29] The Executive Order also tasked the National Institute for Standards and Technology (NIST) to create a cybersecurity framework that helps organizations mitigate risks to the nation's essential systems such as power generation and distribution, the financial services sector, and transportation.[30] NIST released the Framework for Improving Critical Infrastructure Cybersecurity in February 2014, which "consists of standards, guidelines and practices to promote the protection of critical infrastructure."[31]

The second Obama Executive Order titled "Blocking the Property of Certain Persons Engaging in Significant Malicious Cyber-Enabled Activities" gave the administration the option to impose substantial consequences through the tool of economic sanction on any organizations or individuals who launched CEMA at the United States' CI.[32] The intent of Executive Order was to provide a coercive tool to the President against the "significant increase in the frequency, scale, and sophistication of cyber incidents targeting the American people, including everything from large data breaches and significant intrusions to destructive and coercive cyber-attacks intended to influence the way ordinary Americans exercise their constitutional rights."[33] In many cases, these cyber threats came from overseas actors using malicious cyber activities to inflict harm on Americans. Additionally, in May 2011 President Obama launched the International Strategy for Cyberspace which (again) was not a strategy in the classical sense, but rather was "a vision for the future of cyberspace… [and] an agenda for realizing it."[34] The "vision" laid out plans for strengthening partnership, defending key cyber terrain, and building prosperity and security through development. The paper promoted international standards—enhanced security, resiliency, and reliability—while clarifying when and where the United States would use law enforcement and the military to ensure its interests globally. This White House document was not prescriptive like a strategy should be, but offered "a starting point for patient, persistent negotiations between the United States and its allies and partners" according to Secretary of State Hillary Clinton.[35]

The Department of Homeland Security is charged by Presidential Policy Directives (PPD-20 and PPD-21) and Executive Order 13636 (amongst others) to coordinate and synchronize the whole of government cybersecurity activities. The Secretary of Homeland Security "shall provide strategic guidance, promote a national unity of effort, and coordinate the overall Federal effort to promote the security and resilience of the Nation's critical infrastructure."[36] PPD-21 add clarity to the overall governmental role in national cyber defense by stating the policy of the United States.

"It is the policy of the United States to strengthen the security and resilience of its critical infrastructure against both physical and cyber threats. The Federal Government shall work with critical infrastructure owners and operators and SLTT [state, local, tribal, and territorial] entities to take proactive steps to manage risk and strengthen the security and resilience of the Nation's critical infrastructure, considering all hazards that could have a debilitating impact on national security, economic stability, public health and safety, or any combination thereof. These efforts shall seek to reduce vulnerabilities, minimize consequences, identify and disrupt threats, and hasten response and recovery efforts related to critical infrastructure."[37]

The policy clearly focuses on reducing vulnerabilities, minimizing consequences, identifying threats, and hastening response and recovery efforts as they apply to government systems and support for private critical infrastructure operators' own cybersecurity enterprises, while being mindful not to infringe upon private industry's responsibilities. Although praiseworthy, the United States government does not intend to interfere with critical infrastructure cybersecurity efforts directly, nor does DHS possess any significant cyber capabilities or authority to disrupt threats as PPD-21 directs. The Directive further stipulates three strategic imperatives that drive the government's approach to strengthen critical infrastructure security and resilience: "1) Refine and clarify functional relationships across the Federal Government to advance the national unity of effort to strengthen critical infrastructure security and resilience; 2) Enable effective information exchange by identifying baseline data and systems requirements for the Federal Government; and 3) Implement an integration and analysis function to inform planning and operations decisions regarding critical infrastructure."[38] Specifically in regards to relationships across government and unity of effort, PPD-21 directs a national effort be guided and "informed by the expertise, experience, capabilities, and responsibilities of the [sector specific agencies] SSAs, other Federal departments and agencies with critical infrastructure roles, SLTT entities, and critical infrastructure owners and operators."[39] The notion of 'to be guided and informed by' translates into DHS examining what each respective government and private industry does with regard to cybersecurity. To be clear, several of the United States departments and agencies are executing noteworthy actions and operations in cyberspace – both domestically and internationally. With that knowledge, each government department and agency share with and should be knowledgeable about the other entities' cybersecurity actions and operations (at least on the government side). Practicably, this translates into information sharing across governmental organization by placing liaisons in other department and agencies cyber operations centers, which is not synonymous with integrating and synchronizing cyber operations. Under the current structure, a liaison's primary duty is only to pass information – the act of synchronizing and integrating operations requires a far greater degree of interaction than what liaisons are designed or designated to accomplish.

To illustrate the shortcoming of this approach, we can look to an applicable U.S. military analogy. Prior to 1986, the U.S. military suffered from inter-service rivalries and integration complications. Each Service (Army, Air Force, Navy, and Marine Corps) routinely conducted independent operations according to their respective strategies and agendas with little care for coordination or synchronization across the Services. As a result, originating from these inter-service rivalries and lack of integration, the U.S. military experienced significant operational failures, which included: the Vietnam War, the catastrophic disaster of Operation Eagle Claw (the attempted rescue of Iranian hostages) in 1980, and the botched invasion of Grenada in 1983. In 1986, the Goldwater-Nichols Act was passed by Congress to establish an overall structure for joint military strategy, planning and executing of combat operations.[40]

U.S. military joint operations are now well integrated, coordinated and synchronized. The example of the success of Operation Desert Storm in 1991 which involved highly synchronized and coordinated military actions by all four US military Services and 35 other nations to overwhelm and defeat Iraq in only six weeks, as compared to the nine year operational failure of the US involvement in the Vietnam war demonstrate the importance of coordinated, integrated and synchronized joint planning and action. This same methodology should be applied to national cybersecurity operations, or else the United States is sure to experience continued ineffectiveness at best, and potentially significant failure to protect U.S. critical Infrastructure at worst.

Returning to role of DHS in leading national cybersecurity efforts, the U.S. Congress has further defined the role of DHS through the National Cybersecurity and Critical Infrastructure Protection Act of 2013 (H.R. 3696) and amended the Homeland Security Act of 2002. Through this Act, the Secretary of the DHS is to conduct cybersecurity activities on behalf of the federal government and must codify the role of DHS in preventing and responding to cybersecurity incidents involving the IT systems of federal civilian agencies and critical infrastructure in the United States.[41] Specifically, the law directs DHS to lead the Federal government in the management of cybersecurity for critical infrastructure through the development of policies, research and development, and robust partnerships with private industry owners and operators of the infrastructure. Further the legislation directs DHS to establish the National Cybersecurity Communications and Integration Center (NCCIC) to provide broad situational awareness of and to share cyber threat information with the critical infrastructure owners and operators, to include requiring other Federal government entities to contribute to that threat information sharing.[42]

To implement DHS's cybersecurity information sharing responsibility, DHS's NCCIC was created to be a 24/7 cyber situational awareness, incident response, and management center, which strives to the national nexus of cyber and communications integration for the government, the intelligence community, and law enforcement. The NCCIC mission is to reduce the likelihood and severity of incidents that may significantly compromise the security and resilience of the nation's critical information technology and communications networks. The NCCIC is to focus on proactively coordinating the prevention and mitigation of those cyber and telecommunications threats that pose the greatest risk to the nation; pursue whole-of-nation operational integration by broadening and deepening engagement with its partners through information sharing to manage threats, vulnerabilities, and incidents; break down the technological and institutional barriers that impede collaborative information exchange, situational awareness, and understanding of threats and their impact; maintain a sustained readiness to respond immediately and effectively to all cyber and telecommunications incidents of national security; serve stakeholders as a national center of excellence and expertise for cyber and telecommunications security issues; protect the privacy and constitutional rights of the American people in the conduct of its mission.[43] To execute the NCCIC's mission, the United States Intelligence Community provides the NCCIC with current cyber threat information. Portions of that intelligence that can be declassified and shared with private entities across all CI sectors.

As part of PPD-21, President Obama also instructed: (1) the Director of the National Institute of Standards and Technology (NIST) of the Department of Commerce to develop a "Cybersecurity Framework" and (2) the Secretary of Homeland Security to establish a voluntary program that supports the adoption of the Framework by owners and operators of critical infrastructure and other interested entities.[44] The NIST Cybersecurity Framework was completed, but periodically undergoes improvements. PPD-21 further directed the Secretary of the Treasury, along with the Secretary of Commerce and the Secretary of Homeland Security, to each make recommendations on a set of incentives that would promote private sector participation in the voluntary program and improve information sharing. Since the NIST Framework is voluntary, it is up to each private CI owner and operator to adhere to the framework. Consequentially, only those private entities with high profit margins are capable of instituting the guidelines for effective cybersecurity. Outside of law enforcement (detailed below), the government's primary role in FS Sector cybersecurity is in the form of unclassified cyber threat information sharing and advocating for private financial firms' participation in the NIST Framework. The effectiveness of those two activities was discussed earlier.

Shifting to law enforcement, the FBI has a dual responsibility to prevent harm to national security as the United States' domestic intelligence agency and to enforce federal laws as the nation's principal law enforcement agency. "These roles are complementary, as threats to the nation's cybersecurity can emanate from nation-states, terrorist organizations, and transnational criminal enterprises; with the lines between sometimes blurred."[45] Collaborating with other government organizations and private entities is crucial to FBI's success. No single department or agency within the United States government can address cybersecurity threats alone. Consequently, the FBI works with several organizations to execute its mission. "The FBI maintains a presence and close partnership with the National Cyber Forensics and Training Alliance (NCFTA), and shares intelligence with the private sector through FBI-led InfraGard chapters and through various industry-specific Information Sharing and Analysis Centers (ISACs). In partnership with the National White-Collar Crime Center (NW3C), the FBI offers the Internet Crime Complaint Center (IC3) as a means to receive cyber-crime complaints from consumers and businesses for action by authorities, and to disseminate fraud alerts to the public."[46]

The FBI also works closely with several other nations' law enforcement organizations in an effort to fight cyber-crime at the source of the CEMA. Working through multilateral assistance treaties (MLAT), the FBI partners with foreign law enforcement agencies to investigate, attribute, prosecute, and disrupt overseas CEMA directed at United States FS Sector organizations.[47] One hurdle to the FBI's mission centers on the length of time it takes the FBI to execute the MLAT. The MLAT process of working with foreign law enforcement agencies takes a significant amount of time. FBI agents explained to this author that it oftentimes takes the FBI months to work through the investigative process of foreign cyber-crimes.

Further, cyber-criminals are aware of this fact and are able to discretely depart the foreign state before the FBI can complete the investigation and MLAT process. Consequently, foreign cyber-criminals are successful at evading law enforcement.[48]

One other governmental agency that executes law enforcement responsibilities within the FSS is the United States Secret Service (USSS). The Secret Service was created in 1865 to investigate and prevent counterfeiting. Today the USSS's investigative mission evolved from enforcing counterfeiting laws to safeguarding the payment and financial systems of the United States from a wide range of financial and computer-based crimes.[49] To combat cyber-crimes, the USSS adopted a proactive approach, using advanced technologies and capitalizing on the power of task force partnerships. Other USSS directives address the need to combat transnational organized crime that targets the citizens and financial institutions of the United States. The USSS's multi-disciplined forensics experts, cyber investigative experts, and cyber intelligence analysts provide rapid response and threat information in support of financial analysis, infrastructure protection, and criminal investigations.[50] In response to the globalization of technology- based threats, the United States Secret Service's investigative mission abroad is growing and augments the FBI's overseas mission.

In summary, there are several governmental organizations that have some responsibility to assist and/or respond to CEMA directed at the FSS. Currently the government's efforts include unclassified cyber threat information sharing, law enforcement, and advocating for the NIST Framework. Each of the governmental organizations operate in accordance with the authority provided them by United States Legal Code. Cross organizational communication is essential to each entity having familiarity with what the other is undertaking. In interviews I conducted with several of the governmental entities' leaders, cross communication was pointed out as an area for continued emphasis because the ability to effectively relate an organization's cyber activities is largely centered on the liaisons in each

163

organization's cyber operations centers and building relationships based on trust. As is the case even in private industry, a trusting relationship is the key to collaborating across organizations that possess disparate missions and objectives. Noticeably absent from the list of government entities participating in FSS cybersecurity was the Department of Defense. As was previously discussed the DoD struggles to determine when and how it may assist in cybersecurity for CI. The DoD has substantial capability in cyberspace, but executes its mission focused on traditional national defense as encountered in the physical domain.

The U.S. government departments and agencies are guided and directed by United States Code which stipulates what the entity is authorized to execute. With their authorities, the departments and agencies view and conduct their portion of the national cybersecurity effort differently, and often separately, and within the limits of the law; however, that effort is not integrated or synchronized.[51] This fact is highlighted in Government Accounting Office reports and media accounts.[52] One author describes the problem this way, the United States' "organizational structures for cyber defense are incomplete and lack coherence, with gaps and overlaps in responsibility and authority that have yet to be resolved, our structures for controlling attack/response mechanisms are even more immature and have yet to evolve to permit consideration for a 'whole of government response' that would bring to bear all aspects of government power."[53] These national cybersecurity challenges are complicated further by international issues, including inconsistent or nonexistent laws and differing perspectives regarding privacy norms and restrictions, data transferability, and divergent political interests in combatting CEMA.[54] The industrial-aged bureaucracies of the United States government were not designed to contend with the agile and complex information-age threats that transcend government departmental authorities and disciplines.

Given that no single government or private industry organization alone can contend with the cyber threats that instigate CINS, and because a majority of United

States critical infrastructure is owned and operated by private entities, collaboration between the government and private parties is vital to the successful defense of the nation's vital assets. Significant access, expertise, and perspective required to contend with CINS reside in both the private and government sectors; yet despite the importance of securing the nation against cyber-attacks, there is little effective collaboration and synchronization of public/private cyber capabilities due to numerous legal, strategic, and pragmatic issues. Those hindrances to collaboration include: "(1) issues surrounding trust and control of incident response; (2) questions about obligations regarding disclosure and exposure; (3) the evolving liability and regulatory landscape; (4) challenges faced in the cross-border investigation of cybercrime; and (5) cross-border data transfer restrictions that impede the ability of companies to respond nimbly to cyber threats and incidents."[55] Furthermore, there is concern by private industry that government organizations do not share much of what they fully know regarding the cyber threat due to classification issues. The Federal government collects a tremendous amount of data on cyber threats, which is highly classified given the sources and methods by which that information was obtained. Consequently, the Federal government must protect those sources and methods or potentially lose the threat intelligence that is vital to national security in all domains. Given this reality of not sharing classified information, private industry is skeptical that the government will be open with what the government observes in cyberspace, let alone what they may do to protect private sectors.[56] These issues and concerns are understood well by government leaders. Consequently, there is apprehension across corporate America that since private industry can only observe a small portion of the threat picture, they cannot fully comprehend the cyber threat landscape, and therefore, they cannot adequately contend with CEMA that rises to the level of CINS.

Based upon a concern for private industry, the Obama administration tasked the National Security Telecommunications Advisory Committee (NSTAC) in 2014 to examine how private corporations were postured for CEMA and when and how the United States government could aid the defense of the nation's key cyber terrain. In May 2014, the NSTAC concluded that the United States' "policy and doctrine needed to govern a response to cyber events of national significance are incomplete."[57] The NSTAC furthered elaborated that while "government and industry have developed or are currently advancing or evolving programs, practices, and methodologies to share threat information, there exists no effective methodology that currently supports the rapid mobilization and coordination of critical commercial sector assets to respond to a large-scale incident of national security concern [CINS]."[58] Following this discovery, the NSTAC was further tasked to:

> "Identify conditions, triggers, thresholds, and situations that might require increased operational coordination across industry, as well as between industry and Government;
>
> Identify critical commercial assets, functions, and/or capabilities that, if operationally coordinated, would be helpful or are necessary to respond to a cyber-related event of national significance;
>
> Recommend an operational framework that: (1) allows for agile, effective, and distributed implementation across numerous stakeholders, resulting in a coherent, unified, and dynamic national response; and (2) guides, informs, and prioritizes response across the full spectrum of NS/EP events with cyber implications."[59]

The NSTAC's research, which was encapsulated in their November 2014 report, concentrated on addressing how private capabilities or functions could be coordinated to address a CINS. While current information sharing and collaboration across the United States' national cybersecurity enterprise remains unfinished work, this was not the NSTAC's focus. Alternatively, the NSTAC focused on government-private industry collaboration at the highest levels of threat and national emergency (CINS).[60] The NSTAC did not provide a strategy for defending United States critical infrastructure. Their research, however, did identify several observations related to the United States government cybersecurity response efforts.

- "The goal of creating a common operating framework for Government and industry remains elusive, while the Government considers the primary role of the private sector is to serve as a first responder during cyber incidents.

- The Government has identified what it considers to be the Nation's most cyber-dependent critical infrastructures under Section 9 of Executive Order (EO) 13636, Improving Critical Infrastructure Cybersecurity.

- The National Security Council identified four gaps in the Government's ability to effectively execute a cyber response: (1) understanding and identifying the kind of response options and capabilities and courses of action industry has; (2) receiving private sector corroboration of threats and a perspective on the potential consequence of threats; (3) knowing private sector's current posture and ability to handle threats; and (4) identifying what the private sector might expect, request, or need from Government to address threats."[61]

The NSTAC report was clear that solving the problem of cybersecurity for United States' critical infrastructure is complex and complicated. Furthermore, no single entity possesses the full set of authorities, awareness, and disciplines necessary to succeed across the United States' government' systemic responsibilities to the nation. The report further validated what other reports noted, which was that the missing effective collaboration between the government and private industry was essential to the success of national defense and continued economic vitality.

Additionally, there must be a better understanding of when and where the government should either 1) aid private industry during CINS or 2) take the lead. The NSTAC report also examined private industry's ability to response to CEMA and noted that at a high level, the step-phases for current industry response protocol include: if an enterprise detects and cannot mitigate an incident, then, optimally, the enterprise seeks information and/or support from similar enterprise entities within their sector through an ISAC or trust group. In addition, enterprises optimally report on incidents they were able to mitigate, through their ISACs, for dissemination to sector and cross-sector peers.[62]

The NSTAC was clear in defining what the problems are and in explaining the importance of private industry's ability of being the "first responder" while pointing out the limitations and hurdles to successful cyber response. Furthermore, private industry is too largely focused on IT solutions and does not look across the sector to identify vulnerabilities in the seams between entities.[63] Additionally, although the ISACs provide a vital function, the NSTAC report states that the ISACs cannot substitute for a holistic national response.

In July 2016, the White House issued PPD 41, "United States Cyber Incident Coordination" to establish the "principles governing the Federal Government's response to any cyber incident, whether involving government or private sector entities. For significant cyber incidents, this PPD also establishes lead Federal agencies and an architecture for coordinating the broader Federal Government response."[64] PPD 41 established that there be a lead Federal agency aligned to each infrastructure sector (e.g., Department of Treasury for the Financial Services Sector, or the DoD for the Defense Industry Base) to help with cyber incident response activities. Each aligned lead Federal agency is to following five basic principles: establish a shared responsibility for response with the private sector (although that is not explained); take a risk-based approach; respect the affected parties (protect privacy, civil liberties, and the details of the private cyber-attack details; work to coordinate a unified action of the Federal government in support of the private entity; and help enable recovery and restoration activities.[65] As the lead Federal agency, an aligned agency is to ensure response activities include conducting appropriate law enforcement and national security investigative activities; response activities would include technical assistance to protect assets, mitigate vulnerabilities, and reduce impacts of cyber incidents; and Intelligence support and related activities should facilitate the building of situational threat awareness and sharing of related intelligence.

PPD41 further established an architecture of Federal government response coordination for significant cyber-incidents through three central elements: the Cyber Response Group (CRG), national operational coordination, and field-level coordination.[66] First, the CRG is responsible in support of the National Security Council (NSC) Deputies and Principals Committees, to coordinate the development and implementation of U.S. policy and strategy with respect to significant cyber incidents affecting the United States or its interests abroad. Second, national operational coordination will occur through the Cyber Unified Coordination Group (UCG), which "shall serve as the primary method for coordinating between and among Federal agencies as well as for integrating private sector partners into response efforts, as appropriate."[67] The Cyber UCG is made up from all the appropriate Federal Agencies and Departments, each of which is to coordinate responses within their sector. Furthermore, the Cyber UCG will oversee the following agencies that serve as the Federal lead agencies for their specified line of effort:

> "In view of the fact that significant cyber incidents will often involve at least the possibility of a nation-state actor or have some other national security nexus, the Department of Justice, acting through the Federal Bureau of Investigation and the National Cyber Investigative Joint Task Force, shall be the Federal lead agency for threat response activities. The Department

of Homeland Security, acting through the National Cybersecurity and Communications Integration Center, shall be the Federal lead agency for asset response activities. The Office of the Director of National Intelligence, through the Cyber Threat Intelligence Integration Center, shall be the Federal lead agency for intelligence support and related activities."[68]

As the third aspect of the Federal cyber architecture, PPD 41 directs the field-level representatives of each sector specific agency or threat response lead agencies to ensure they effectively coordinate their activities within their respective lines of effort with all other Federal Agencies or Departments, along with the affected private entity. Through my research and interaction with these cyber organizations, only limited coordination is achieved through a combination of placing liaisons in their operations centers to pass relevant information, as well as conducting on-site agency-to-agency information sharing of the activities that were taken of a specific response. Finally, PPD 41 specifies that when CEMA affects a private entity, the Federal government "typically will not play a role in this line of effort, but it will remain cognizant of the affected entity's response activities, consistent with the principles above and in coordination with the affected entity."[69] The sector-specific agency is to coordinate the government's efforts to understand the potential business or operational impact of the CEMA on private sector critical infrastructure. This directive confuses and limits the aligned Federal agency in fully supporting private industry, not to mention hampering the defense of U.S. critical infrastructure by keeping the Federal government on the sidelines of national defense when CINS occur against privately owned and operated critical infrastructure. Moreover, PPD 41 falls well short of providing any meaningful ways to achieve the specified directives President Obama laid out. Although notable in its architecture, PPD 41 intends for the Cyber UCG to create unity of effort, which can occur at the national Agency and Department head level; however, since PPD 41 does not to alter agency authorities or command responsibilities, each Federal Department and Agency will maintain operational control over their respective agency assets, thereby not being mandated to integrate or synchronize Federal government cyber operations.

In 2017, President Trump continued the tradition of articulating general cyber guidance to the United States government through his Executive Order on "Strengthening the Cybersecurity of Federal Networks and Critical Infrastructure," albeit in a slightly different way. In this Executive Order, President Trump took the stance that the Federal government must first properly protect its computer networks if it is going to effectively defend the nation. "The executive branch operates its information technology (IT) on behalf of the American people. Its IT and data should be secured responsibly using all United States government capabilities. The President will hold heads of executive departments and agencies (agency heads) accountable for managing cybersecurity risk to their enterprises."[70] The Executive Order goes on to call for a list of reports that the White House requires specific governmental departments to author – specifically, about whether the government is adequately prepared to defend the nation against CEMA. The Order's required reports include an assessment of the United States' critical infrastructure, the electrical grid, and the Department of Defense's warfighting capabilities.[71] As with the prior administration, although assessing United States' status and capabilities is important, looked at from a national strategy perspective, this Executive Order did little to further or steer the nation in countering the ever-growing cyber threat trend.

In September 2018, the Trump Administration published the "National Cyber Strategy of the United States of America." In this document, President Trump lays out the goals of the strategy: "Defend the homeland by protecting networks, systems, functions, and data; Promote American prosperity by nurturing a secure, thriving digital economy and fostering strong domestic innovation; Preserve peace and security by strengthening the ability of the United States — in concert with allies and partners — to deter and, if necessary, punish those who use cyber tools for malicious purposes; and Expand American influence abroad to extend the key tenets of an open, interoperable, reliable, and secure Internet."[72] The document further states four pillars that define the objectives of the "cyber strategy," which include: Protect the American People, the Homeland, and the American Way of Life; Promote American Prosperity; Preserve Peace through Strength; and Advance American Influence. These four pillars are vital objectives that should be achieved.

Additionally, noteworthy in this document is the fact that defending critical infrastructure is paramount, as is the inclusion of the use of coercion. These two aspects are of great consequence to developing a coercive cyber strategy. Although acknowledging that the United States critical infrastructure is largely privately owned and operated, there is very little tangible action suggested or means offered to integrate public/private capabilities and responses to secure those centers of gravity. Furthermore, it is commendable to state that the United States "will also deter malicious cyber actors by imposing costs on them and their sponsors by leveraging a range of tools, including but not limited to prosecutions and economic sanctions, as part of a broader deterrence strategy."[73] Arguably, that is the correct approach; however, once again, there is a paucity of detail describing how the nation's vast cyber organizations will unite to accomplish this, not to mention with what means they will obtain these goals. Furthermore, the threat of litigation in international court does not carry much deterrent effect to most cyber threat actors since prosecution rates are extremely low. Throughout the document there are several significant statements that aptly define what the nation is to do in and through cyberspace, but there is a striking absence of how and with what resources the nation is to achieve the prominent objectives. As with other Administrations' strategy documents, the Trump Administration's National Cyber Strategy is simply a directive policy manuscript that lacks the elements of a complete national coercive cyber strategy.

In November 2018, Trump signed into law the establishment of the Cybersecurity Information Sharing Agency (CISA Title 22). The bill, known as the CISA Act, reorganized and retitled DHS's National Protection and Programs Directorate (NPPD) as the lead federal agency in charge of overseeing civilian and federal cybersecurity programs. The NPPD, which was first established in 2007, contends with most of the DHS' cyber-related issues and projects. Now as CISA, although the agency's directives will remain unchanged, it will benefit from increased funding and more authority in imposing Federal cyber directives. "Elevating the cybersecurity mission within the Department of Homeland Security, streamlining our operations, and giving NPPD a name that reflects what it actually does will help better secure the nation's critical infrastructure and cyber platforms. The changes will also improve the Department's ability to engage with industry and government stakeholders and recruit top cybersecurity talent."[74] CISA is expected to improve the cyber-security defenses across other Federal agencies, coordinate cybersecurity programs with states, and bolster the government's overall cyber-security protections. More than a year later, however, very little changed regarding public-private information sharing or actual imposition of consequences on malicious cyber actors. Furthermore, there still remains confusion as to which Federal entity corporations should interact with.

For years, U.S. policymakers voiced their concern that jurisdictional confusion between the FBI and DHS was inhibiting the U.S. government from effectively countering CEMA. The evolution of U.S. Cyber Command and CISA was supposed to help clarify that confusion. Many policymakers assert that CEMA directed at the private sector from foreign intelligence services seems to be a national defense issue for the DoD; however, both the FBI and DHS each claim to be the lead agency for companies to contact when they fall victim to CEMA. Although each is correct, the confusion lies in the fact that based upon their legal mandates, CISA should take the lead on incident response duties, while the FBI should handle any criminal investigations. Meanwhile, DoD is responsible for securing the Defense Industrial Base. Further compounding the jurisdictional confusion, the NSA and U.S. Cyber Command now have information-sharing programs with several critical infrastructure sectors. So, it is no wonder the private sector, along with policymakers remain confused as to which Federal entity should engage and help defend U.S. critical infrastructure in times of cyber crisis.

In 2018, the United States Congress weighed in to help the nation and passed the 2019 National Defense Authorization Act (NDAA), which directed the President to develop a new cybersecurity policy for the nation, which amongst other things, is to alter its previously defensive-only posture for defending U.S. critical infrastructure.[75] Specifically Section 1636 stated:

"(a) IN GENERAL—It shall be the policy of the United States, with respect to matters pertaining to cyberspace, cybersecurity, and cyber warfare, that the United States should employ all instruments of national power, including the use of offensive cyber capabilities, to deter if possible, and respond to when necessary, all cyber-attacks or other malicious cyber activities of foreign powers that target United States interests with the intent to—

(1) cause casualties among United States persons or persons of United States allies;

(2) significantly disrupt the normal functioning of United States democratic society or government (including attacks against critical infrastructure that could damage systems used to provide key services to the public or government);

(3) threaten the command and control of the Armed Forces, the freedom of maneuver of the Armed Forces, or the industrial base or other infrastructure on which the United States Armed Forces rely to defend United States interests and commitments; or

(4) achieve an effect, whether individually or in aggregate, comparable to an armed attack or imperil a vital interest of the United States."[76]

The 2019 NDAA shifted focus away from terrorism as the primary threat to the nation and now focused statecraft on nation-states – specifically, Russia, China, and others. This new and more aggressive cyber posture directed by Congress was in response to increasing actions taken by Russia during the 2016 election to interfere with the United States' established democratic processes. With this new NDAA, Congress directed the creation of a national strategy that includes coercive elements and the clarification of roles and responsibilities within the Federal government. The question remains, will that strategy be developed and will it include all coercive aspects required to defend the nation against cyber incidents of national significance?

US Department of Defense Cyber Strategy

Turning back to the United States government organizations and the quest for a national cyber strategy, the U.S. military possesses documents labelled as a cyber strategy. The United States Department of Defense Cyber Strategy 2018 is the primary unclassified department-level strategy or a visionary directive. The Department of Defense is responsible for defending the United States homeland and United States interests from attack, including attacks that may occur in cyberspace. According to the 2018 Strategy, the

"Department must take action in cyberspace during day-to-day competition to preserve U.S. military advantages and to defend U.S. interests. Our focus will be on the States that can pose strategic threats to U.S. prosperity and security, particularly China and Russia. We will conduct cyberspace operations to collect intelligence and prepare military cyber capabilities to be used in the event of crisis or conflict. We will defend forward to disrupt or halt malicious cyber activity at its source, including activity that falls below the level of armed conflict. We will strengthen the security and resilience of networks and systems that contribute to current and future U.S. military advantages. We will collaborate with our interagency, industry, and international partners to advance our mutual interests."[77]

To this end the Defense Department has developed capabilities for cyber operations and is integrating those capabilities into the full array of tools that the United States government uses to defend United States national interests, including diplomatic, informational, military, economic, financial, and law enforcement tools. Upon examination of this document, it becomes obvious that it lacks most of the details necessary to guide and/or develop the action and operations necessary to defend the homeland against malicious cyber threats.

Although not actually a strategy to tie ends, ways, and means together while focusing on deterring or defeating a particular adversary, the DoD Cyber Strategy does set general strategic goals and objectives for their cyber activities and missions. It focuses on building capabilities for effective defense and offensive operations to defend DoD networks, systems, and information, to defend America against cyberattacks of significant consequence; and support operational and contingency plans. DoD set five strategic objectives for its cyberspace strategy:

"1. Ensuring the Joint Force can achieve its missions in a contested cyberspace environment;

2. Strengthening the Joint Force by conducting cyberspace operations that enhance U.S. military advantages;

3. Defending U.S. critical infrastructure from malicious cyber activity that alone, or as part of a campaign, could cause a significant cyber incident;

4. Securing DoD information and systems against malicious cyber activity, including DoD information on non-DoD-owned networks; and

5. Expanding DoD cyber cooperation with interagency, industry, and international partners."[78]

Determining whether or not the DoD meets its cyber strategy objectives year after year has been subject of repeated Congressional inquiries and governmental audits. In one such audit, the General Accounting Office (GAO) issued a report to Congress in 2016 outlining the failings of the DoD to meet its cyber strategy objectives. In this report, the GAO assessed the DoD's ability to provide cybersecurity assistance in times of CINS. The GAO evaluated DoD's guidance, policies, and plans and determined that DoD lacked clarity in: roles and responsibility and command structure for response to civil authorities. Although the military has plans to protect its own cyberspace, it does not have plans to protect other government organizations or United States critical infrastructure. In numerous interviews that I conducted with DoD and United States Cyber Command leaders, it was clear to all that this remains a gap. [79]

The 2018 DoD Cyber Strategy is more of a conceptual cyber document for the United States military and discusses how the department will build its forces in order to implement its objectives. The document does acknowledge the necessity to work with private entities, which is a noteworthy improvement from previous versions of the same strategy. The DoD Cyber Strategy, however, is overly IT focused and does not address the defense of the military's weapon systems or the defense of United States critical infrastructure. The DoD document still leaves many questions unanswered concerning how, when and where the DoD will use its cyber capabilities.[80] This lack of focus on U.S. critical infrastructure is indicative of all U.S. 'strategies' that I found and was further confirmed in interviews conducted with United States Cyber Command planners.[81] Given that the United States has deferred critical infrastructure cybersecurity largely to private industry, we should also examine its cybersecurity strategies.

The U.S. Private Critical Infrastructure Sector

The private critical infrastructure sector entities possess its own cybersecurity capabilities and strategies to secure its own organizations. It is beyond the scope of this book to describe a typical private industry cybersecurity enterprise or strategies in detail since they all are different. However, one can gleam generalities about the private sector cyber capability from industry/sector-wide surveys of private leaders responsible for cybersecurity. Of note, individual critical infrastructure owners/operators have different levels of capabilities and funding to devote to building robust cyber capabilities and processes. In one such cybersecurity survey conducted in 2018 by Ernst and Young LLC., 1,400 global private organizations participated.[82] When asked about the maturity of their cybersecurity programs, the private leaders responded:

- 55% of organizations do not make 'protecting' part of their strategy;

- 53% have seen an increase in their security budget this year;

- 22% say phishing their #1 threat;

- 33% of organizations see careless/unaware employees as the biggest vulnerability;

- 53% have no program – or an obsolete one – for one or more of the following: threat intelligence, vulnerability identification, breach detection, incidence response, data protection, and identity and access management;

- 17% of organizations say their top fear is loss of customers' information.[83]

Of the 1,400 organizations that responded to the survey, 92% of firms are concerned about their information security function in key areas. 30% of the company leaders are struggling with skills shortages, while 25% cite budget constraints. 28% of the smaller organizations say their information security function does not currently meet their company needs or is to be improved, and

56% say they have talent shortages or fiscal constraints.[84] When examining the data by sector, no single sector had greater than 12% of its survey participants who rated their organization as possessing a "very mature" cybersecurity program.[85] Very few private industry entities can contribute substantially to the nation's ability (government and private together) to have cybersecurity programs that are truly resilient with the necessary redundancies, or that can provide a formidable cyber defense to contribute to the deterrence quotient for the country. Given this general deficiency in the private sector's cyber capabilities, along with a realization that corporate cybersecurity strains to contribute (from an individual organization viewpoint) to a state's ability to coerce the cyber threat, the United State government must reevaluate its homeland cyber defense plan which primarily relies on private cybersecurity enterprises to counter the adversaries who commit CINS.

CEMA Cases Against the United States

Following are cases in which the United States was the victim of a major CEMA. The level of sophistication, impact, and/or magnitude of the attack was beyond that for which a single critical infrastructure company could contend, and the malicious actor was a state or state-sponsored entity, making it the responsibility of the United States to respond.

Operation Ababil to Operation Cleaver

Since the early 2000's, the information security industry as a whole, tracked nefarious cyber actors such as the Iranian Cyber Army, which early on, mainly focused on patriotic hacking (website defacements). Operation Ababil to Operation Cleaver denotes a demonstrative change in scale and intent of Iranian sponsored cyber actors that targeted United States critical infrastructure. Operation Ababil to

Operation Cleaver began in 2012 and culminated with the targeting of a United States water dam in New York State in 2016. Since at least 2009, Iran witnessed debilitating and advanced malware campaigns against its nuclear, oil, and gas industries; the most famous which was the industrial sabotage via Stuxnet (2009 - 2010) discussed earlier. Since Stuxnet, Iran's motivations shifted. Retaliation for Stuxnet began almost immediately in 2011.[86] "A major retaliation came in the form of 2012's Shamoon[87] campaign, which impacted RasGas and Saudi Aramco. It is estimated that Shamoon affected over 30,000 computer endpoints and cost the affected companies tens-of-thousands of hours recovering from the attacks."[88] The direct financial setback from this retaliation and amount of downtime experienced were significant. Shamoon was a watershed event for security defenders and was the first glimpse into the real capability and intention of Iranian cyber operations.

On September 18, 2012 (the initiation of Operation Ababil),[89] the Cyber fighters of Izz Ad-Din Al Qassam also known as Qassam Cyber Fighters announced their cyber-attacks on Pastebin where they criticized Israel and the United States and justified the attacks as a response to the "Innocence of Muslims" video released by controversial American pastor Terry Jones.[90] Their targets included the New York Stock Exchange as well as a number of major banks, including J.P. Morgan Chase and Bank of America.[91] The nature of the CEMA included DDoS incidents, which proved to be only minor. The attacks ceased on Oct 23, 2012 because of the Muslim holiday, Eid al-Adha, at which time the hackers offered to speak to the media through e-mail.[92] According to United States Senator Joseph Lieberman, the Iranian government was sponsoring the group's attacks on US banks in retaliation for Western economic sanctions. Specifically, he said "I think this was done by Iran and the Quds Force, which has its own developing cyberattack capability." [93] The Quds Force is a special operations unit of Iran's Revolutionary Guard Corps. Michael Smith, a senior security evangelist at Akamai, found the size of the attacks—

65 gigabits of traffic per second—to be consistent with that of a state actor (such as Iran) and agreed with Senator Lieberman.[94]

On December 10, 2012, the Qassam Cyber Fighters announced the initiation of phase two of Operation Ababil, which included an increased number of DDoS incidents on United States financial institutions.[95] In that statement, they specifically named United States Bancorp, J.P. Morgan Chase, Bank of America, PNC Financial Services and SunTrust Bank as targets. Again, the motive for the CEMA was the disrespect of the Prophet Mohammed in the above-mentioned video. Once again, cybersecurity experts pointed to Iran as backing the DDoS attacks and indicated the DDOS operations "generated up to 100 gigabits per second of data — 10 to 20 times more than what it usually takes to knock a site offline. The attackers overwhelmed routers, servers, and server applications all at once; typical DDoSers target just one. They specifically targeted the banks' Domain Name Server architecture, which translates website names ("cash.com") into numerical internet-protocol addresses. And their traffic largely came from legitimate IP address, making it tough for the banks to filter."[96]

On February 12, 2013, the Qassam Cyber Fighters issued a warning that the other copies of the movie referenced in their January 29 posting must be removed.[97] They followed this with a "serious warning"[98] and then an "ultimatum"[99] after the additional copies of the video were not removed. On March 5, 2013, they announced the beginning of Phase 3 of Operation Ababil on their Pastebin page.[100] Again several United States financial institutions experienced noteworthy DDoS attacks.

In September 2013, the United States Navy announced that their Navy/Marine Corps Internet was hacked by Iran.[101] The sophistication of the CEMA originating from Iran increased. By 2014, as reported by the cybersecurity firm Cylance, Iran was responsible for CEMA targeting over 50 targets in 16 countries.[102] Cylance called the attacks "Operation Cleaver" because the word cleaver frequently appeared in the attackers' malicious code. The New York Times was able to independently corroborate the firm's findings with another security firm, Crowdstrike, which said it had been tracking the same group of Iranian hackers for the past nine months under a different alias, "Cutting Kitten;" kitten is the firm's naming convention for attack groups based in Iran, a nod to the Persian cat.[103] The hackers used a set of tools that can spy on and potentially shut down critical control systems and computer networks, aiming them at targets in the United States, Canada, Israel, India, Qatar, Kuwait, Mexico, Pakistan, Saudi Arabia, Turkey, the United Arab Emirates, Germany, France, England, China and South Korea.

Cylance said the most severe incident was that of CEMA targeting transportation networks, including airlines and airports in South Korea, Saudi Arabia and Pakistan. Researchers said they had found evidence that hackers had gained complete remote access to airport gates and security control systems, "potentially allowing them to spoof gate credentials."[104] It became apparent that Iran was retaliating against the U.S. for its perceived role in Stuxnet and Iran now had access to various systems from which it could place at risk - airline travel, Industrial Control Systems (ICS)/Supervisory Control and Data Acquisition (SCADA) systems, and Critical Infrastructure and Key Resources (CIKR).

These nefarious acts also demonstrated Iran's cyber capabilities to gain geopolitical leverage with potential allies, of which they had little. Due to the breadth and depth of Iran's global targets, there soon was a growing focus on CIKR companies in South Korea, which gave Iran additional clout in their burgeoning partnership with North Korea. To that end, in September 2012, Iran signed an extensive agreement for technology cooperation agreement with North Korea, which allowed for additional partnerships on various projects related to IT and security.[105]

On March 24, 2016, the FBI announced the indictment of seven Iranians, believed to working on behalf of the Iranian government, for a series of cyber-crimes that cost America financial institutions tens of millions of dollars.[106] The FBI cited CEMA began in December 2011, and by September 2012 were occurring on nearly a weekly basis. On specific days, hundreds of thousands of customers were cut off from the online access to their bank accounts. "According to court documents, one of the hackers who helped build the botnet used in some of the attacks received credit for his computer intrusion work from the Iranian government toward completion of his mandatory military service requirement."[107] Other defendants claimed responsibility for hacking servers belonging to NASA and for intrusions into thousands of other servers in the United States, the United Kingdom, and Israel. In addition to targeting the United States financial sector, one of the Iranian defendants repeatedly gained access to computer systems of the Bowman Dam in Rye, New York in 2013. Although the cyber-criminal never gained control of the dam, his access allowed him to understand the key details about the dam's operation, including information about gates that control water levels and flow rates. The CEMA highlighted the vulnerabilities of the nation's critical infrastructure to Iranian hackers, which were a danger to the public health and safety.[108]

Significance and Consequences of the CEMA

The Iranian hackers were overt about their DDoS attacks on the United States financial institutions. The sophisticated CEMA employed by the Iranians allowed for persistent access and potential exploitation at a later time. The unauthorized access could potentially be leverage against the United States or other victim states when Iran chooses to unleash hidden cyber payloads. Compared with the previous Chinese case (Titan Rain – Byzantine Hades), one can see a much lower threshold for the Federal government to come to the aid of private critical infrastructure owners. In the Operation Cleaver case, "tens of millions of dollars" were spent by the owners of the United States financial institutions to respond and mitigate the malicious effects of the Iranians hackers. Several sources in the FBI and DHS opined, that maintaining the American populace's confidence in the United States' financial institutions was a motivating force for the Federal government's action. Some administration officials said that the unsealing of the indictment against the Iranian hackers eased the way for the imposition of economic sanctions. As a result, President Obama in April 2015 issued an executive order creating the authority to impose such sanctions specifically for malicious cyber-activity. That authority has not been used yet. [109]

Findings

The United States knew who perpetrated the CINS as evidenced by the FBI indictment and several private cybersecurity firms' reports. There was a clear understanding of the malicious cyber actor's intent or objective within the larger geopolitical landscape. Moreover, the evidence showed that the United States comprehended the nature of the interests at stake or the risks involved prior to the event given how overt the Iranians were about their DDoS attacks on the United States financial institutions. The more sophisticated CEMA executed by the Iranians allow for persistent access and potential exploitation at a later time. I submit that the unauthorized access could potentially be leverage against the United States or other victim states when Iran chooses to unleash hidden cyber payloads, thereby potentially pressuring the victim states in costly ways.

Was there a clearly established threshold for which the United States would take action? Yes, but it is unclear to national leaders when to intercede given the type of attack (DDoS) and slow comprehension of the impact on the financial sector. In the Operation Cleaver case, "tens of millions of dollars" were spent by the owners of the United States financial institutions to respond and mitigate the malicious effects of the Iranians hackers. Through my research, I heard from several sources in the FBI and DHS, who stated that maintaining the American populace's confidence in the United States' financial institutions was a motivating force for the Federal government's action, albeit just federal law enforcement, which could hardly be thought of as significant pressure on Iranian decision makers.

As to the political will to take action, very little was stated by U.S. national leaders about Federal government counter options, other than FBI investigation involvement. Some administration officials said that the unsealing of the indictment against the Iranian hackers could ease the way for economic sanctions to be imposed. President Obama in April 2015 issued an executive order creating the authority to impose such sanctions specifically for malicious cyber-activity. That authority was not been used against Iran for this cyber event. [110]

In summary, for years, the United States government treated CEMA carried out by foreign states as matters of national security and kept that information classified. Some (limited) cyber threat information was passed to private industry, but it was too little and not specific. United States officials were reluctant even to acknowledge a major intrusion by a foreign country either for political or intelligence reasons. But as the scope and severity of the intrusions grew between 2011 and 2015, that reluctance changed and the United States began openly identifying and indicting state-sponsored cyber actors. As earlier explained, the indictment against the Chinese 3 PLA officers was the first example. By January 2015, the United States instituted new financial sanctions on North Korean officials and government agencies in response to a cyberattack on Sony Pictures Entertainment[111] and in 2016 the FBI indicted seven Iranians for CEMA targeting United States critical infrastructure. The indictments in national security cyber cases reflect a "new approach" that borrows from counterterrorism, said Assistant Attorney General John Carlin.[112] "It demonstrates a continued commitment to raising the cost of cybercrime and to demonstrating that the United States government can uncover the tradecraft of cybercriminals and attribute their activities with confidence," said Zachary Goldman, executive director of New York University School of Law's Center on Law and Security.[113] However, indictments can hardly be considered truly credible capability that would pressure state-sponsored cyber threat actors against their nefarious intentions, especially if none of those indictments yielded the incarceration of the perpetrators responsible.

When examining the trend of United States coercive actions against the nation's malicious cyber adversaries, there is a positive trend to the activity. Unfortunately, in this Iranian case, there was again little more than law enforcement and bolstering of private industry's defense. The United States' actions adhere to its existing policies, but indicate a lowering of the threshold for action, which includes a concern for the perception by the American populace of the security and availability of United States critical infrastructure. However, if the Iranians (or any other potential adversary) could gain unauthorized and persistent access to the nation's vital systems, then those systems would be at risk of not functioning in times of crisis, should the adversary choose to execute their hidden payloads.

Was there more that the United States could have done to thwart the Iranians? Potentially, there could have been deliberate targeting of Iranian national decision makers to put greater pressure on them through targeted sanctions and freezing of financial assets, thereby sending a much stronger signal that the CEMA witnessed was not acceptable. Precise targeting of the responsible Iranian forces' cyber capabilities also could have taken place in an effort to set back their means. However, no such "signaling" was accomplished, which sent another message that the United States implicitly was stating that this level of national cyber-attacks would not be countered with truly punitive counterpunches. If this logic is indeed accurate, then other nations may be similarly emboldened to strike the United States without fear of serious repercussion when they see the need to challenge the world's sole superpower. This reality is not in line with established U.S. national security policy;

and therefore, implies the need for the development of a better cybersecurity strategy and policy that clearly defines an appropriate threshold for United States government action when critical infrastructure sectors are vulnerable to national foes. That strategy must include more instruments of power than just law enforcement along with private industry cyber defense if the United States is to ensure the defense and vitality of the nation.

Office of Personnel Management Theft of 21.5 Million Security Files

In 2015, the United States' Office of Personnel Management (OPM) discovered two separate but related cybersecurity incidents that impacted the data of Federal government employees, contractors, and others organizations. In June 2015, OPM discovered that the background investigation records of current, former, and prospective Federal employees and contractors were stolen. Through its investigation, OPM and the interagency incident response team concluded with high confidence that sensitive data, including the Social Security Numbers (SSNs) of 21.5 million individuals, were taken from the background investigation databases. "This includes 19.7 million individuals that applied for a background investigation, and 1.8 million non-applicants, primarily spouses or co-habitants of applicants." [114] Some of the records included findings from interviews conducted by background investigators and approximately 5.6 million include fingerprints. Usernames and passwords that the background investigation applicants used to fill out their background investigation forms also were stolen.[115]

J. David Cox, president of the American Federation of Government Employees, a union that represents more than 670,000 workers in the executive branch, stated in a letter to OPM: "We believe that the Central Personnel Data File was the targeted database, and that the hackers are now in possession of all personnel data for every federal employee, every federal retiree, and up to one million former federal employees."[116] The letter addressed to OPM Director Katherine Archuleta, further listed an alarming array of information that the union believed to be compromised. "We believe that hackers have every affected person's Social Security number, military records and veterans' status information, address, birth date, job and pay history, health insurance, life insurance, and pension information; age, gender, race, union status, and more."[117]

Upon detecting that intrusion, OPM launched an investigation – in partnership with the Department of Homeland Security's United States Computer Emergency Readiness Team (US-CERT) and the FBI – to determine its full scope and impact. On June 8, as the investigation proceeded, the incident response team confirmed to relevant Federal agencies that there was a high degree of confidence that OPM systems containing the sensitive information had been exfiltrated.[118] DHS official, Andy Ozment testified that the attackers had gained valid user credentials to the systems they were attacking, likely through social engineering. The breach also consisted of a malware package which installed itself within OPM's network and established a backdoor. From there, attackers escalated their privileges to gain access to a wide range of OPM's systems.[119] Dr. Ozment reiterated that when the malware activity behind the breach was discovered, "we loaded that information into Einstein (DHS' government-wide intrusion detection system) immediately. We also put it into Einstein 3 (the intrusion prevention system currently being rolled out) so that agencies protected by it would be protected from it going forward."[120]

Several sources leaked statements that the perpetrator of the CEMA was most likely China. The Wall Street Journal reported that United States government officials deduced that Chinese hackers perpetrated the breach.[121] The Washington Post reported that the attack originated in China, citing unnamed government officials.[122] Whether the attacks were motivated by commercial gain remains unclear, but it was suggested that hackers working for the Chinese military intend to compile a database of American citizens using the data obtained from the breach.[123] Even more alarming than the theft of personnel information, there is the grave potential that the hackers could have added false data into the OPM database. I was told by FBI agents familiar with the case that it is unknown if new, false personnel data was entered into OPM's database, which if true, could mean individuals not actually investigated for a security clearance may now appear to be cleared for classified data.[124]

Significance and Consequences of the CEMA

Prior to the event, OPM was alerted multiple times of their security vulnerabilities and failings. A March 2015 OPM Office of the Inspector General semi-annual report to Congress warned of "persistent deficiencies in OPM's information system security program," including "incomplete security authorization packages, weaknesses in testing of information security controls, and inaccurate Plans of Action and Milestones."[125] Leaders of OPM struggled to contend with the breach in the face of intense Congressional scrutiny.

Given the scale and duration of the data breaches, it may not be possible for the United States government to fully know the exact extent of the damage done just by the CEMA targeting OPM's systems. When considering the aging infrastructure of many agencies in Washington, one could ask, are there other vulnerabilities that the government faces in securing its networks? Is OPM's data breach simply the only data breach discovered to date that was publicly announced? There is a good possibility there are more breaches since the OPM systems are linked electronically to other agencies and databases. According to a 2007 White House report on OPM security clearance performance, checks of State Passport records and searches of military service records are now conducted electronically.[126] According to this report, there are electronic linkages between the OPM Security Clearance files, Department of Defense service records, and State Department Passport records.[127]

At the time of this writing, there was no known (unclassified) response or counter-action taken to impose consequences on the malicious cyber actor, largely because it is not known with even medium certainty as to who conducted the CEMA. If the government sources that leaked the information about China are accurate, then attribution with enough certainty may be available to take some action, but that information is likely classified. The issue remains however, without a strategy, some certainty of attribution, and a specified threshold for which a response should be initiated, the United States government did not take appropriate action to rectify the situation or impose costs on the malicious actor.

Russian CEMA targeting the Commercial Retail Sector and United States Government

In 2015, former Director of National Intelligence James Clapper stated to the Senate Armed Services Committee –

"Cyber threats to United States national and economic security are increasing in frequency, scale, sophistication and severity of impact; [and] the ranges of cyber threat actors, methods of attack, targeted systems and victims are also expanding...Politically motivated cyberattacks are now a growing reality, and foreign actors are reconnoitering and developing access to United States critical infrastructure systems, which might be quickly exploited for disruption if an adversary's intent became hostile. In addition, those conducting cyber espionage are targeting United States government, military and commercial networks on a daily basis."[128]

Similarly to China, Russia possesses a sophisticated cyber capability that until recently was not overt. Currently Russian CEMA, as Clapper points out, is unabashedly obvious. My research indicates that the lack of consequences imposed upon other malicious cyber actors set the condition whereby Russian hackers now are willing to take greater risks to reap the spoils of CEMA against the United States without concern for attribution.

In a Washington Times article, Bill Getz revealed that United States intelligence agencies recently identified a Russian cybersecurity firm with expertise in testing the network vulnerabilities of the electrical grid, financial markets and other critical infrastructure, as having close ties to Russia's Federal Security Service (FSB – the Russian civilian intelligence service). The relationship between the company and the FSB heightened fears among United States intelligence officials that Russia is stepping up cyber efforts to infiltrate computer networks that control United States critical infrastructure.[129] The CEMA appears to be part of FSB and Russian military cyber-espionage program, potentially in preparation for future cyberattacks. "The Russian company is [even] taking steps to open a branch office in the United States as part of the intelligence-gathering effort."[130]

Frank J. Cilluffo, Director of the Center for Cyber and Homeland Security at The George Washington University stated in testimony before the United States House of Representatives Committee on Homeland Security Subcommittee on Cybersecurity, Infrastructure Protection, and Security Technologies, that Russia's cyber capabilities are more sophisticated than those of China, and Russia has been particularly adept at integrating cyber into its strategic plans and operations.[131] Cilluffo further stated, in 2009 cyber-spies from Russia had penetrated the United States electrical grid, leaving behind software programs, but did not cause damage to United States infrastructure. The hackers sought to navigate the systems and their controls, which Cilluffo believed to be some sort of preparation for a future attack.[132] Russian CEMA continued to elevate in scale and intensity in 2010.

In October 2010, an FBI system monitoring U.S. Internet traffic picked up an alert from the NASDAQ Exchange indicating malware penetrated the company's central servers.[133] A five-month investigation by the FBI, NSA, DHS, Treasury Department, CIA, and DoD concluded that Russia had used two zero-day vulnerabilities in combination to take remote control of a Nasdaq computer. NSA believed that Russia was behind the CEMA because they had seen a version of this malware before.[134] The investigators (both law enforcement officials and private contractors hired by the company) found the presence of several other groups operating freely, some of which may have been in the exchange's networks for years, including criminal hackers and Chinese agents.[135] The evidence of other foreign nations in the NASDAQ gave pause to determining who was behind the initial FBI alert. "Investigators also discovered that the website run by One Liberty Plaza's building management company had been laced with a Russian-made exploit kit known as 'Blackhole,' infecting tenants who visited the page to pay bills or do other maintenance."[136] The investigators were surprised by how vulnerable the NASDAQ was to cyber intrusion and CEMA. The investigators suspected that the hackers first broke into NASDAQ's computers at least three months before the initial notice of infection. There were indications that a large cache of data was stolen, though proof was scarce. By mid-2011, investigators began to conclude that the Russians were not trying to sabotage NASDAQ, but wanted to replicate it, either to incorporate its technology directly into their exchange or as a model from which to learn. Some of the FBI investigators did not agree since there was malware found that was destructive in nature.[137]

On July 25, 2013, the FBI announced the unsealing of an indictment against a Russian hacker, Aleksandr Kalinin for hacking certain computer servers used by the NASDAQ Stock Market. In a separate indictment also unsealed the same day, Kalinin and another Russian hacker, Nikolay Nasenkov, were charged with an international scheme to steal bank account information by hacking United States-based financial institutions and then using the stolen account information to withdraw millions of dollars from the victims' bank accounts. Kalinin also was charged in a separate indictment unsealed in federal court in Newark, New Jersey with the theft of millions of dollars from more than 800,000 victim bank accounts from Citibank and PNC Bank.[138] According to the FBI, the CEMA and theft of greater than $7.8 million dollars from United States banking customers began as early as 2005.

Russia has a history of merging crime, business, and politics—and there are few, if any, signs that things are changing today. In fact, now there is an increase in joining of Russian intelligence community and cyber-criminals as a result of the deteriorating relations between Russia and the West over Ukraine conflict.[139] Evidence of the complicity between the Russian government and its cyber-criminals and hackers became obvious when the Russian Foreign Ministry issued "a public notice advising `citizens to refrain from traveling abroad, especially to countries that have signed agreements with the United States on mutual extradition, if there is reasonable suspicion that United States law enforcement agencies' have a case pending against them."[140]

In September 2015, Finnish cybersecurity firm F-Secure asserted that Russia sponsored systematic cyber-espionage in Europe, the United States, and Asia has been ongoing for at least several years. F-Secure's report "links a number of state-sponsored cyber-attacks to a hacking group engaged in Russian intelligence gathering."[141] F-Secure identified a group of hackers called "the Dukes" that uses a family of unique malicious cyber tools to steal information by infiltrating computer networks and sending the data back to the hackers. The attribution was based upon Russian Federation support to the Dukes due to several facts that include: Dukes family of malware possessed coding comments in Russian; the assertion of timestamps found in many GeminiDuke samples, suggested the group works in the Moscow Standard Time zone; the known targets of the Dukes are Eastern European foreign ministries, western think tanks, and western governmental organizations; the malware conforms to publicly-known Russian foreign policy and security policy interests; and Dukes appear to have targeted governments all over the world, but none targeted the Russian government.[142] Based on the their evidence and analysis,

F-Secure "believes, with a high level of confidence, that the Duke toolsets are the product of a single, large, well-resourced organization (which we identify as the Dukes) that provides the Russian government with intelligence on foreign and security policy matters in exchange for support and protection."[143] F-Secure's report was not the first to accuse Russia of sponsoring cyber-espionage.

In 2014, separate teams of cybersecurity researchers asserted that the Russian government was likely behind the widespread cyber-espionage and CEMA that hit victims in the United States and elsewhere. United States security firm Symantec, reported in 2014 the discovery of a highly-sophisticated CEMA tool called "the Regin," which had been employed since 2008 to steal information from governments and businesses.[144] A separate report by the United States cybersecurity firm FireEye stated that a long-running effort to hack into United States defense contractors was "likely sponsored by the Russian government."[145] In early 2015, Russian hackers targeted the State Department with a sophisticated cyber intrusion tool, which was later used to penetrate the sensitive unclassified computer system of the White House.[146] Both United States government organizations were victims of cyber exploitation of their unclassified systems, which held and processed sensitive information. Later in 2015, Russian hackers again instigated CEMA against another United States government department – the DoD. The Russian CEMA directed at the Chairman of the Joint Chiefs of Staff unclassified servers was detected around July 25, 2015, officials said. The Pentagon immediately disabled the email system (which is used by about 4,000 military and civilian personnel) in an attempt to contain the damage.[147] In 2015, Reuters reported that the FBI initiated an investigation prompted by a 2014 announcement by Milwaukee-based cybersecurity firm Hold Security that it obtained information that a Russian hacker group dubbed "CyberVor" ("Vor" translates to thief in Russian) stole the 1.2 billion credentials and more than 500 million email addresses.[148]

Government cyber-espionage is conducted by most states around the world, but not to the level, scale, and impact witnessed by the United States from Russia, largely because the CEMA was not strictly espionage. When entire cyber systems are shut down, the effect is debilitating to organizational processes and functions. Oftentimes, it takes days to weeks to restore the functionality of those systems. Furthermore, the widespread effects of the Russian CEMA on the commercial sector included: the theft of personally identifiable information, state secrets, proprietary corporate information, and currency.

Significance and Consequences of the CEMA

Russia continues to raise the sophistication of its CEMA and is routinely targeting United States critical infrastructure, some of which are air gapped (not connected to a network). In early 2014, unknown hackers succeeded in penetrating United States electrical, water, and fuel distribution systems. In November 2014, DHS revealed that Russian hackers infiltrated several critical infrastructure sectors in the United States.[149] A destructive "Trojan Horse" malware program penetrated the software that runs much of the nation's critical infrastructure and is poised to cause an economic catastrophe, according to the Department of Homeland Security. National Security sources told ABC News there is evidence that the malware was inserted by hackers believed to be sponsored by the Russian government, and is a very serious threat.[150] The DHS experts speculated that the Industrial Control Systems (which controls critical processes for the operation of critical infrastructure, including power transmission grids, wind turbines, nuclear plants and oil and gas pipelines) in many plants were infected with the Russian BlackEnergy malware. DHS revealed that the hacking campaign has been running at least since 2011, despite the detection of nefarious activity.[151] DHS sources stated that this was no random attack and they fear that the Russians have torn a page from the old Cold War playbook to place the malware in key United States systems as a threat and/or as a deterrent to a United States cyber-attack on Russian systems.[152] The Moscow connection troubles United States leaders because Russia is the only country to date that combined CEMA with physical conventional military operations, as was elaborated on previously.

Evidently, Russia invests considerable resources into its cyber program and enterprise. In a separate statement, James Clapper told the Senate Armed Services Committee in March 2015 that Russia's Ministry of Defense is "establishing its own cyber command" responsible for "conducting offensive cyber activities."[153] The Russian government appears to be stepping up its research and development of cyber technology at first-rate computer science institutions such as the prestigious St. Petersburg Polytechnic University and Samara State University, according to Taia Global.[154] The Russian government values its cyber capabilities and endeavors to stay at the forefront of sophistication and global cyber primacy.

To summarize, Russian cyber-criminal organizations, in coordination with or at the direction of the Russian government, executed CEMA against a plethora of commercial corporations, critical infrastructure sectors, and United States government organizations over the last ten years in an overt fashion to achieve national objectives. It is likely much more is known by the United States government with regard to classified Russian CEMA directed at the United States. The effects inflicted upon the United States include exploitation, disruption, destruction, and coercion. Russian CEMA aimed at the United States constitutes some of the most sophisticated cyber incidents to date by any country and Russia remains a cyber force to be reckoned with.

In spite of not having a national cyber strategy and despite to presence of coercive tools of statecraft, the United States repeatedly endured malicious incident after malicious incident across both private and government sectors without responding to the Russian CEMA and aggression. United States government leadership in both the Executive and Legislative branches were acutely aware of the scale, frequency, and severity of the Russian CEMA over the past decade, but failed to respond meaningfully with any tool of statecraft except law enforcement. As James Clapper notes, "We foresee an ongoing series of low-to-moderate level cyber-attacks from a variety of sources over time, which will impose cumulative costs on U.S. economic competitiveness and national security."[155] The cumulative effect over time for the United States will be devastating if allowed to continue. Given no real imposition of consequences by the United States on Russian cyber-attacks, the United States is again implicitly stating that it will not respond with any significant response for cases of state-sponsored CEMA, thereby allowing nefarious cyber actions against core critical infrastructure assets. Consequently, Russia remains undeterred from conducting CEMA and its motivation to continue will likely remain strong due to the relative ease of their operations, lack of repercussions, along with the gains they realized. Once again, counter to stated national security strategies, the United States is implicitly allowing Russia a permissive environment in which CEMA can be used as a coercive tool short of war, with relatively low risk of retaliation. In the political game of "chicken" conducted in and through cyberspace between two nuclear super powers, the United States "blinked" and Russia is capitalizing on that fact.

CEMA Targeting U.S Healthcare Institutions

Among all of the United States critical infrastructure sectors, healthcare is the most beleaguered by persistent CEMA from numerous (and oftentimes unknown) malicious cyber actors, who exploit vulnerabilities in insecure and antiquated healthcare networks and systems in order to exfiltrate patient health records.[156] According to the cybersecurity firm Gemalto's report, "2015 First Half Review: Findings from the Breach Level Index," of the 16 critical infrastructure sectors, the

Healthcare sector suffered from the most data breaches, an estimated 21% (186 out of 888 reported events).[157] According to the United States Department of Health and Human Services (HHS), data from more than 120 million United States citizens was compromised in more than 1,100 separate breaches at organizations handling protected health data from 2009 to 2014.[158] According to a 2014 SANS institute report, of the CEMA targeting the healthcare sector, approximately 94% of United States medical institutions claimed their organizations were victims of CEMA; 72% of the total targeted were healthcare providers, ~10% healthcare business associates, 6% health plan organizations, and the remaining 12% were pharmaceutical companies, healthcare information clearinghouses, and other healthcare entities.[159] One could argue that the healthcare sector is rapidly becoming the prime target for malicious cyber actors – and the sector the most susceptible to successful CEMA. The healthcare sector is a lucrative target because organizations do not invest seriously in cybersecurity and surveys of the healthcare support the lack of cybersecurity capability or focus.

In KPMG's 2015 "Health Care and Cyber Security" survey, 81% of the participating 223 healthcare most senior cybersecurity leaders stated that systems were "compromised by one or more cyberattacks within the last year," while the remaining 19% stated that their organizations "remained secure," or did not admit willingly that CEMA breached their system, or "did not know whether their system had been compromised."[160] In all cases, the possibility of an undiscovered or unreported breach was likely because only 75% of the respondents felt that their organization possessed the capability to detect a compromise. Moreover, only 53% of the healthcare providers assessed themselves capable of defending themselves from CEMA after detection.[161] The healthcare sector is so lucrative a target because these organizations manage extremely sensitive and diverse data which ranges from personal identifiable information (PII) to financial data.

Healthcare data is stored digitally as electronic Protected Health Information (ePHI). An electronic health record (EHR) contains a patient's PII, their private health information, and their financial information. Systems belonging to the healthcare sector and the Federal government (OPM) were targeted recently because they contain vast amounts of sensitive personal information. "EHRs enable greater access to patient records and facilitate sharing of information among providers, payers, and patients themselves. However, with extensive access, more centralized data storage, and confidential information sent over networks, there is an increased risk of privacy breach through data leakage, theft, loss, or cyber-attack [CEMA]."[162] Both the Federal government and healthcare sector collect, store, and protect data concerning United States citizens and government employees. Healthcare however, is behind the government in cybersecurity capabilities, which is alarming when one considers the fact that most American's have EHRs in the healthcare sector. According to Rob Bathurst, Professional Services Director of Cylance, "[w]hile working and consulting in the healthcare sector, we have noted the sector is currently lagging behind other sectors in deployed prevention, detection, and reactive technologies."[163] Furthermore, many healthcare organizations lack properly trained cybersecurity personnel capable of operating security technologies.

Malicious cyber actors spend and develop significant resources to steal EHRs and identities, while other hackers seek information about specific high-profile patients, and still others want to harm the healthcare providers. Consequently, due to the wider variety of personal information available about a larger selection of victims, a greater variety of malicious cyber actors now target healthcare systems.[164] A healthcare organization accrues a wide amount of information and stores it in a single, often-vulnerable system. Healthcare databases are prime targets for cybercriminals because hackers recognize that healthcare organizations lack the resources, processes, and technologies to prevent and detect CEMA, and thus protect patient data.

A single healthcare database may contain over 18 PII identifiers (name, address, social security number, etc.), a patient's private health information (PHI), and a patient's financial payment information (insurance and credit card information), and other patient personal information, such as address, social security numbers, spouse, children, etc. The FBI's Jim Trainor stated that on the black market, cybercriminals pay much more for personal health information (PHI) than stolen credit card data. "Credit cards can be say five dollars or more where PHI records can go from $20 say up to -- we've even seen $60 or $70."[165] The PHI is valuable because it can be utilized to create a realistic false identity or even sold to other criminals for insurance and billing scams. Unlike credit card identity theft, where card issuers are liable for customer losses of $50 or more, medical identity theft often leaves its victims with no automatic recourse to recoup their losses.

The malicious cyber actors gain access to healthcare data through poorly protected medical endpoints, including personal health devices, which become gateways that expose consumers' personal computers and information to cybercriminals. According to SANS, the top three cyberspace culprits that are vulnerable to CEMA are: connected medical endpoints, Internet-facing personal health data, and security systems and edge devices. The first – connected medical endpoints – include radiological imaging software, video conferencing systems, and digital video systems. "Connected medical devices, applications and software used by health care organizations providing everything from online health monitoring to radiology devices to video-oriented services are fast becoming targets of choice for nefarious hackers taking advantage of the IoT [Internet of Things] to carry out all manner of illicit transactions, data theft and attacks."[166] This is especially worrisome because securing devices, such as network printers, faxes and surveillance cameras, is often ignored.

The second area – Internet-facing personal health data – relates to areas where PII is vulnerable to theft because of where that data is located and its exposure to unauthorized access. Internet-facing personal health data may be exposed in a web-based call center's website or in a compromised personal health record (PHR) system. In a PHR system, consumers' personal health records are not necessarily tethered to an electronic health record system and, therefore, are neither certified under the United States standards nor regulated under healthcare legislation. Consumers may find that they have no recourse under the law if PII in an untethered PHR is compromised, leaving the consumers to bear the costs.[167]

The third area of vulnerability is security systems and edge devices. This category includes virtual private network (VPN) applications and devices, improperly configured firewalls, and enterprise network controllers. These security devices and applications can become compromised thanks to CEMA, which is a common target for malware and can lead to times when these systems are not detecting malicious traffic coming from the network endpoints inside the protected perimeter—inside the firewall or behind the VPN. If these "systems and devices are not detecting, they are not reporting—and that means they are out of compliance with privacy and security regulations for patient data."[168]

Compliance does not equal security. Organizations may think they are security compliant, but oftentimes they are not secure. Tom Turner from Bitsight Technologies told CBS News that he rated healthcare companies on cybersecurity and he "absolutely" worries about the security of his own health care records. "Healthcare is absolutely performing at the bottom of the other industries," and oftentimes organizations spend less than 3% of their operating budget on cybersecurity.[169] The amount spent on cybersecurity is low especially when compared to what the healthcare industry is expected to lose to CEMA over the next five years…an estimated $305 billion from coordinated CEMA.[170]

The amount spent on healthcare cybersecurity also is insignificant when compared to the costs Americans and the United States government spend on healthcare. The United States spends just short of 18% of its Gross Domestic

Product (GDP) on healthcare.[171] In fact, that figure rose consistently in a number of areas over that last five years. Healthcare costs statistics from 2018 reveal the magnitude of the rise for America. The overall national health expenditure (NHE) costs grew 3.9% to $3.5 trillion in 2017, or $10,739 per person, and accounted for 17.9% of Gross Domestic Product.[172] Furthermore in 2017, Medicare spending grew 4.2% to $705.9 billion in 2017, or 20 percent of total NHE; Medicaid spending grew 2.9% to $581.9 billion in 2017, or 17 percent of total NHE; Private health insurance spending grew 4.2% to $1,183.9 billion in 2017, or 34 percent of total NHE; Out of pocket spending grew 2.6% to $365.5 billion in 2017, or 10 percent of total NHE; Hospital expenditures grew 4.6% to $1,142.6 billion in 2017, slower than the 5.6% growth in 2016.[173]

An examination of the amount spent by the United States government on healthcare as compared to all other spending reveals that healthcare is the single largest category of Federal spending (see Figure 4.1). More than $1.71 trillion will be spent by the United States government on healthcare in 2019 – more than any other nation – and more than is spent on United States defense.[174] Yet despite this exorbitant spending and the high costs to American citizens and healthcare organizations, healthcare remains vulnerable to CEMA and a lucrative target for malicious cyber actors to further inflate those costs. Additional examination of the actors involved and examples of significant CEMO directed at the healthcare sector elucidates the magnitude of the problem to the nation.

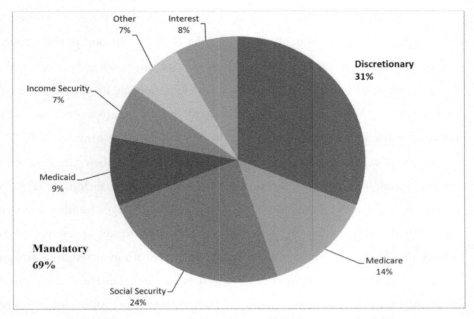

Figure 4.1 – 2018 United States Federal Spending Comparison[175]

Malicious cyber actors can use the PII stolen in healthcare breaches for insurance fraud, identity theft, financial gain, or targeted attacks. Hackers can sell information on the Dark Web or use the information themselves. An adversary or their client may use stolen insurance information to create fake insurance credentials and then create appointments, undergo surgery, or have other medical procedures performed at the expense of the victim and healthcare organizations.[176] The nefarious actor could also use the information to obtain prescription medicine under the victim's identity. According to Computer World, fraudulent billing accounts for 3-10% of annual United States health expenditures.[177] Similarly, the PII, PHI, and EHR can be used to steal patients' and employees' identity. The malicious cyber actor can access financial accounts, take out loans, or apply for credit in the victim's name. If unnoticed, the criminal can assume the identity of the victim for an extended period of time. In addition to identity theft, the stolen medical information can be used for targeted attacks on individuals or hospital devices. In one public example, during his tenure as Vice President, Al Qaeda operatives allegedly attempted to compromise Dick Cheney's pace maker by exploiting an unsecured Bluetooth connection.[178] All of these examples highlight various negative outcomes cyber-criminals can achieve with the theft of individuals' personal information.

Malicious cyber actors can be categorized according to their target selection, tactics, techniques, malware, and procedures. Any of the malicious cyber actors (hacktivists, cybercriminals, and nation-state actors) will target healthcare systems based on the vulnerability of the system and the opportunity presented to the adversary. "Hacktivists retaliate against opposing political and ideological platforms or against organizational action deemed unsatisfactory or offensive. Cybercriminals attack systems in an attempt to generate a profit through the exploitation or auction of victim data. Finally, nation-state actors operate in accordance with geopolitical agendas."[179] Of these groups of actors, the state-sponsored actor is the most concerning and leverages extremely sophisticated CEMA techniques and malware obfuscation methods so that they can conduct effective, long duration operations. Their malware often incorporates rootkits for persistent presence, encryption to prevent reverse engineering, and code to mask the presence of malware from the system user.[180]

State-sponsored actors may seek intelligence for use in espionage operations, collect intellectual property, or desire to disrupt critical services. They tend to be well funded and generally do not conduct cyber campaigns solely for financial gain.[181] Stolen PII usually is not collected to harm individuals financially (that is not to say that the information will not be exploited or sold on underground markets), but is sought to burden the data owner and the United States government, who must investigate the breach and compensate civilians for the personal and fiscal harms of the compromise.

One Chinese government-sponsored group called "Deep Panda" began targeting the healthcare sector, the United States government, and energy sectors around 2012. In the United States healthcare sector, Deep Panda attacked VAE, Anthem, Empire Blue Cross Blue Shield, and Premera Blue Cross.[182] The information stolen from the healthcare organizations included social security numbers and other PII. Deep Panda conducted the CEMA against OPM, Anthem healthcare network, and Premera Blue Cross simultaneously. Deep Panda also is suspected of attacking United Airlines shortly thereafter and may be behind attacks against American education institutions.[183] The healthcare, OPM, and travel information can be aggregated by China to impact the United States government negatively over time. It is not known exactly what purpose China has in mind for the stole data. One option would be to study the information to improve their critical infrastructure sectors. An alternative purpose may be to create a database of United States citizens for political and corporate espionage objectives.

Health Data Management tracked ten major CEMA incidents announced during 2015, with the single largest one victimizing 78.8 million individuals. Some of the attacks began in 2014 or even earlier, but were not discovered until later. The total number of victims from these hacks (not counting a newly disclosed one that may be substantial) is 109,671,626, which represents about one-third of the population of the United States.[184] Each victim organization paid credit and/or identity theft protection services. First, Anthem insurance disclosed the theft of 78.8 million customer records compromising PII. Second, 11 million customer records were stolen from Premera Blue Cross. Third, 10 million records were stolen from Excellus Blue Cross. Fourth, hackers gained access to 4.5 records at UCLA Health. Fifth, malicious cyber actors stole 3.9 customer records from Medical Informatics Engineering. Sixth, CareFirst Blue Cross and Blue Shield announced that hackers accessed 1.1 customer records. Seventh, malicious cyber actors gained access to 220,000 employee and customer records at Beacon Health Systems in Indiana.

Eighth, hackers penetrated and stole 151,626 records from Advantage Dental in Oregon. Ninth, the FBI informed Muhlenberg Community Hospital that hackers compromised 84,681 patient records. Tenth, an unspecified number of customer records were stolen at Maine General Health.[185]

Healthcare organizations rely on legacy systems, and some entities do not invest in cybersecurity at a rate that matches the urgency of the threats faced today. Dave Kennedy, the chief executive of TrustedSEC said, "[t]he medical industry is years and years behind other industries when it comes to security."[186] The healthcare industry is working to coordinate such incidents through groups designed to share information about the cyber threats – such as the National Health Information Sharing and Analysis Center, or NHISAC. The NHISAC is one of several critical infrastructure ISACs that work with the DHS to share threat data, such as tactics used in CEMA and forensic information about hackers.

Significance and Consequences of the CEMA

In this case, numerous malicious cyber actors repeatedly outpaced the United States healthcare industry's capability to contend with that threat, while the Federal government did little to nothing to impose consequences or influence the malicious cyber actors' decision-making. Healthcare is overwhelmed with the malignancy of the cyber pathogen. Furthermore, although the individual instances of CEMA and CEMO did not cross this administration's threshold of national significance, the combined effect of the series of cyber incidents should have triggered a response from the Federal government due to sheer magnitude of theft of United States' citizens' personal information. The reason for no response may be in part due to the fact that there was only a fiscal impact, which many in government believe is the responsibility of each private healthcare organization to contend with. However, when one examines the totality of the various healthcare incidents/operations along with the potential information that was lost, it is not difficult to envisage where and how an adversary can use the stolen personal information at scale against the United States in times of conflict or heighten tension. For example, the ill-gotten PII can be utilized to identify weakness of United States political, intelligence, and military members as a means of exploiting them in the run up to a conflict. From an economical perspective, the relatively simply CEMA directed at the healthcare sector costs both private and government sectors hundreds of millions (or billions) of dollars each year and this adversarial approach would be within the strategy of a foe that wishes to force the United States to spend its wealth on cybersecurity means, mitigation measures, and law suits in lieu of investing that money in more value-driven ways that advance the sector.

Additionally, when one considers the vulnerability to the United States as a whole from the healthcare cyber threat, one is struck by the magnitude this problem. The total costs to America (costs to citizens, private healthcare organizations, and Federal spending) combined with how little is spent on healthcare cybersecurity, juxtaposed against the potential loses to the sector in dollars along with the theft of personal identifiable information/identities and the risk of exploitation by foreign nations based upon that stolen PII, healthcare cyber threats place both the United States economic security and national security at considerable risk. In summary, the United States is susceptible to considerable negative influence and/or effects through the loss of hundreds of millions of United States citizens' personal health records/PII and the loss of billions of dollars. The threat combined with the vulnerability and risk that an adversary may leverage with this vital information against the United States can raise this series of CEMA to the level of CINS, now and in future conflicts. As such, United States political policy must evolve to contend with this evolving threat and national strategy should include the healthcare sector security as part of a holistic coercive national cyber strategy – or suffer the fate of poor foresight.

Comprehending Why the United States Took Little to No Action

From the great number of statements made by the past and present President, members of Congress, and other politically appointed U.S. leaders, there appears to be a disconnect between what the leaders are stating as their concern for the United States economic and national security and the actions of the nation to combat the malicious cyber actors who threatened that security. These cases clearly demonstrate several examples where sophisticated adversaries undertook repeated nefarious cyber operations targeting U.S. critical infrastructure sectors; however, little to nothing was done (other than indictments) to stop, dissuade, or influence the malicious cyber actors' decision making. Are these instances of CINS not significant enough to warrant a more concerted effort to protect the nation or a dramatic evolution in national cybersecurity? Must the critical infrastructure sectors experience even worse malicious effects before the government acts in a more decisive way? Or, is it possible that the United States government simply chose not to impose consequences? Are there other reasons for inactivity on the United States government part? An aggregated examination of the cases highlights several aspects of a more complex answer.

First, from a systemic and national level, there are several factors that shape perspectives and approaches to national cybersecurity of critical infrastructure. Those factors are: 1) a strong counter-argument for restraint in cyberspace; 2) growing foreign influence through on-line and social media channels to shape national narratives; and 3) inability of the U.S. national political apparatus to effectively build consensus to define and implement a national cybersecurity strategy.

Beginning with the strong counter-argument for restraint, we may understand how national dialogues shape political decision-makers' perspectives on the issue.

The counter-argument is often built upon three central themes: offensive cyber operations are hardly ever decisive, so we should focus on defense and deception; there is fear that United States counter-cyber operations could escalate tensions with global partners; and these same counter-cyber operations do not perpetuate proper acceptable norms of state behavior in cyberspace. Let us dissect and dispose of the counter-argument.

The notion that the United States should avoid offensive cyber operations because they rarely yield decisive results is true when viewed only through a military and wartime lens. Even this book's cases studies of Russia show that during war, cyber operations are complimentary to kinetic operations are most successful when integrated with other instruments of power. Furthermore, proponents of the counter-argument limit this part of their argument to just wartime operations where cyber operations are targeting an adversary's networks, key military communication equipment, and weapon systems.[187] This argument falls well short of actually considering the reality and vast magnitude of CEMA seen across critical infrastructure attacks that are not part of war or physical conflict between international protagonists. As this book has illustrated, a great majority of CEMA witnessed today falls well short of an act of war. Consequently, by presenting an argument to avoid the offensive in lieu of the defense and deception incorrectly ties national cyber strategies to physical wartime strategies, which misses the realities of the conflict in and through the virtual domain. Hackers do not think in terms of offense and defense, but rather in terms of exploiting vulnerabilities to achieve his objectives. By injecting a notion that the U.S. should avoid the offense (or any actions outside of defense and deception) is counterproductive success within conflict in the virtual domain. Defense through hardening of U.S. cyber capabilities is vitally important, as is resilient processes and capabilities to gracefully degrade while under attack. However, an effective national cyber strategy should also look at ways to proactively deny the adversary his ability to succeed and if necessary, impose consequences on that nefarious actor in ways to pressure him to alter his behavior. This not the same thing as offense in the proponent's counter argument. I would suggest a better construct to advocate is "proactive defense" rather offense. Any activities to proactively work to identify and prevent cyber-attacks is a prudent construct to help ensure the vitality of national infrastructure. Proactive defense implies the notion that the United States is seeking to prevent the attack, where offense implies the United States is the aggressor. Proactive defense seeks to limit the adversary's cyber objectives in ways that stop or reduce his ability to strike. Proponents of the counter-argument of no offense do not understand the possibilities and nuances of counter-options within cyberspace and therefore advocate for notions that are counterproductive to national cybersecurity. More importantly, a proper cyber approach (proactive defense when combined with other instruments of national power) will best reflect the conceptual methodology to change the national narrative on cybersecurity.

As to the fear of escalating a potential conflict with international adversaries during a cyber conflict, there is always concern that this remains a distinct possibility. Furthermore, proponents of the counter-argument suggest that cyber operations may lead to a security dilemma (a tit for tat exchange of actions and capabilities that continually raises the actions of both sides of a conflict to an unacceptable level). History is replete with cases where this has occurred. This perspective is valid...without a coherent national strategy...cyber or physical. This is a primary purpose of this book...to explain how to proper define the domain and build a strategy that effectively imposes consequence on cyber foes in a way that is favorable to the United States, which would include controlling the escalation of the cyber conflict. Without such a strategy, either nothing happens to coerce adversaries or what does happen is not controlled in such a way as to ensure a constructive outcome for America.

Next, the proponents of the counter-argument postulate that if the United States countered our adversaries through the virtual domain, it would not be setting the example of acceptable norms for cyberspace. This argument falls short for two reasons. First, to do nothing is an unacceptable course of action…why continue to allow cyber-criminal and state-sponsored cyber actors freedom to conduct their nefarious deeds without imposition of consequence? Or why only rely on defense and deception when what the above case studies show that this course of action has only emboldened our adversaries. The point is that continuing with the nation's current path is not working…something more must be done. Second, as will be illuminated in the next chapter, there are several acceptable courses of action based upon international law that provide the United States with avenues for action (even proactive defense). These internationally legally acceptable avenues actually perpetuate customary norms of state behavior and not the opposite. So, by not acting in accordance with internationally acceptable law, the United States is essentially not setting the example for proper behavior…the proponents for the counter-argument have their logic exactly backwards.

Next, let us turn to how on-line news and social media entities are shaping the national narrative on this and other issues of significance, which in turn shapes how Congressional members respond to their constituents' perspectives (rightly or wrongly) and arrive at an opinion as to how to plot a course for the nation on many topics, including cybersecurity. Digital news has gained prominence lately in the way societies are gathering information about numerous national topics to include political candidates and election agendas. Now, information and disinformation through the virtual domain are subjects of contest for numerous players on the national and international stage…a battle to determine what is fact and what is "fake news." With the advent of technologies to alter recorded video and voice, combined with easily created false personas to instigate untrue narratives, it is increasingly difficult to decipher truth from fiction.

211

If the United States is going to be successful in cyberspace, it must accept that the battle of the narrative on-line is real (and part of the strategic battle in the virtual domain) and that it must incorporate plans to confront false reports with fact while working to uncover the instigators of falsehoods. Improper influence in elections is the most serious case of how external actors shape democratic processes and manipulate national perspectives. Documented malign influence in elections has been documented in not only the United States in 2016 and 2018, but also in elections in Germany, France, Brazil, Nigeria, Taiwan and elsewhere.[188] Many on-line viewers have lost trust in established news outlets and tend to consume information that affirms, rather than informs, their views. The United States, along with Western governments and private industry should take strong measures to mitigate foreign influence operations. Successful false narratives are able to sway public attention and propel action in ways that are counter the good order and discipline of properly functioning nations. Furthermore, adversaries that are effective at building and implementing false narratives are able to control global messages during international conflict, as was shown in the Russian cases against Georgia, Ukraine, and Estonia. This similar power to create false narratives and control messages sway and divide national leaders against the United States' desire to advance national objectives that are truly in the best interest of the country, which include electoral reform, gun control, and national security objectives (cybersecurity). Specifically, the United States should denounce foreign disinformation campaigns as soon as they are identified, and should define quantitative means to measure the effectiveness of those foreign methods. On-line news agencies and social media corporations must aggressively monitor their sites for nefarious state-sponsored content, and work to advance verified and fact-checked content.[189] The result is a nation unlikely to construct an effective national cybersecurity strategy.

Another aspect of the American reality of little to no action against adversaries that commit CINS (and closely related to the previous) has to do with the political realities of the United States national political situation. Currently within the United States, there is an extremely divisive environment between political parties that places political allegiance ahead of national concerns. There have been and are several legislative proposals put forth to contend with the national cyber threat. Unfortunately, most do not make it through the Congress to the President for approval because bi-partisan politics shut down the initiative simply because one party works to defeat the opposite party's proposals. Not until a bi-partisan proposal comes forth and/or each party places the nation before political party objectives will Congress actually pass meaningful legislation to direct the creation and implementation of cyber policy and strategy.

There is No National Cyber Strategy

Returning to the task of assessing the United States' current strategy to defend the nation, we must ask: in general, how well does the United States currently address (or not) the element of strategy in the cyber defense of U.S. critical infrastructure? Currently, in the academic sense of connecting ends, ways, and means, the United States does not have a declared national strategy to defend the nation's critical infrastructure from cyber-attack. As was mentioned earlier, cyberspace and the Internet now connect threats directly to corporations and Americans, and the disintermediation of the government as the responsible agent of national defense has left the United States government struggling to deter cyber threats that routinely target private critical infrastructure entities. The inability to architect a true national strategy to defend critical infrastructure allows nefarious cyber actors free reign in executing their CEMA. Despite decades of Presidential policies and numerous directive documents masquerading as "Strategy" (e.g., DoD's

2018 Cyber Strategy – see previous chapter), the United States still only possesses policy statements rather than having a fully coherent and readily applicable national cyber strategy. Several administrations articulated policy for the Executive Branch of government (via Presidential directives and orders) and the Congress mandated requirements to develop national cyber strategy, yet the United States continues to fail to create such a national strategy. Every Administration over the last three decades lacked the direction and ability to connect ends, ways, and means in any consequential way to adequately secure the United States critical infrastructure against cyber-attacks. Several decades of good intent do not make up for a lack of results.

Federal government leaders acknowledge a role in defending the United States against malicious cyber actors, but struggle to understand fully when and how the government should respond beyond law enforcement, threat information sharing, and private industry's cybersecurity advocacy – no strategy exists that directs the Federal government to synchronize and integrate their capabilities, resources, and authorities in cases of CINS to influence the decision-making of the malicious cyber actors. Referring to a national cyber strategy, Paul Rosenweig stated "most observers would agree that the United States has yet to develop a stable solution."[190] Without a national cybersecurity strategy, the United States will continue to endure virtual blow after blow in the cyber conflicts that the nation currently experiences – and suffer the cumulative costs imposed upon United States economic competitiveness and national security. Moreover, without a national strategy that incorporates coercive effects, the United States at best, will continue to react and respond instead of proactively defend and counter adversarial cyber actions.

A number of other reasons also help explain why the United States is where it is currently with regard to lacking a national coercive cybersecurity strategy. First, the evolutionary nature of cyberspace, the complexities involved in cyber defense and attribution, the disintermediation of governmental defense and law enforcement organizations, the reliance on private critical infrastructure owners/operators, and the difficulty in distinguishing between probe and attack in cyberspace present challenges that may appear overwhelming to policymakers and national strategists. Second, despite the proliferation of numerous cybersecurity studies, the U.S. government simply has not devoted enough sustained attention to the present cyber storm along with creating the organizational structures needed to support our cyber deterrence activities...there is no concerted national cybersecurity strategy making process. Finally, as a result of the evolutionary nature of CEMA, from unauthorized access, exploitation, disruption, to destruction, the United States and private industry efforts are incorrectly focused on defensive and resiliency-only responses. These limited options (that are largely private industry based) are insufficient to contend with the threat. Malicious cyber actors' benefits outweigh their costs and risks. More significantly, state and state-sponsored cyber actors understand this lack of consequences and are now actively executing CEMA against the United States for their nefarious motives and objectives at a much greater scale and severity.

Returning finally to the reasons why the United States government may not have taken a more robust and effective action in the above case studies, one could also argue that the United States deliberately chose the very limited action witnessed in the above cases and elected not to coerce the cyber adversaries. If that were true, however, then national leaders would be deliberately acquiescing to cyber threats, which appears to be counter to national objectives and numerous Administrations. One might then postulate that the disconnect between stated national objectives and past ineffective action to deter cyber threats is not likely intentional, but rather based on a lack of knowledge on how to properly build a national counter-cyber strategy.

Summary

The above case studies demonstrate that the United States' cybersecurity policies are lacking specifically as a result of no national coercive strategy. Furthermore, the United States is unable to create the necessary unity of effort in the form of a credible integrated cybersecurity organization/framework to effectively influence the nation's cyber adversaries. Consequently, in instances of CINS, the Federal government must have a national strategy and capability that habitually works with private industry to plan and execute cyber actions and operations to deny, deter, and influence malicious cyber actors who threaten United States economic and national security. Malicious actors are attacking with impunity.

Through my years of research, I have concluded that the reason for a lack of robust action from the many organizations in the Federal government is the absence of the structure or framework to integrate and synchronize all of the instruments of power together effectively to combat the nation's cyber foes. Despite several initiatives within both the government and private sectors, there is still a lack of unity of effort across the operational level of U.S. government and between government and private entities. The reason lies squarely within the White House Administrations in that "existing structures tend to conflate two distinct operational functions – those of policy decision-making and those of implementation."[191] The function of setting coercive policy and adopting a strategy resides with the White House, while implementing cyber actions and operations should reside squarely in the Executive Branch's departments and agencies.

Within the White House, the National Security Advisor and his/her staff assists the President with the creation of cyber policy and strategy. At the operational level of Federal government cyber response actions, DHS is the lead entity for coordinating implementing the National Cyber Incident Response Plan[192] through the DHS's National Cybersecurity and Communications Integration Center (NCCIC) as was discussed earlier. Since the types of actions and operation to effectively contend with national cyber threats require options beyond threat

216

information sharing and advocating for private industry's defense. The NCCIC and the National Cyber Incident Response Plan are wholly insufficient. Currently there is no single, unified organization that possesses all of the necessary authorities, capabilities, and disciplines to develop and execute a "whole of government" cybersecurity strategy that utilizes all the instruments of power. Furthermore, none of the United States governmental cyber operations centers incorporate private sector partners in the planning and implementation phases of their actions and operations. Consequently, the United States must create an effective national and international organizational construct/framework for the development and implementation of cyberspace actions and operations as part of an overall national cyber strategy. The United States' cyber organizations and capabilities will be expounded upon in the next chapter. The next step in fighting this plague is to develop the national coercive cybersecurity strategy.

---

[1] NSTAC Report to the President, Nov 21, 2014.

[2] Richard L. Kugler, "Deterrence of Cyber Attacks," in *Cyberpower and National Security*, Franklin D. Kramer, Stuart H. Starr, and Larry K Wentz, eds., (National Defense University Press, Washington D.C., 2009), pg. 310.

[3] For more the guidance, see the National Security Act of 1947 at: http://legcounsel.house.gov/Comps/National%20Security%20Act%20Of%201947.pdf and the 1986 Goldwater-Nichols Act (PUBLIC LAW 99-433-OCT. 1, 1986) at: http://history.defense.gov/Portals/70/Documents/dod_reforms/Goldwater-NicholsDoDReordAct1986.pdf.

[4] Donald J. Trump, the *National Security Strategy* of the United States, (The White House, Washington DC, December 2017), pg. ii, found at: https://www.whitehouse.gov/wp-content/uploads/2017/12/NSS-Final-12-18-2017-0905.pdf.

[5] Ibid. p1.

[6] Ibid, pg. 4.

[7] Nathan J. Lucas and Kathleen J. McInnis (Congressional Researchers), "The 2015 National Security Strategy: Authorities, Changes, Issues for Congress," (Congressional Research Service, Washington DC, April 5, 2016), pg. 1, found at: https://www.fas.org/sgp/crs/natsec/R44023.pdf.

[8] Lamont Colucci, "The Post-Strategic Presidency: Obama's National Security Strategy shows he's unwilling or unable to take decisive action," *United States News and World Report*, Feb 24, 2015, found at: http://www.usnews.com/opinion/blogs/world-report/2015/02/24/obamas-national-security-strategy-shows-hes-a-post-strategic-president.

[9] Ali Wyne, "Assessing the New US National Security Strategy," PS21 - Project for the Study of the 21st Century, March 26, 2015, found at: https://projects21.org/2015/03/26/assessing-the-new-us-national-security-strategy/.

[10] Trump, 2017 NSS, pg. 12.

[11] Ibid, pg. 13.

[12] Ibid, pg. 13.

[13] Ibid, pg. 32.

[14] Ibid, pg. 32.

[15] Ibid, pg. 32.

[16] Barack Obama, *The 2011 International Strategy for Cybersecurity*, (The White House, Washington DC, May 2011), pg. 8, found at: https://www.whitehouse.gov/sites/default/files/rss_viewer/international_strategy_for_cyberspace.pdf.

[17] Ibid, pg. 10.

[18] Barack Obama, "Executive Order -- Improving Critical Infrastructure Cybersecurity," (The White House, Washington DC, Feb 12, 2013), found at: https://www.whitehouse.gov/the-press-office/2013/02/12/executive-order-improving-critical-infrastructure-cybersecurity.

[19] See Presidential Policy Directive 21 (PPD 21) -- Critical Infrastructure Security and Resilience, found at: https://www.whitehouse.gov/the-press-office/2013/02/12/presidential-policy-directive-critical-infrastructure-security-and-resil.

[20] Presidential Decision Directive 63, *Critical Infrastructure Protection* (The White House, May 22, 1998), found at: http://ww.fas.org/irp/offdocs/pdd-63.pdf.

[21] Ibid.

[22] Ibid.

[23] Ibid.

[24] See ISAC Council White Book, "The Integration of ISACs into Government and Departments of Defense and Homeland Security Exercises," (Jan 2004), found at: http://www.isaccouncil.org/whitebooks/files/Integration_of_ISACs_Into_Exercises_013104.pdf.

[25] For a complete list of ISACs see: http://www.isaccouncil.org/.

[26] The White House, *The National Strategy to Secure Cyberspace*, (Washington D.C., February 2003), found at: http://www.us-cert.gov/reading_room/cyberspace_strategy.pdf .

[27] Ibid.

[28] The White House, Press Releases (Washington D.C., March 2010), Obama administration partially lifts secrecy on classified cybersecurity project, found at: http://www.whitehouse.gov/the_press_office/Statement-by-the-Press-Secretary-on-Conclusion-of-the-Cyberspace-Review .

[29] The White House, *Improving Critical Infrastructure Cybersecurity*, (Washington D.C., Feb 2013) found at: https://www.gpo.gov/fdsys/pkg/FR-2013-02-19/pdf/2013-03915.pdf.

[30] Ibid.

[31] Evelyn Brown, "NIST Establishes National Cybersecurity Center of Excellence," National Institute of Standards and Technology, (Feb 21, 2012), found at: http://www.nist.gov/itl/csd/nccoe-022112.cfm.

[32] The White House, "Executive Order: Blocking the Property of Certain Persons Engaging in Significant Malicious Cyber-Enabled Activities," (Washington D.C., April 1, 2015), found at: https://www.whitehouse.gov/the-press-office/2015/04/01/executive-order-blocking-property-certain-persons-engaging-significant-m.

[33] Lisa Monaco, White House Blog, "Expanding Our Ability to Combat Cyber Threats," (Washington D.C., April 1, 2015), found at: https://www.whitehouse.gov/blog/2015/04/01/expanding-our-ability-combat-cyber-threats.

[34] Barak Obama, *International Strategy for Cyberspace* (Washington D.C, May 2011), pg. i, found at: https://www.whitehouse.gov/sites/default/files/rss_viewer/international_strategy_for_cyberspace.pdf.

[35] William Jackson, "White House sets strategy for international cyber behavior," GCN Online, May 16, 2011, found at: https://gcn.com/articles/2011/05/16/international-strategy-cyberspace.aspx.

[36] See PPD 21, and Executive Order -- Improving Critical Infrastructure Cybersecurity (13636) found at: https://www.whitehouse.gov/the-press-office/2013/02/12/executive-order-improving-critical-infrastructure-cybersecurity, and Fact Sheet on Presidential Policy Directive 20 found at: https://fas.org/irp/offdocs/ppd/ppd-20-fs.pdf.

[37] PPD 21.

[38] PPD-21

[39] PPD-21

[40] For more on the 1986 Goldwater-Nichols Act, see https://history.defense.gov/Portals/70/Documents/dod_reforms/Goldwater-NicholsDoDReordAct1986.pdf.

[41] H.R.3696 - National Cybersecurity and Critical Infrastructure Protection Act of 2014, 113th Congress (2013-2014), July 29, 2014, found at: https://www.congress.gov/bill/113th-congress/house-bill/3696.

[42] Ibid.

[43] Department of Homeland Security National Cybersecurity and Communications Integration Center website located at: https://www.dhs.gov/national-cybersecurity-and-communications-integration-center.

[44] Barack Obama, PPD-21.

[45] Federal Bureau of Investigations website, "Addressing Threats to the Nation's Cybersecurity," see https://www.fbi.gov/about-us/investigate/cyber/addressing-threats-to-the-nations-cybersecurity.

[46] Ibid.

[47] Statements taken from an interview by the author with SSA Donald Freese, Director of FBI's National Cyber Investigative Joint Task Force (NCIJTF) on March 12, 2016 in Chantilly, VA.

[48] Ibid.

[49] See the United States Secret Service website "The Investigative Mission," found at: http://www.secretservice.gov/investigation/.

[50] Ibid.

[51] This observation was explained to the author by numerous senior leaders in the DHS, FBI, NSA, DoD (United States Cyber Command) during various interviews conducted from 4-7 May 2015.

[52] For more on this observation, see GAO Report: "Critical Infrastructure Protraction - DHS Action Needed to Enhance Integration and Coordination of Vulnerability Assessment Efforts."

[53] Paul Rosenweig, pg. 2.

[54] Judith H. Germano, "Cybersecurity Partnerships: A New Era of Public-Private Collaboration," (New York University School of Law, New York, 2014), pg. 1.

[55] Ibid, pg. 3.

[56] Statements derived from an interview conducted by the author on 4 May 2015 with Financial Services – Information Sharing and Analysis Center President, Bill Nelson.

[57] The President's National Security Telecommunications Advisory Committee (NSTAC), *NSTAC Report to the President on Information and Communications Technology Mobilization*, November 19, 2014, pg. 1, found at: https://www.dhs.gov/sites/default/files/publications/NSTAC%20-%20Information%20and%20Communications%20Technology%20Mobilization%20Report%2011-19-2014.pdf. In November 2013, the Executive Office of the President requested the President's National Security Telecommunications Advisory Committee (NSTAC) examine the implications of the operational coordination of critical commercial assets or capabilities to facilitate a coordinated information and communications technology (ICT) response to a cyber-related event of national significance.

[58] Ibid, pg. ES-1-2.

[59] Ibid, pg. ES-2.

[60] Ibid, pg. ES-2.

[61] Ibid, pg. ES-2.

[62] Ibid. pg. ES-2-3.

[63] This statement originated from a Securities Industry and Financial Markets Association (SIFMA) "Quantum Dawn 3 Cybersecurity Exercise" as an observation of the exercise participants in which the author contributed, on 16 Sep 2015, New York City, NY. For more on Quantum Dawn 3 and other SIFMA cybersecurity exercises, see: http://www.sifma.org/quantum-dawn-3/.

[64] Barak Obama, "Presidential Policy Directive 41 – United States Cyber Incident Coordination," the White House, Washington D.C. July 26, 2016, found on-line at: https://obamawhitehouse.archives.gov/the-press-office/2016/07/26/presidential-policy-directive-united-states-cyber-incident.

[65] Ibid.

[66] Ibid.

[67] Ibid.

[68] Ibid.

[69] Ibid.

[70] President Donald J. Trump, Executive Order 13800, "Executive Order on Strengthening the Cybersecurity of Federal Networks and Critical Infrastructure," May 11, 2017, found at: https://www.whitehouse.gov/presidential-actions/presidential-executive-order-strengthening-cybersecurity-federal-networks-critical-infrastructure/.

[71] Ibid.

[72] Donald J. Trump, "National Cyber Strategy of the United States of America," The White House, Washington D. C., September 2018, pg. 1, found on-line at: https://www.whitehouse.gov/wp-content/uploads/2018/09/National-Cyber-Strategy.pdf.

[73] Ibid, pg. 8.

[74] Christopher Krebs (Director of CISA), CISA's Homepage accessed on-line at: https://www.cisa.gov/.

[75] 115th U.S. Congress, 2nd Session, Public Law 115-874, "JOHN S. MCCAIN NATIONAL DEFENSE AUTHORIZATION ACT FOR FISCAL YEAR 2019," July 25, 2018, found at: https://www.govinfo.gov/content/pkg/CRPT-115hrpt874/pdf/CRPT-115hrpt874.pdf.

[76] Ibid.

[77] United States Department of Defense, *DoD Cyber Strategy*, (Washington DC, Sep 2018), pg. 2, found at: https://media.defense.gov/2018/Sep/18/2002041658/-1/-1/1/CYBER_STRATEGY_SUMMARY_FINAL.PDF.

[78] Ibid.

[79] United States Government Accounting Office Report to Congressional Committees, "Civil Support – DoD Needs to Clarify its Roles and Responsibilities for Defense Support of Civil Authorities during Cyber Incidents," (Washington DC, April 2016), pg. 1.

[80] Danny Vinik, "America's Secret Arsenal," *The Politico – The Agenda Cyber Issue*, Dec 12, 2015, found at: http://www.politico.com/agenda/story/2015/12/defense-department-cyber-offense-strategy-000331.

[81] Interviews conducted by author in Feb 2016 with United States Cyber Command Deputy J5 and with other United States Cyber Command leaders between Mar 2016 and Nov 2018.

[82] Ernst and Young LLC., "Is cybersecurity about more than protection? EY Global Information Security Survey 2018–19," found at: https://www.ey.com/Publication/vwLUAssets/ey-global-information-security-survey-2018-19/$FILE/ey-global-information-security-survey-2018-19.pdf.

[83] Ibid.

[84] Ibid.

[85] Ibid.

[86] Brian Wallace, "Operation Cleaver," Cylance, 2014, pg. 6, found at: https://cdn2.hubspot.net/hubfs/270968/assets/Cleaver/Cylance_Operation_Cleaver_Report.pdf.

[87] The Shamoon virus behaves differently from other malware attacks intended for cyber espionage. Shamoon can spread from an infected machine to other computers on the network. Once a system is infected, the virus continues to compile a list of files from specific locations on the system, upload them to the attacker, and erase them. Finally, the virus overwrites the master boot record of the infected computer, making it unbootable. See Symantec Security Report at: http://www.symantec.com/connect/blogs/shamoon-attacks.

[88] Brian Wallace, pg. 6.

[89] The group's moniker, Izz ad-Din al-Qassam, was a Muslim preacher who lead in the fight against British, French and Jewish nationalist organizations in the Levant in the 1920s and 1930s. "Operation Ababil" was also the name of a failed Pakistani military operation in April 1984.

[90] See Pastebin Post at http://pastebin.com/mCHia4W5.

[91] Adam Samson and Matt Egan, "Chase, NYSE Websites Targeted in Cyber Attacks," *Fox Business News,* Sep 19, 2012, *accessed online 22 May 2016, found at: http://www.foxbusiness.com/features/2012/09/19/chase-website-experiences-intermittent-troubles.html.*

[92] See Pastebin Post at http://pastebin.com/QWXkfPhG.

[93] Ellen Nakashima, "Iran blamed for cyberattacks on United States banks and companies," *The Washington Post,* Sep 21, 2012, found at: https://www.washingtonpost.com/world/national-security/iran-blamed-for-cyberattacks/2012/09/21/afbe2be4-0412-11e2-9b24-ff730c7f6312_story.html.

[94] Antone Gonsalves, "Bank attackers more sophisticated than typical hacktivists, expert says," *CSO Online,* Sep 28, 2012, found at: http://www.csoonline.com/article/2132319/malware-cybercrime/bank-attackers-more-sophisticated-than-typical-hacktivists--expert-says.html.

[95] See Pastebin Post: http://pastebin.com/E4f7fmB5.

[96] Noah Shachtman, "Bank Hackers Deny They're Agents of Iran," *Wired,* Nov 27, 2012, found at: https://www.wired.com/2012/11/bank-hackers-deny-theyre-agents-of-iran/.

[97] See Pastebin Post at: http://pastebin.com/KDQkBngL.

[98] See Pastebin Post at: http://pastebin.com/r4k1u8kQ .

[99] See Pastebin Post at: http://pastebin.com/EEWQhA0j.

[100] See Pastebin Post at: http://pastebin.com/kXSsVScS.

[101] Nicole, Perlroth, "Report Says Cyberattacks Originated Inside Iran," *The New York Times*, Dec 2, 2104, found at: http://www.nytimes.com/2014/12/03/world/middleeast/report-says-cyberattacks-originated-inside-iran.html?_r=0.

[102] Brian Wallace, pg. 7.

[103] Nicole Perloth.

[104] Ibid. pg. 11.

[105] Ibid, pg. 11.

[106] Federal Bureau of Investigations, "International Cyber Crime Iranians Charged with Hacking United States Financial Sector," Mar 24, 2016, FBI Website found at: https://www.fbi.gov/news/stories/2016/march/iranians-charged-with-hacking-us-financial-sector.

[107] Ibid.

[108] Ibid.

[109] Ellen Nakashima and Matt Zapotosky, "United States charges Iran-linked hackers with targeting banks, N.Y. dam," *The Washington Post*, 24 Mar 2016, found at: https://www.washingtonpost.com/world/national-security/justice-department-to-unseal-indictment-against-hackers-linked-to-iranian-goverment/2016/03/24/9b3797d2-f17b-11e5-a61f-e9c95c06edca_story.html.

[110] Ellen Nakashima and Matt Zapotosky, "United States charges Iran-linked hackers with targeting banks, N.Y. dam," *The Washington Post*, 24 Mar 2016, found at: https://www.washingtonpost.com/world/national-security/justice-department-to-unseal-indictment-against-hackers-linked-to-iranian-goverment/2016/03/24/9b3797d2-f17b-11e5-a61f-e9c95c06edca_story.html.

[111] Ibid.

[112] Ibid.

[113] Ibid.

[114] Office of Personnel Management Website, "Cybersecurity Resource Center Cybersecurity Incidents," accessed 22 May 2016, found at: https://www.opm.gov/cybersecurity/cybersecurity-incidents/.

[115] Ibid.

[116] Robert Hackett, "A product demo may have revealed what could be the biggest ever government data breach," *Fortune*, Jun 12, 2015, found at: http://fortune.com/2015/06/12/cytech-product-demo-opm-breach/.

[117] Ibid.

118   See   Federal   Bureau   of   Investigations   website,   found   at: https://www.fbi.gov/news/news_blog/fbi-investigating-opm-cyber-intrusion.

119 Sean Gallagher, "Encryption "would not have helped" at OPM, says DHS official," *Ars Technica*, Jun 16, 2015, found at: http://arstechnica.com/security/2015/06/encryption-would-not-have-helped-at-opm-says-dhs-official/.

120 Ibid.

121 Barrett, Devlin, Danny Yadron, and Damian Paletta, "United States Suspects Hackers in China Breached About four (4) Million People's Records, Officials Say," *Wall Street Journal*, 5 June 2015, accessed 22 May 2016, found at: http://www.wsj.com/articles/u-s-suspects-hackers-in-china-behind-government-data-breach-sources-say-1433451888.

122 Sam Sanders, "Massive Data Breach Puts 4 Million Federal Employees' Records At Risk," *National Public Radio*, Jun 4, 2015, found at: http://www.npr.org/sections/thetwo-way/2015/06/04/412086068/massive-data-breach-puts-4-million-federal-employees-records-at-risk.

123 Kevin Liptak, Theodore Schleifer and Jim Sciutto, "China might be building vast database of federal worker info, experts say," CNN Politics Online, Jun 6, 2015, found at: http://www.cnn.com/2015/06/04/politics/federal-agency-hacked-personnel-management/.

124 Interview by author of an FBI Supervisory Special Agent from the Cyber Division on 18 April 2016 in Houston, Texas.

125 Office of Personnel Management, "Office of the Inspector General, Semiannual Report to Congress: October 1, 2014–March 31, 2015," found at: https://www.opm.gov/news/reports-publications/semi-annual-reports/sar52.pdf.

126 Michael Adams, "Why the OPM Hack Is Far Worse Than You Imagine," *Lawfare Blog*, Mar 11, 2016, accessed online 22 May 2016, found at: https://www.lawfareblog.com/why-opm-hack-far-worse-you-imagine.

127 Ibid.

128 Guy Taylor, "James Clapper, Intel chief: Cyber ranks highest on worldwide threats to United States," *The Washington Times*, Feb 26, 2016, found at: http://www.washingtontimes.com/news/2015/feb/26/james-clapper-intel-chief-cyber-ranks-highest-worl/?page=all.

129 Bill Getz, "Russian cybersecurity intelligence targets critical United States infrastructure," *The Washington Times*, Dec 16, 2015, found at: http://www.washingtontimes.com/news/2015/dec/16/inside-the-ring-russia-cyberspace-intelligence-tar/?page=all.

[130] Ibid.

[131] Frank J. Cilluffo, Director of the Center for Cyber and Homeland Security, "Testimony Before the United States House of Representatives Committee on Homeland Security Subcommittee on Cybersecurity, Infrastructure Protection, and Security Technologies," Feb 25, 2016, found at: http://docs.house.gov/meetings/HM/HM08/20160225/104505/HHRG-114-HM08-Wstate-CilluffoF-20160225.pdf.

[132] Ibid.

[133] Michael Riley, "How Russian Hackers Stole the Nasdaq," *Bloomberg News*, July 21, 2014, found at: http://www.bloomberg.com/news/articles/2014-07-17/how-russian-hackers-stole-the-nasdaq.

[134] Ibid.

[135] Ibid.

[136] Ibid.

[137] See Federal Bureau of Investigations website: "Manhattan United States Attorney and FBI Assistant Director in Charge Announce Charges Against Russian National for Hacking NASDAQ Servers," found at: https://www.fbi.gov/newyork/press-releases/2013/manhattan-u.s.-attorney-and-fbi-assistant-director-in-charge-announce-charges-against-russian-national-for-hacking-nasdaq-servers.

[138] Ibid.

[139] Culluffo.

[140] Kevin Poulsen, "Russia Issues International Travel Advisory to its Hackers," *Wired*, September 3, 2013. http://www.wired.com/2013/09/dont-leave-home/.

[141] "The DUKES: 7 years of Russian cyberespionage," F-Secure, pg. 3, found at: *https://www.f-secure.com/documents/996508/1030745/dukes_whitebook.pdf.*

[142] Ibid, pg. 26.

[143] Ibid, pg. 27.

[144] See Symantec Report, "Regin: Top-tier espionage tool enables stealthy surveillance," found at: http://www.symantec.com/content/en/us/enterprise/media/security_response/whitebooks/regin-analysis.pdf.

[145] See FireEye Report, "Russia Again?" found at: https://www.fireeye.com/blog/products-and-services/2015/08/in_case_you_missedi0.html.

[146] Evan Perez and Shimon Prokupecz, "How the United States thinks Russians hacked the White House," *CNN News*, April 8, 2015, found at: http://www.cnn.com/2015/04/07/politics/how-russians-hacked-the-wh/.

[147] Craig Whitlock and Missy Ryan, "US suspects Russia in Pentagon hack," *The Washington Post*, Aug 8, 2015, found at: http://columbiadailyherald.com/news/local-news/us-suspects-russia-pentagon-hack.

[148] Nate Raymond, "FBI has lead in probe of 1.2 billion stolen Web credentials: documents," *Reuters*, Nov 24, 2015, found at: http://www.reuters.com/article/us-usa-cyberattack-russia-idUSKBN0TD2YN20151124.

[149] Pierluigi Paganini, "Russian hackers infiltrated many US critical infrastructure," *Security Affairs*, Nov 8, 2014, found at: http://securityaffairs.co/wordpress/29977/cyber-warfare-2/russia-hacked-us-critical-infrastructure.html.

[150] Ibid.

[151] Ibid.

[152] Ibid.

[153] Ibid.

[154] Ibid.

[155] Frank Vernuccio, "The Cyber Threat," *New York Analysis of Policy and Government*, Sep 2, 2015, found at: http://www.usagovpolicy.com/nyanalysis/the-cyber-threat/.

[156] Institute for Critical Infrastructure Technology (ICIT), "Hacking Healthcare IT in 2016: Lessons the Healthcare Industry Can Learn from the OPM Breach," January 2016, pg. 1, found at: http://icitech.org/wp-content/uploads/2016/01/ICIT-Brief-Hacking-Healthcare-IT-in-2016.pdf.

[157] Gemalto, "2015 First Half Review: Findings from the Breach Level Index," (Gemalto, NV, 2015), pg. 11, found at: http://www.gemalto.com/brochures-site/download-site/Documents/Gemalto_H1_2015_BLI_Report.pdf.

[158] United States Department of Health and Human Services, Office for Civil Rights, "Breach Portal: Notice to the Secretary of HHS Breach of Unsecured Protected Health Information," accessed 11 Jun 2016, found at: https://ocrportal.hhs.gov/ocr/breach/breach_report.jsf.

[159] Barbara Filkins, "Health Care Cyberthreat Report: Widespread Compromises Detected, Compliance Nightmare on Horizon," (SANS Institute InfoSec Reading Room, Feb 2014, sponsored by Norse), pp. 2-3, found at: https://www.sans.org/reading-room/whitebooks/analyst/health-care-cyberthreat-report-widespread-compromises-detected-compliance-nightmare-horizon-34735.

[160] Greg Bell and Michael Ebert, "HEALTH CARE AND CYBER SECURITY: Increasing Threats Require Increased Capabilities," (KPMG LLP, 2015), pp. 1-3, found at: http://www.kpmg-institutes.com/content/dam/kpmg/healthcarelifesciencesinstitute/pdf/2015/cyber-healthcare-survey.pdf.

[161] Ibid. pg. 4.

[162] ICIT, pg. 4.

[163] Ibid. pg. 4.

[164] Ibid, pg. 4.

[165] Kris Van Cleave, "Anthem hack highlights desirability of stolen health records," *CBS News*, Feb 5, 2015, found at: http://www.cbsnews.com/news/do-hackers-have-your-health-records/.

[166] Barbara Filkins, pg. 7.

[167] Ibid, pg7.

[168] Ibid, pg.7

[169] Kris Van Cleave.

[170] Mike Miliard, "Cyberattacks could cost providers $305B," *Healthcare IT News*, Oct 19, 2015, found at: http://www.healthcareitnews.com/news/cyberattacks-could-cost-providers-305b.

[171] ICIT, pg. 1.

[172] Centers for Medicare and Medicaid Services website accessed Mar 30, 2019, found at: https://www.cms.gov/research-statistics-data-and-systems/statistics-trends-and-reports/nationalhealthexpenddata/nhe-fact-sheet.html.

[173] Ibid.

[174] "The United States Government Spending," accessed on Mar 30, 2019, found at: https://www.usgovernmentspending.com/.

[175] Ibid.

[176] SANS, pg. 8.

[177] Stacy Collett, "How to Stop Fraud," *Computer World*, Jul 6, 2009, found at: http://www.computerworld.com/article/2526450/security0/how-to-stop-fraud.html.

[178] ICIT, pg. 10.

[179] Ibid, pg. 11.

[180] Ibid, pg. 18.

[181] Ibid, pg. 19.

[182] See FBI Flash on Deep Panda located at: http://krebsonsecurity.com/wp-content/uploads/2015/02/FBI-Flash-Warning-Deep-Panda.pdf.

[183] ICIT, pg. 20.

[184] Health Data Management Report, "10 Largest Healthcare Cyber Attacks of 2015," Jan 6, 2016, found at: http://www.healthdatamanagement.com/slideshow/10-largest-healthcare-cyber-attacks-of-2015#slide-1.

[185] Ibid.

[186] Andrea Peterson, "2015 is already the year of the health-care hack — and it's only going to get worse," *The Washington Post*, Mar 20, 2015, found at: https://www.washingtonpost.com/news/the-switch/wp/2015/03/20/2015-is-already-the-year-of-the-health-care-hack-and-its-only-going-to-get-worse/.

[187] Brandon Valeriano and Benjamin Jensen, "The Myth of the Cyber Offense: The Case for Restraint," The CATO Institute, Jan 15, 2019, found at: https://www.cato.org/publications/policy-analysis/myth-cyber-offense-case-restraint.

[188] For information on the disinformation wars targeting elections, se Council for Foreign Relations, at: https://www.cfr.org/influence-campaigns-and-disinformation.

[189] Keir Giles, "Countering Russian Information Operations in the Age of Social Media," Council on Foreign Relations, Nov 21, 2017, found at: https://www.cfr.org/report/countering-russian-information-operations-age-social-media.

[190] Paul Rosenweig, pg. 2.

[191] Ibid, pg. 2.

[192] For more on the National Cyber Incident Response Plan, see: http://www.federalnewsradio.com/wp-content/uploads/pdfs/NCIRP_Interim_Version_September_2010.pdf.

CHAPTER FIVE

DEVELOPING A NATIONAL CYBER STRATEGY: INTEGRATING COERCION INTO U.S. CRITICAL INFRASTRUCTURE DEFENSE

The United States uses the word "Strategy" in dozens of national documents that prescribe some form of a policy initiative rather than a plan for the Federal government. Broadly speaking, a strategy should refer to how a specific goal or set of goals is to be realized...it is the logic behind the plan. Ideally, national strategy is the correlation between ends, ways, and means...and between the results the nation desires and the capabilities and resources at its disposal.1 Strategy and tactics are both focused on developing and then executing actions and operations designed to attain particular objectives in relationship to an adversary. Generally speaking, strategy involves how an organization structures and/or allocates the resources at its disposal; whereas tactics relates to how the organization employs them. Together, strategy and tactics bridge the gap between ends, ways, and means.

According to noted Harvard business strategy scholars, Martin Reeves, Knut Haanaes, and Janmejaya Sinha, general or corporate strategy defines the markets and environment in which an organization will operate, and competitive strategy defines the basis on which it will compete.[2] Typically, strategy is decided in the context of defining the entity's mission and vision…defining what the entity does, why it exists, and what it is wanting to become. Alternatively, competitive strategy hinges on an organization's capabilities, strengths, and weaknesses in relation to environmental and market characteristics and the corresponding capabilities, strengths, and weaknesses of its competitors.[3] Oftentimes, an organization may need a hybrid approach to strategy development – an approach that deliberately charts an initial path knowing that, at a specified point and upon reaching interim goals, the organization would shift strategies to then attain its broader, long-term goals in order to gain the advantage in the environment.

I believe that this methodology also applies to U.S. national cyber strategy. One approach that best aligns with a comprehensive national cyber security strategy is a two-pronged or hybrid strategy, initially of "renewal" and then shifting to a "shaping" strategy. A "renewal" approach to strategy "aims to restore the vitality and competitiveness of a firm (or in this case nation) when it is operating in a harsh environment."[4] Oftentimes, the harsh situation may be the result of a strategic mismatch between organizational plans and the approach to the external environment. When the external geopolitical circumstances are so overwhelming that the United States' way of conducting cybersecurity cannot be sustained, decisively changing course is the only way for the United States to not only survive, but also to secure another chance to succeed at deterring the cyber threat.[5] Consequently, the United States must recognize and react to the worsening geopolitical realities and act decisively to reinstate its viability. The geopolitical cyber environment will remain unpredictable; however, the conditions can be established through effective strategies to shape how the nation works with private industry and other nations to chart a viable path towards curbing the cyber threat.

Once the United States' cybersecurity strength is established, then the United States should alter approaches to a "shaping" strategy...an approach that allows the United States to collaborate with other key stakeholders in the global endeavor to deter the cyber threat. Because the cyber threat is so complex and pervasive, the United States requires the partnership of others to "share the risk [and] contribute complementary capabilities" that will build the requisite conditions to dominate the cyber landscape before the threat can adapt.[6] A shaping strategy must be effective in the uncertain and ambiguous geopolitical cyber realities witnessed today. This is essential given the early phase of global cybersecurity progress and success, and the lack of effective public-private cybersecurity integration. In the shaping approach, key partners "engage other stakeholders to create a shared vision of the future at the right point in time. They build a platform through which they can orchestrate collaboration and then evolve that platform and its associated stakeholder ecosystem by scaling it and maintaining its flexibility."[7] The current critical infrastructure cyber threat landscape is volatile and the external circumstances are challenging; consequently, unless something changes within the Federal government, the United States' current way of conducting national cybersecurity cannot be sustained. Deliberately changing course is the way to survive and alter the current cybersecurity paradigm. This hybrid approach would, ideally address the global cyber ecosystem and threat, rather than just a single nation or industry. This chapter lays out that hybrid strategy.

The Role of Coercion

In the most general sense, coercion in cyberspace is built upon the following arguments. First, the application of a coercive cyber strategy within the art of statecraft must be based primarily on the current global cyber threat and the geopolitical landscape. Rarely will CINS occur in the absence of some broader conflict. Every situation or conflict is different and has unique factors that shape the political environment. Some low-level CEMA may be launched for a singular purpose such as financial gain, and may or may not be part of a wider conflict. However, in order to better understand the motives behind CINS, the CEMA that is manifested during a CINS should not be viewed in isolation, but examined within the context of the larger geopolitical landscape.

Second, to properly employ coercive means, the coercer must possess a robust discernment of the adversary along with the other actors' involvement in the conflict. Understanding the nuances of the participating protagonists and their alliances helps build the insights necessary to perceive their motives, values, and strategies. Armed with a richer comprehension of the adversary and geopolitical landscape, the strategist can craft an appropriately tailored coercive plan that will either deny that foe success in his objectives and/or place the adversary's pressure points at risk for cost imposition campaigns. One must remember that each adversary is an adaptive and reactive opponent who wants to triumph in the developing conflict; consequently, the coercer must adapt more quickly in order to ensure victory.

Third, with the above knowledge, the strategist can then establish what adversarial behavior and actions are unacceptable or require modification and then construct a coercive strategy that utilizes the appropriate instruments of national power to influence the foe. National decision makers must use these instruments of power in a way that influences or compels the threat to change its unwanted behavior or action. A central purpose for designing a defensive coercive strategy is to influence the adversary's decision making in ways that are beneficial to the coercer.

Fourth, effective coercion requires possessing the political will and employing credible capabilities. Consequently, the coercer must amass sufficient physical, financial, and political capabilities both for defending against CEMA and engaging in the cyber actions necessary to impose unacceptable costs on an adversary or to defeat his strategy. Equally important, cyber coercion also "involves a psychological and cognitive component: like other forms of [coercion], it requires the capacity to influence the motives, cost-benefit calculations, and risk-taking propensities of adversaries, in order to convince them that launching a cyber-attack would not serve their interests and objectives and that the costs and risks would outweigh any sensible calculation of benefits."[8] Crafting the proper blend of influential physical cyber tools and psychological capabilities to achieve one's aims is the foundation of a successful coercive strategy.

Finally, the coercer must possess the necessary command and control structure and processes to implement the national coercive strategy, and then execute actions, options, and operations quicker than the enemy in order to gain and maintain the advantage. Understanding the adversary, developing a tailored strategy, and employing credible capabilities alone are not sufficient to succeed in the art of statecraft and coerce an adversary. The coercer also must be able to direct, employ, react, assess, adapt, redirect, and continue to dominate the foe on every possible effort involved in the conflict. "A one-size-fits-all approach to deterrence will not work because of the multiplicity and diversity of potential adversaries and cyber-attacks, and because [the coercer's] goals and actions may shift from one situation to the next."[9] Consequently, the strategist must build a custom coercive strategy that considers each type of adversary, category of CEMA, and type of friendly response based upon its own merits. Ultimately, coercion is a game of the mind...it is convincing your adversary to choose to "do or not do" as the coercer desires.

Coercion is the necessary missing element beyond defense that pressures the adversary to change his behavior.

For the purposes of this chapter, the inclusion of coercion as one tool of statecraft will be applied primarily in reference to CINS, which is the threshold where the federal government should involve the "whole of government" to actively partner with private industry or should lead the overall response (private industry in support), given the elevated nature and significance of the CEMA and the conflict.

A Framework of Coercive Cyber Effects

Whether or not one believes that cyberspace changed the form of conflict, cyber-enabled malicious activity directed at the United States' critical infrastructure has become a reality. The cyber threat to economic and national security along with global stability is no longer confined to states, but also includes sophisticated malicious cyber entities (state-sponsored or not) and individuals (hacktivists, terrorists, and criminals). The cyber domain possesses certain characteristics that strategists and policymakers must understand if they are to apply coercion effectively. In cyberspace, "networks are inherently unbounded, infinitely scalable, and abstract. Space and time are collapsed; all potential attackers are your next-door neighbor [think disintermediation] and there are no discrete, observable phase shifts or transitions (a probe can become an attack instantaneously). Identities are difficult to discern, and actions ambiguous."[10] Consequently, it is important to appreciate how the contributions of cyber effects should be thought of within the broad activities of economic and national security.

Generally speaking, one can envision coercive cyber effects across a spectrum of national cybersecurity activities as a framework that spans four interrelated areas: the resiliency/redundancy of each organization involved as well as systemically across sectors and the nation; the cyber defense of critical infrastructure sectors and broadly across the nation; the way instruments of national power induce adversarial decision making through coercive diplomacy, and when all else fails, through forceful coercion. Any national cybersecurity policy or strategy that only considers one area of the spectrum is incomplete. A holistic national strategy encompasses the entire spectrum of activities as a framework to affect adversarial decision making while simultaneously encouraging cooperation of all parties to a conflict (see Figures 5.1 and 5.2). Furthermore, a complete coercive strategy considers inducements and entanglements, all within the context of international law for acceptable behavior. These aspects of a coercive strategy will be explained in detail below.

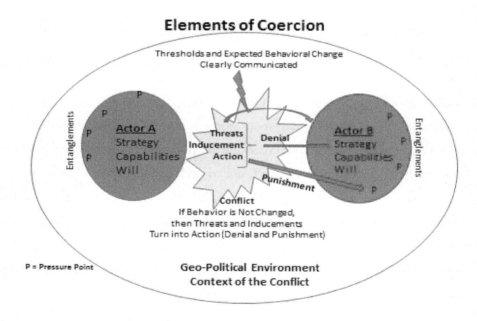

Figure 5.1 – The Elements of Coercion

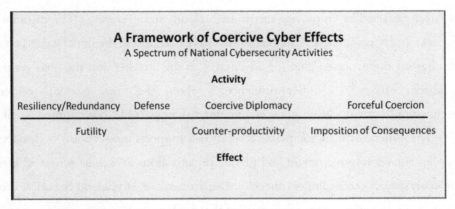

Figure 5.2 – A Framework of Coercive Cyber Effects

The first area of the framework is resiliency and redundancy, which refers to the ability of organizations to continue functioning after suffering a significant debilitating or destructive event.[11] The coercive effect the adversary is envisioned to perceive is a sense of frustration by eliminating any gain or benefit from his CEMA. Resiliency and redundancy have long been recognized as possessing deterrent effects (the primary effect being survival).[12] DHS's 2013 National Infrastructure Protection Plan defined resilience as "the ability to resist, absorb, recover from, or successfully adapt to adversity or a change in conditions."[13] In a homeland security context, a "change of conditions implies a terrorist attack, a natural hazard, such as hurricane or earthquake, or a technological failure, such as a dam collapse or a serious accident at a nuclear power plant."[14] Resiliency in the corporate world means possessing the necessary back-up and restoral capabilities of vital data, systems, and processes required for continued operations in times of crisis. Resiliency reduces the implications of a successful attack and ensures the organization continues to function as designed. In the physical domains, resiliency is oftentimes expensive; however, in cyberspace resiliency can be achieved quickly. For example, information systems can be rebooted or restored from a back-up and services restarted by employing distributed (cloud) architectures. "The capacity to recover assets, resources or capabilities that have been lost in the initial [cyber] attack diminishes the expected gain (or advantage) to the attacker and thus has residual deterrent effects."[15]   Cyber resilience is about the "management—not the elimination—of risk. Not only is eliminating risk impossible, but it impedes agility; an environment with an acceptable level of risk supports innovation."[16] Resilience applies equally to government and private organizations as well as across all layers of cyberspace. According to the U.S. Department of Homeland Security, cyber resilience is developed through measures that are based upon three core principles: automation – enabling rapid incident detection and response; interoperability – enabling distributed threat detection across an organization's cyberspace; and authentication – enabling trusted communication for automated collaboration in a secure manner.[17]

An additional and complementary aspect to resiliency is redundancy. Redundancy (which includes robustness and reconstitution) refers to possessing adequate and appropriate duplicative technologies and processes to mitigate the negative effects of a potential attack. An organization with a properly designed and sufficiently redundant cyberspace environment would be able to collaborate effectively in a distributed environment, respond with agility, and recover rapidly.[18] Referring back to our CINS cases, had Estonia and Georgia or Ukraine possessed resilient systems with redundant bandwidth capacity, the DDoS attacks may have made the CEMA futile. Resiliency and redundancy are derived by building cyber capabilities and processes that improve the organization's cybersecurity during each phase of CEMA: pre-disruption (through an ability to sense and resists threats), during the disruption (by reacting rapidly to threats, mobilizing effective responses that minimize the negative impacts), and post-disruption (by absorbing shocks while working to maintain the functionality of access to cyberspace while reconstituting the operating systems).[19]   From a cyber domain and U.S. national security perspective, resiliency and redundancy are the obligation of the owners and operators of critical infrastructure. During a CINS, the government has little authority (in most cases currently) to direct the resiliency or redundancy capabilities of U.S. CI, and as such relies on private industry to design capable cyber networks, systems, and processes that will be resilient and redundant. Resiliency and redundancy help to create a sense of futility in the adversary by eliminating the potential for benefit or gain – even if successful. Resiliency and redundancy aid the organization in overcoming the cyber-attack; and if that is not possible, then helps the organization to degrade gracefully in such a way that the effects of the attack are reduced.

The second area of the framework is defense, which includes the capabilities designed to reduce the effectiveness of the adversary's attack. Defense works against the adversary's plans and capabilities, preventing or defeating the attacks that the foe initiates. As mentioned in the previous chapter, defense has an enduring deterrent effect because it raises the actual costs of the attack (monetary expenditures are required to overcome formidable defenses) and reduces the prospect for victory by making success less certain – in a sense also creating the effect of futility. Why bother to attack when one knows the defenses are so formidable? In the physical domain, defense refers to surveillance configurations, guards, security fences and systems, etc. In the cyber domain, defense refers to intelligence gathering, intrusion detection systems, network security, malware protection, firewalls, etc. The actual actions involved in defense may be executed by either private cyber defenders or government organizations. For example, in the energy sector, nuclear power cyber defense will be primarily private sector enabled, but with government nuclear oversight governing the security, network architecture, and procedures.[20] As mentioned in Chapter Two, The United States National Military Strategy for Cyberspace Operations defines cyber defense as those "[d]efensive cyberspace operations [that] direct and synchronize actions to detect, analyze, counter, and mitigate cyber threats and vulnerabilities; to outmaneuver adversaries taking or about to take offensive actions; and to otherwise protect critical missions that enable U.S. freedom of action in cyberspace."[21] Defense is related to coercion in that an effective defense will influence the adversary's decision making through his perceived likelihood of succeeding in carrying out his offensive strategy. In the physical domain, the better the defense, the more likely an adversary will be deterred (futility). That same notion generally applies to cyberspace; however, given the hyperconnectivity of cyberspace, no matter how robust the cyber defense, a determined adversary may find a way to gain access and initiative his CEMA (e.g., Stuxnet). Regardless, building a formidable cyber defense with resiliency and redundancy contributes to deterrence by creating a sense of futility in the adversary.

The third conceptual area of the framework is coercive diplomacy or statecraft and includes elements of deterrence (capabilities and policies designed to convince the adversary not to launch an attack)[22] and compellence (capabilities and policies designed to change the actions of an adversary through the fear of consequences) through the use of diplomacy, international negotiation, informational campaigns, and international law and organizations, just to name a few. This conceptual area is the point where governmental actions begin within a national coercive effort and should complement private actions, if properly constructed. With the use of the instruments of statecraft, the coercer may institute several coercive effects to raise the costs to the adversary and create a sense of counter-productivity. This area is, by design, the responsibility of the federal government and activities undertaken in this layer are outside private entities' obligation or responsibility.

Broad areas to which a counterproductive effect may be implemented include: international norms for responsible state behavior, international law, undermining or delegitimizing another state's strategy, bilateral or multilateral agreements for cyber response and law enforcement, and public attribution of hackers (public shaming) or transparency, just to name a few. These effects are designed to raise costs to the adversary in various ways (sometimes outside the cyber domain) such that the potential or actual adversary's decision makers perceive that continuing or initiating CEMA would be counter-productive to their overall goals and objectives. Multilateral agreements such as the Budapest Convention define and reinforce what acceptable behavior for responsible states should be (at least for those states that ratify the treaty). Other global efforts to enforce international norms include actions such as those proposed in 2009 by U.N. Secretary General Ban Ki-moon to add cyber-weapons to the list of arms falling under the jurisdiction of the United Nations' Advisory Board on Disarmament Matters.[23] A state that chooses to violate bi- or multilateral agreements and international norms, is a state that is open to the application of pressure and risks being ostracized by the greater international community. "Counter-productivity can be normative, for example, where an attack might be tactically successful but is strategically counter-productive because it undermines the attacker's motivational goals, political or moral legitimacy, or general support."[24] Furthermore, engaging in a public information campaign through social media and other communications channels to expose an adversary's hackers may pressure the decision makers to cease CEMA, which could contribute to the counter-productive effects in a coercion strategy.[25] This was the tactic used by former President Obama against China in 2015 to reduce the corporate espionage levels at that time. Cyber actors prefer to work under a condition of anonymity. Revealing the activity and identity of the hacker(s) may influence or limit the actions that hacker or his supporting organization may take. Likewise, using communication channels to demonstrate greater transparency in one's own strategy may empower the defender to rally international support and thereby increase the deterrent effect of the coercer's strategy and objectives.

The final area is forceful coercion (employed either unilaterally or as part of a coalition or alliance), which also includes elements of deterrence and compellence through the threat or actual use of force against the adversary. When the other areas of the framework fail to provide the necessary behavioral changes, sometimes punitive or forceful coercion is required. Forceful coercion is the might behind the other three areas and is designed to impose or threaten consequences and penalties. The desired effect is an increase in costs in the perception of the decision makers up to the point where those decision makers choose that acting as demanded is better than continuing with the CEMA. In the physical domain, the military (along with other elements of statecraft) is used across a spectrum of activities to exert force against an adversary's pressure points or to deny or degrade the foe's strategy and objectives. The military is postured to be a formidable force that stands ready to repel any attack – and is a deterrent force. So too do federal law enforcement entities (FBI, U.S. Marshals, U.S. Secret Service, U.S. Coast Guard, etc.) impose consequences through the employment of cyber and cyber-related capabilities. Federal law enforcement activities include: investigation, attribution, prosecution, and disruption of criminal cyber activities. Additionally, the President, working with the State Department and the Department of the Treasury may elect to impose economic punishment in response to unacceptable cyber behavior through such actions as the initiation of sanctions. A recent example of this approach was the 2019 U.S. threat of tariffs on Mexican goods entering the United States, if the Mexican government did not change its policy of allowing immigrants passage through Mexico to the U.S. border. Responding to the threat, the Mexican government "shifted into an enforcement-first policy of detention, deportation and sending National Guard forces to block migrants' passage from southern Mexico."26 Acceding to U.S. pressure to stop the migrant flow is a classic case of coercion in practice. In cyberspace, the applicable U.S. government organizations could implement similar forceful coercive cyber actions as part of a national cyber strategy. This area of the framework is the sole responsibility of the government and is not currently legal or proper for private cyber organizations.[27]

There are two lines of effort that the coercer may take in the area of forceful cyber coercion. Both lines of effort require varying levels of certainty as to who is behind the attack (attribution). With greater certainty of attribution, more coercive options are available. The first line of effort – denial of the cyber-attack and/or adversary's strategy – focuses on the CEMA and the objectives behind the CEMA. In this case, the coercer may initiate cyber response options designed to deny the success of the CEMA being targeted against the coercer. For example, the coercer (working with cyber defenders, Internet Service Providers (ISPs), and others) may filter, redirect, or block the actual CEMA at the gateway to the nation, negate the CEMA entirely (sandbox the threat[28]), or intrusively counter-attack the computer initiating the CEMA in order to stop the malware at its source along with the bots that may be supporting the host. Outside the cyber domain, the coercer also may take diplomatic, law enforcement, informational, or economic actions to strike at the broader geopolitical strategy of the attacker. For example, as mentioned in Chapter Three, the United States used diplomatic, informational, and law enforcement tools to pressure China for its corporate espionage as a way to target China's strategy at the state level. Although not totally successful, the United States' activities were intended to target China's strategy. Both the cyber and non-cyber responses intended to target the CEMA or the attacker's strategy risk the possibility of escalating the situation, and consequently care must be given to the actions taken based upon the interests and stakes of the conflict. In cases of CINS, the notion of escalation dominance becomes of greater importance. Conversely, there may be times where doing nothing may be the best option.

The second line of effort under forceful coercion is compelling the adversary to change his behavior through punitive measures that substantially impose consequences by raising his costs to an unacceptable level. This line of effort requires a high degree of certainty for attribution. The actions taken in this effort may be executed in the cyber domain or the physical, and include all instruments of national power. The defender must possess a great degree of adversarial understanding in order to know what interests are susceptible to pressure, what motives are at play, and what the foe intends as his broader strategy. Not all adversaries are subject to pressure or counter-attack in the cyber domain; however, all adversaries do value something that is vulnerable to pressure. Although a terrorist may not value his life, he often does value his cause, his associates, his family, and his reputation. The key to successful coercion is applying pressure in a way that adversarial decision makers respond (up to and including military force if warranted...although the threat of military force is usually unnecessary and not the first course of action in cases of CEMA below an act of war). Each area of the above framework supplements the other by making up for limitations in the other areas. If each area were effective by itself, there would no need for the other layers. Successfully contending with conflict in both lines of effort is contingent upon using all four areas mentioned above to varying degrees depending upon the context of the conflict and the adversary encountered.

There are concerns with implementing forceful coercion that must be considered proactively. A poorly crafted coercive cyber response could have unintended effects such as spillage into the global cyberspace (i.e., affecting other users beyond the intended foe). A cyber response could be reverse-engineered to be used against the coercer. A perceived benefit of a cyber response may be outweighed by the risk of having the coercer's pressure points being vulnerable to a foe's cyber retaliation. Further, a cyber response may not target the desired adversarial pressure point if his vulnerabilities were unknowingly patched or if previous access opportunities disappeared. As was mentioned previously, cyberspace is comprised of several layers which constantly change and maintaining the necessary situational awareness on those layers for vulnerabilities and access opportunities is demanding. Finally, the asymmetry of constraints, as Byman and Waxman call it, is the characteristic where a less powerful country may be more interested in upsetting the status quo and may not be inhibited by international norms and laws.[29] Even relatively minor conflicts in the eyes of powerful states (like the United States) may appear overwhelming to small states and they may disregard law and norms in the interest of their relative stake in the conflict. Strategists and policymakers must be aware of these factors related to crafting forceful coercive strategies and plan accordingly. With an understanding of the differences in the physical and virtual domains and the effects cyber actions may have on a target state, the strategist can contemplate how coercion may be applied in the cyber domain.

National Cyber Strategy

Strategy is the tying together of ends (goals), ways (method to achieve the goals) and means (the capabilities required to achieve the goals) while evaluating the risks inherent in the actions taken against a specific foe. Strategy is a dynamic process, constantly evolving for a thinking reactive adversary who is also relentlessly seeking his own goals. Strategy must properly contend with an ever-shifting geopolitical landscape across several actors, each with distinct motives present simultaneously. Coercion is an integral tool of statecraft and is often found in international political strategies. The art of developing an appropriate coercive strategy involves balancing the correct coercive tools with the other instruments of national power. As Byman and Waxman state, "the analytical emphasis on threatening costs must be balanced with an equal emphasis on adversary countermoves in response to threats."[30] As in the physical domain, coercion in cyberspace can occur in the absence of a national political cyber strategy; however, at the higher end of the spectrum of conflict, a national cyber strategy is critical to coercing an adversary successfully (in both domains) who threatens the United States' critical infrastructure, and therefore its economic and national security.

245

Previous cases explained where victim states did not have a national strategy to contend effectively with the CINS inflicted upon it. In each case, the victim state reactively developed actions and operations in order to contend with the coercive pressure experienced with varying degrees of success. Had these victim states possessed a national cyber strategy, they could have crafted the ends, ways, and means necessary to create the effects that span futility, counter-productivity, and the imposition of consequence tailored to each threat. For instances of CINS, it is important to have first thought through how the instruments of statecraft can be postured to maximize resiliency/redundancy, defense, coercive diplomacy, and if needed, forceful coercion in order to ensure the vitality of the state's key resources and critical infrastructure. Failure to do so places the state's economic and national security at risk. Effective strategy applies coercion in cyberspace with all three cyber effects.

A national cyber strategy cannot be created as a fixed provision, but rather as a continuous interplay of forces at the diplomatic, economic, scientific, military, and cultural levels of the state. Consequently, any state that proposes to create and manage a national cyber strategy, must also develop the necessary associated policies to support the respective activities and organizations that would undertake such a strategy. For the United States, the White House is where national strategies and policies originate; however, history has proven how difficult good national strategy development actually is. "The creation and management of national policy require investments of scarce intellectual, political, and, ultimately, material resources. From the White House perspective, there are many claimants for this kind of investment, and they are often in competition with each other. The odds of survival are steep in part because of the structure and mindset of the White House itself: in an age of specialists, the White House is a redoubt of generalists. In a policy field such as cyberpower, there will be a short supply of policymakers who have the requisite blend of technical and political acuity."[31] To effectively construct a national cyber strategy, the United States must shift its paradigm to the digital age and embrace its role alongside its private partners to lead the nation against the cyber threats that threaten CINS against its critical infrastructure and functions. America currently possesses all of the elements necessary for national cyber strategy development – it needs now to step into that leadership role.

Actors – Understanding the Adversary

Successful coercive strategy development and implementation is about changing the behavior of the adversary in a manner favorable to the coercer. Understanding the opponent fully is vital to determining his motives, objectives, capabilities, values, and pressure points. To coerce in cyberspace, the coercer requires just as much knowledge about the adversary in cyberspace as in the physical domain. The difference is that knowing and locating that foe may be more difficult in cyberspace. As was described in the previous chapters, attribution with certainty may not occur or may take time to determine (with moderate certainty). In the cases of CINS, there is a clear demarcation of quantity and quality of capabilities between the actors who can and cannot execute the CINS required to effectively attack U.S. critical infrastructure. Nation-states currently represent the most capable cyber threat. The sophisticated CEMA required to attack critical infrastructure is expensive and labor-intensive to create, and it is less likely that lower-end malicious cyber actors possess the requisite skill, capacity, or motivation to carry out such an attack. State or state-sponsored cyber organizations "are likely to be very well organized and industrialized, with vast resources at their disposal; they seek to improve the strategic capabilities of their host nation sponsors by providing them with information about products, current views, plans, and other data, which can lead to long-term strategic losses."[32] Unfortunately, sophisticated cyber actors are typically those best able to conceal their methods and identities.

No matter what coercive effect (futility, counter-productivity, imposition of consequence) is desired, the coercer in cyberspace will have to know who to coerce. Once the degree of certainty rises to the point that the coercer's intelligence agencies may begin their tradecraft, then the necessary and lengthy effort of comprehending the foe may begin. A framework called Behavioral Influences Analysis (BIA) is one approach for analysis that provides a methodical list of questions or concepts that guide the strategist to study the desired individual or group.[33] Behavioral Influences Analysis is a methodical process that provides intelligence to strategists, policymakers, and operators to facilitate understanding and exploitation of the perceptual and behavioral context of the adversary. Using this approach, analysts combine sociology, anthropology, psychology, and operations research to best comprehend a threat actor's motives, perspectives, and potential behaviors. Through a deep-dive into an actor's influences, the strategist can be better positioned to understand the cultural, organizational, and cognitive foundations, which would lead to a constructive analysis of that threat actor.[34]

The United States military intelligence community developed and uses this framework to understand the adversary in every domain. Regardless of the type of actor encountered, BIA contributes to a necessary and comprehensive understanding of the decision makers involved and their susceptibility to coercion in cyberspace. With the developed adversarial intelligence, the strategist may then craft the coercive campaign to defend against, deter, degrade, or deny the foe's strategy; and if necessary, compel him to alter his nefarious behavior through correctly identifying and imposing costs on adversarial pressure points. Additionally, this framework will identify the opponent's entanglements that may be exploited while also suggesting areas ripe for inducement.

Interests and Risks

How does the United States factor interests and risks into the coercive effects of futility, counter-productivity, imposition of consequence for the United States' critical infrastructure which is owned and operated primarily by private entities? Without a national strategy, the United States currently only identifies the interests and risks the nation possesses and does not factor the use of coercion into defending its key cyber terrain. Although the 2014 NSTAC report did not offer a national strategy for the United States, the report presented a "unified risk assessment approach that suggests when increased operational coordination within industry, as well as between industry and Government, might be required, and highlights the level of Government support and collaboration in a five-level cyber condition graphic."[35] A national risk assessment model is useful for determining the potential or actual impact of CEMA and the likelihood that the CEMA may escalate to CEMO or CINS. With a national strategy, the United States could implement the NSTAC's risk assessment model which includes the following three criteria/parameters (see Figure 5.3 below):

- "Event Characteristics: Does the potential or actual event (or series of events) manifest characteristics that could result in substantive disruption, corruption, or destruction of critical infrastructure, EO 13636 Section 9 entities, and sector resources?"[36] Substantial exploitation as was explained in the Titan Rain – Byzantine Hades case study in Chapter Three should be added to this list.

- "Intelligence Sources: Do the perpetrators (i.e., threat actors) have the means, intent, or ability to escalate the potential or actual event to an event of national significance?"[37] We should also add: what is the larger geopolitical context of the conflict, what are the motives of the opponent, and do we know his motives? Use the Behavioral Influences Analysis methodology to determine this.

- "Capability to Respond: Based upon prior knowledge, does industry have the capability to respond and address the incident, without changes in legal authority, rules of engagement, or operating framework?"[38] Also, what is the nature of the U.S. cyber target and do we understand the inherent vulnerabilities in that network or system? Both government and private industry must jointly understand what is to be defended.

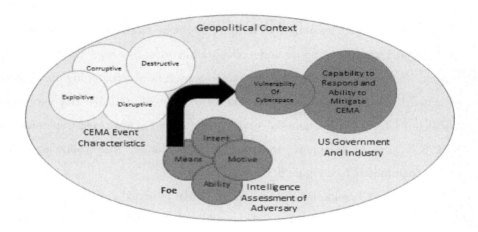

Figure 5.3 – Risk Assessment Model[39]

With this risk assessment model or framework, cyber defenders (both government and private), strategists, and policymakers may estimate the likelihood of a particular event escalating to a point beyond the level that private industry can contend with alone (more on thresholds below). In order to successfully mitigate and coerce in cyberspace, credible capabilities are necessary.

Credible Capabilities

In order to coerce effectively, the adversary must believe the coercer can and will either defeat his strategy or injure him unacceptably if he continues with the unwanted behavior. Coercion "takes effect in the mind of the opponent – he ultimately determines whether he is [coerced]. What matters is his concluding that the harm will be 'unacceptable'."[40] The perceived credibility of the capabilities behind a coercive threat determines the likelihood that the adversary believes his nation, organization, or strategies are at risk. Coercion requires the possession of credible capabilities to impose consequences or costs. Possessing credible capability applies equally to the physical and virtual domains. As in the physical domain, credible cyber capabilities must include: the means to deliver the effects that contribute to implementing coercion (futility, counter-productivity, imposition of consequence), effective capabilities for authorizing and directing the cyber effects (the military refers to this as command and control – C2), and with the "means and C2 being sufficiently survivable and effective to do that unacceptable harm after the opponent has launched his best attack and puts up his best defense."[41] One can use portions of the spectrum of national cyber security activities (resiliency/redundancy, defense, coercive diplomacy, and forceful coercion) to describe how credible capabilities can be used in cyberspace. Specifically, credible capabilities fall under the areas of resiliency/redundancy, defense, and coercive response options of denial and punishment (offense).

Most cybersecurity analysts and leaders conclude that there is no silver bullet solution to possessing credible capabilities. There is no one-size-fits-all answer and no single methodology that will protect an organization from sophisticated CEMA, and consequently, most capable organizations rely on several tools and methods of cyber capabilities in which to protect their organization. "Cyber resilience is about managing security with a multi-layered approach that encompasses people, processes, and technology. Correlating security intelligence is important, but just as important is increasing your employees' security IQ so they can make better decisions and reduce risky behavior. Instead of continually putting security measures in place, businesses need to identify their most important business assets and how current security measures relate to them. It's a paradigm shift that uses security intelligence to guide decisions and support agility."[42] Cyber resiliency can be thought of as a series of multi-layered concepts, processes, and frameworks to help an organization either mitigate the risk of cyber threats or gracefully degrade during the CEMA in a way that allows for redundant systems to be brought on line. As threats evolve and organizational security needs progress, cyber resilience is about continual refinement. The evolutionary process can be thought of as a methodology with five pillars: prepare/identify, protect, detect, respond, and recover.[43]

One research firm, Forrester, conceptualizes cyber resiliency and redundancy similar to Abraham Maslow's Hierarchy of Needs for self-actualization, but altered for an organization's network. Their framework focuses on the core needs required for defending the organization's cyberspace environment against CEMA as laying the foundation for a resilient cybersecurity strategy. The needs in order of importance are: "an actual security strategy; a dedication to recruiting and retaining staff; a focus on the fundamentals; an integrated portfolio that enables orchestration; prevention; and detection and response."[44] The United States government approaches cyber risk and critical infrastructure resiliency through education and by providing the voluntary NIST framework mentioned previously.

Next, cyber defense and coercive cyber capabilities concepts can be discussed simultaneously since many of the capabilities and tactics are similar. Actual cyber capabilities and tactics are beyond the scope of this monograph, but a framework for quantifying the capabilities is presented here in order to comprehend how national cybersecurity professionals evaluate their capabilities and tactics. Cyber capabilities should not be thought of only as the technical aspects of a government's or private industry's cyberspace, but rather should be considered across the totality of the layers of cyberspace. In fact, the foundations of a successful coercive strategy also consider all the layers of cyberspace in time and location, and appears similar to this capability's framework.

When quantifying an organization's cyber capabilities, one can think of those capabilities across six broad areas that contribute to the nation's ability to defend its critical infrastructure and to conduct coercive cyber actions. The range of actions that the organization's cyber capabilities can undertake include defense, denial of adversarial CEMA, and execution of compellent or offensive cyber operations. The six areas are: doctrine, organization, materiel, training, personnel, leadership, and facilities.[45] One should distinguish between Strategy (informs what objectives should be achieved) and Doctrine (constitutes a description of how to achieve those objectives).[46] Organization includes the presence of a national level leadership or coordinating authority (Presidential or Secretarial level of direction) and an operational level cybersecurity organization, which includes law enforcement, intelligence, and the military at a minimum. Materiel includes both the government and private industry's technical tools and systems required to protect critical infrastructure. Training/Experience refers to cybersecurity concepts being included in each organization's education/training syllabi and the operational level professional trade or skill.[47] Personnel refers to the requirement of having an enough cyber expert. Specifically, the recruitment and retention of cyber specialists is regarded as an important factor in determining cyber capability. Leadership refers to having qualified individuals at the operational level and tactical levels who understand the strategic authorization process for cyber operation. Qualified leaders also comprehend the possible unintended consequences of cyber operations and the need for clear understanding at a senior level about how to respond to national level incidents.[48] It is important that leaders also possess detailed knowledge about the escalation mechanisms for national cyber security incidents. Finally, facilities refer to the possession of national level security operations centers in which to conduct cyber operations across the spectrum of activities, centers to manage forensic investigations, malware laboratories, and research and development organizations. The six areas together constitute the range of capabilities needed to develop and execute cybersecurity operations at the national level.

To partially answer the question of how the United States implements the element of credible capabilities for coercion, one can look to the amount of money the government spends on cybersecurity capabilities and the proficiency of those cybersecurity capabilities. The 2019 United State Presidential budget, section 21 proposes investing over $14.98 billion in resources for cybersecurity.[49] That is a sizeable investment by anyone's standard and much of that funding will go to a wide range of capabilities. The United States government is often perceived as possessing some of the most credible cyber capabilities in the world, although due to secrecy, it is impossible to know accurately.[50] "In part this secrecy is integral to the whole concept: a cyberattack is useful insofar as the enemy is unaware of it. The more the government reveals about what's in its arsenal, the more our adversaries can do to protect themselves."[51]

It is also instrumental to examine in which organization the United States government spends its cybersecurity money. Although the government spends a small portion of its overall budget on cybersecurity (for 2014 spending see Figure 5.4), when one considers that spending as an actual dollar amount, the money spent is considerable. For the Department of Defense (DoD), the money goes toward standing up the 133 cyber teams and over 6,200 personnel U.S. Cyber Command is authorized to have in order to defend the nation.[52] Cybersecurity experts also agree that the United States possesses the most sophisticated intelligence apparatus in the world along with "pre-eminent offensive cyberspace capabilities."[53] The United States employs "all-source" intelligence capabilities and personnel to build a comprehensive understanding of its cyber adversaries. The actual expenditures for cyber operations are classified and therefore, not known to us. Suffice it to say, substantial capabilities exist within the DoD and its sister intelligence and law enforcement agencies such as CIA, NSA, and FBI.

With these considerable cyber capabilities come several considerations that potentially may limit their employment. Some cyber capabilities can only be used one time and then the capability is known to the world, which would then allow defenders to construct viable defenses for that capability. "The use of a cyber capability is often a one-time deal: if the government has a piece of malicious software and uses it to exploit a flaw in an enemy's code, it could render future uses of that capability ineffective, since the adversary could just patch it. It could also compromise intelligence-collection activities that use the same exploit."[54] Credible capabilities are useful if the government understands when and where those capabilities (especially "one and done" tools) should be used.

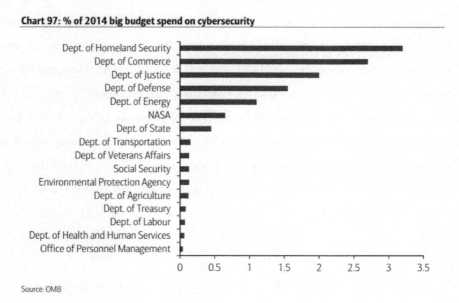

Chart 97: % of 2014 big budget spend on cybersecurity

Source: OMB

Figure 5.4 – Percentage of Budget Spent on Cybersecurity by U.S. Departments[55]

Pressure Points

For coercion to succeed, the threats must be directed at the source of the power by which a foe derives his capability, control, or influence. The determination of pressure points is as equally important from a cyberspace perspective as it is in the physical domain. With a robust understanding of the adversary's pressure points, the coercer may craft campaigns that create the effects of futility, counter-productivity, and the imposition of consequences. Conversely, the coercer also must be equally aware of what his pressure points are and be prepared to defend those.

From a defense of United States critical infrastructure perspective, the "Government has identified what it considers to be the Nation's most cyber-dependent critical infrastructures under Section 9 of Executive Order 13636, Improving Critical Infrastructure Cybersecurity. It has begun to mature, identifying high-level cyber functions—in both the private sector and Government—that should be the focus of protection or restoration efforts before, during, or after a cyber incident."[56] These identified "Section 9" portions of each sector are the privately owned "key cyber terrain" and are the pressure points that the United States must ensure continue to function as they were designed, even if the nation is attacked. As evident by the many policy documents and Executive Orders, the United States is acutely aware of its pressure points and should provide for their defense.

Thresholds and Expected Behavioral Changes Clearly Communicated

According to noted deterrence theorist Thomas Schelling, thresholds are finite steps in the enlargement of a conflict and are conventional stopping places or dividing lines. They have some quality that makes them recognizable, and they are somewhat arbitrary. Apparently, any kind of conflict needs a distinctive restraint that can be recognized by both sides, conspicuous stopping places, conventions and precedents to indicate what is within bounds and what is out of bounds, or ways of distinguishing new initiatives from just more of the same activity.[57] The element of threshold and expected behavior also applies to the cyber domain. The opponent in cyberspace also must clearly understand what the bad behavior is or what the desired change in behavior should be. The endeavor is simply not coercive if the adversary does not perceive a threat to his current action nor know the coercer desires a change in behavior. For cyber coercion to be effective, the coercer must establish what constitutes bad behavior and the consequence for unacceptable conduct.[58]

The notion of thresholds is vitally important in a United States defensive cybersecurity strategy because both private and government entities will be involved in CINS. Thresholds help identify when CEMA rises to the point where private critical infrastructure sectors may require assistance from the government. With an understanding of U.S. pressure points, inherent vulnerabilities, and cyber capabilities (both friendly and hostile), one could devise a threshold framework that delineates when private industry should act on its own, when collaboration between private and government is essential to successful cybersecurity, and when the government must take the lead in defending the EO Section 9 key cyber terrain. "Combining this assessment protocol with the NCCIC impact criteria, the NSTAC generated a means to characterize the Cyber Condition (CyberCon) at any given time, reflecting the increased level of collaboration and/or support required for enterprises and sectors to respond to cyber incidents, as well as when an incident would likely warrant increased coordination between industry and Government."[59]   The five CyberCon tiers are labeled as colors and described as follows:

- GREEN: The enterprise/entity (with vendors) alone can address the cyber event.

- BLUE: The enterprise can address the cyber event with support from sector resources, such as Information Sharing and Analysis Centers (ISACs) and trust groups. One example of this level would be an Internet service provider (ISP) requesting short-term rate limiting support from fellow ISPs.

- YELLOW: At this level, support to mitigate an event is drawn from resources outside an individual sector using current legal authorities.

- ORANGE: At this level, the assessment suggests that industry can mitigate and respond; however, new or incremental Government support would likely be indicated, which may take various forms. At the same time, at this level, the Government would enhance its own attention and response to the incident at hand, which would likely yield increased Government-industry coordination.

- RED: At this level, industry is unable to mitigate the incident fully, even with additional authorities. If the incident cannot be fully mitigated, industry would want recommendations or direction on the priorities for protection (e.g., pre-incident) or recovery (e.g., post-incident). Specification of national security priorities is a responsibility inherent to Government.[60]

These thresholds provide a general criterion by which both government and private industry might classify the significance and sophistication of the CEMA being targeted at U.S. critical infrastructure and then better discuss when, why, and how might the government aid private industry in those cases where a CINS reached an "orange" level. For level Green, Blue, and Yellow, it is assumed that corporate cyber defenses and sector capabilities are sufficient to contend with CEMA. At the orange level, a whole of government effort could focus on the touch-points or intersections where government support, collaboration, or coordination might better enable private sector response. Next, in cases where a CINS reached a "red" level, the government should consider the transition from "industry-led mitigation with government support" to "government-led mitigation with industry support."[61] With this threshold framework, the United States government could develop a conceptual understanding of the types of CINS for which they would either provide a greater level of support or take the overall lead for the response to a CINS. The case studies in Chapter Three help define examples where government actions to assist and/or lead cybersecurity efforts are necessary.

Will

"Will" at the national level is the political determination, motivation, and ability to follow through with an action when a coercer deems it necessary.[62] "Will" applies to both the physical and virtual domains. In the cyber domain, political will varies in strength depending on which part of the national cybersecurity spectrum of activity one references. As was described above, there is strong political will in both private industry and government organizations to improve individual cybersecurity programs – both resiliency/redundancy and defense. The president's policy decision and Executive Orders constantly refer to improving both. Political will is high because those activities are conservative, are not a threat to the international order, and are threat agnostic in that an organization has the right and obligation to protect itself. No one questions the requirement to execute these measures. However, the farther right on the spectrum the discussion moves, the lower the political will falls. For example, during minor incidents that affect only one private corporation and a cyber-criminal in nature, there is ample political will to direct the Justice Department to indict the cybercriminal. If, on the other hand, the malicious cyber actor is a sophisticated criminal organization with extremely close ties to a state with nuclear weapons (assuming the United States knows who perpetrated the CEMA) and has executed a multi-billion dollar theft of multiple financial organizations, then the response to the CEMA is complicated and requires weighing the options of acting (or inaction) against the larger geopolitical context of the entanglement the United States has with the state that sponsors the sophisticated criminal organization. Political will may wane in these more complicated cases due to fear of escalation, fear of potential cyber collateral damage on unintended targets, and other non-cyber explanations.

Additional reasons for the decline in political will revolve around three issues. First, attribution is a difficult and timely process and attribution may not yield definite proof of who perpetrated the CEMA. Oftentimes, politicians will not have enough information with regard to adversary's capabilities, objectives, and intentions in order to direct coercive cyber actions.[63] Second, despite political rhetoric to hold malicious cyber actors accountable, politicians are disinclined (rightly) to use offensive cyber options in foreign territories or through "neutral" states without prior permission due to sovereignty concerns. Consequently, government cyber investigators must work within bi- or multi-lateral agreements to investigate, attribute, and apprehend the malicious cyber actors.[64] Third, U.S. political decision makers also are disinclined to approve coercive cyber operations if the second/third order effects or estimated collateral damage is not known or knowable. Without this level of fidelity of information, the approval to begin cost-imposition cyber operations wanes.[65]

Without a national cybersecurity strategy to articulate when and why risk should be accepted by national decision makers, "political will" may not be sufficient to initiate coercive cybersecurity actions to alter the current negative trend in cyber threats. Although the United States and some private organizations possess competent cyber power, the United States lacks the conceptual orientation to apply its cyber strength and inflict costs. The question to be asked is, when will the U.S. take more risk to protect the nation from CEMA? It took the sinking of the Titanic and the loss of over 1,500 people to change maritime safety laws.[66] It took the terrorists attacks of 9/11 to institute the Patriot Act. In prior instances, it took a considerable loss of life to compel legislative action. What will it take to induce the U.S. to protect the nation from CEMA? Where "will" should improve however, is in the motivation to evolve the current cybersecurity paradigms that were constructed by industrial-age bureaucracies. This evolution is necessary to overcome the many hurdles that hinder national cybersecurity strategy development in order to create the effects of futility, counter-productivity, and cost imposition in a digital world.

Inducements

Any competent coercive cyber strategy will not only look for cost imposition strategies, but will also look for ways to encourage the foe to act in the way the coerce desires. Inducement is the act of influencing through positive motivational incentives or "carrots." Inducements in coercion and international relations are the counters to hostile threats. "Instead of raising costs of defiance, inducements increase the value of concessions."[67] Inducements apply equally well in both domains. Most of the inducements used in the physical domain also work well for cases of CINS. In the cyber domain, there are several international efforts that reinforce what "normal" or acceptable behavior is in the hopes of inducing states' compliance to the norms. The Budapest Convention on Cybercrime, discussed in previously, is an excellent example of an international program. The 50 signatories of the convention have agreed to adhere to the established thresholds of unwanted behavior (cybercrime or attack) and the obligation of each signatory to aid the others in the investigation, attribution, and extradition of perpetrators.[68] Simply by being part of the Budapest Convention, the signatories are induced to act responsibly. There is some reassurance in the assumption that each signatory will follow the treaty rules. The large number of signatories also adds to a broader degree of international deterrence or futility since each of the 50 participants agreed to enforce the treaty, thereby adding noteworthy cyber capabilities to the global cyber domain.

By nature, inducements do not contribute to the cyber effects of counter-productivity and cost imposition. Since there is no national cybersecurity strategy in the United States, inducements have not been implemented as part of a coercive stratagem. Additionally, private industry does not provide appreciable inducements to aid the nation's ability to induce favorable behavior from malicious cyber actors. Conversely, there are inducements for private industry to improve their cybersecurity programs in the form of Federal grants. Recently, the Department of Energy committed $25 million in grants over the next five years to support cybersecurity education. A new grant, for example, will support the creation of a new cybersecurity consortium consisting of 13 Historically Black Colleges and Universities (HBCUs), two national labs, and a K-12 school district.[69] Other Federal government agencies also provide grants to help improve cybersecurity professionals' ability to defend key cyber terrain. Pace University's Seidenberg School of Computer Science and Information Systems was awarded a 2.5 million grant from the National Science Foundation (NSF) to help educate cybersecurity students. Additionally in 2015, NSF also awarded $74.5 million in research grants through the NSF Secure and Trustworthy Cyberspace program to improve cyber education.[70] If the United States establishes a national cyber strategy, then the government also may choose to induce private organizations that do not comply with NIST's voluntary cybersecurity framework to improve their programs through the implementation of Federal grants. For those EO 13636 Section 9 organizations that are non-compliant because of budgetary constraints, the United States government may decide that a grant is necessary due to national and economic security reasons.

Entanglements

Beyond cost imposition and inducement approaches, the coercer may also find that the adversary's allies may provide a point of leverage, for which pressure can be applied. Political entanglement is the interweaving of states' interests, motives, processes, and concerns such that each state relies on the other for economic, political, and/or security reasons. Entanglement with other states or alliances can bring improved security or a lack of freedom to do as the state wishes. An adversary's entanglement can provide a source of leverage for a coercer in either the physical or virtual domain. However, given the borderless nature of cyberspace and the anonymity of actions in the virtual domain, entanglement is a lesser factor (compared to the other elements of coercion) in the lower end of the spectrum of CEMA. In cases of CINS (CyberCon Orange and Red) where the United States increases its role in national cybersecurity or takes the lead, entanglement becomes an additive and important element to coercing adversaries and identifying pressure points in which to impose costs. From a cyber effect point of view, entanglement contributes to futility, counter-productivity, and cost imposition from both a friendly and enemy perspective.

From a private international corporate perspective, entanglement is a complex problem that should be carefully examined to be thoroughly understood. Several United States critical infrastructure owners/operators are international corporations that must relate and work equally well with the governments in which they conduct business. For example, in the telecommunications sector, CenturyLink owns and operates not only a major portion of the United States' Internet service, but also controls 20% of the world's Internet.[71] Consequently, from a business standpoint,

CenturyLink must function equally well with the governments in which they provide Internet service. If they are seen as taking cyber defense actions that favor the United States while leaving another country vulnerable, CenturyLink could lose business and stock prices could fall. Since corporate board members have a fiduciary responsibility to their shareholders, corporate executives will work to ensure business does not falter. Therefore, the entanglements of private global corporations can be a hurdle to success for the United States in gaining full collaboration or cooperation before and during CEMA. Of import and given the international operations of many of the corporations involved, any involvement between government and corporate organizations should be respectful and transparent of the activities undertaken so as to not jeopardize the corporations' ability to operate overseas.

At the levels needed for effective public/private partnerships, any cyber cooperation becomes an international undertaking with global implications and consequences, especially considering the hyperconnectivity of cyberspace. Therefore, any successful cyber actions should be a multi-stakeholder, multi-jurisdictional enterprise. Entanglements can add to the United States' security or they can complicate it. For example, some states with which the United States is entangled are also states that possess the most sophisticated cyber capabilities and conduct CEMA directed at the United States. Applying coercion against a state with which the United States is entangled will limit the selection of tools of statecraft that the United States can use effectively. In the cases of China or Russia, the United States would not lightly choose military force to coerce those opponents for fear of escalating a conflict. Conversely, the United States could choose cyber, financial, or diplomatic tools (cost imposition or inducement effects) to influence adversarial decision makers, as the United States did in the 2018 sanctions against China in the U.S. – China Trade Wars. Nevertheless, entanglement (government and private) is a reality that must be factored into a comprehensive national coercive cybersecurity strategy and policies. The strategy and policy can take coercive actions that are founded in international law.

International Law

In each of the cases described in Chapter Three, one could ask which international law should govern the actions and responses of the attackers and defenders. Which international law to use is a widely debated and an unresolved dilemma. When analyzing the various instruments of national power (statecraft) that are available for use in a coercive strategy, each instrument may lead to a different interpretation on which law to use. Most contemporary legal examinations of state response to CEMA focus on activities involved in the response rather than on the responsibility of the state. For example, some experts[72] have written about the use of the military in response to CEMA and resorted to a discussion on international law grounded in the law of self-defense (or law of armed conflict). The use of military force is useful dialogue for cases that clearly rise to an act of war. However, as I have demonstrated earlier, this may not be realistically applicable to the majority of cyber conflict encountered over the last three decades and may not be indicative of future cyber conflict. "A customary law paradigm reflected in Article 51 of the U.N. Charter, the right of self-defense, permits States to respond forcefully to 'armed attacks,' including cyber operations qualifying as such. This self-defense centric analytical framework reflects state fears of a possible 'cyber 9/11' in which another state or a transnational terrorist group mounts a cyber operation producing devastating human, physical, or economic consequences. Yet, preoccupation with cyber armed attacks is counter-experiential."[73] Some scholars refer to cases of CINS as cyberwarfare; however, few, if any, CEMA incidents have crossed the war threshold. The law of self-defense only would provide a useful legal framework for those cases where CEMA amounts to an armed attack or use of force.[74]   Conversely, as previous described, a great majority of the types of CEMA encountered currently fall below that level.   Alternatively, I believe that the international legal discussion should center on the states' obligation to act responsibly toward other states and to allow victim states the unhindered right to ensure the operational functionality of its vital societal and governmental components (governmental bodies, military, law enforcement, critical infrastructure, etc.).   Consequently, the international law of State Responsibility most appropriately applies to CEMA in cases most often seen currently.[75]

According to the International Court of Justice (ICJ), nations bear "responsibility" for their internationally wrongful acts pursuant to the law of State Responsibility.[76] The IJC confirmed this principle on several occasions. "It is the foundation upon which the authoritative, albeit nonbinding, Draft Articles on Responsibility of States for Internationally Wrongful Acts (Articles on State Responsibility) have been constructed."[77] For all international interactions and states' legal responsibilities, a prominent customary norm must be considered in this discussion – the principle of sovereignty. As noted in the "Island of Palmas" legal case, sovereignty indicates independence. "Independence in regard to a portion of the globe is the right to exercise therein, to the exclusion of any other state, the functions of a state."[78] In the cyber domain, sovereignty grants a state the right (and in some cases the obligation) to regulate and control cyber activities and infrastructure within its national boundaries.[79] The legal construct of territorial sovereignty specifies the protection of critical infrastructure located on a state's territory. Consequently, CEMA directed at the critical infrastructure of another state amounts to a violation of that state's sovereignty.[80]

The principle of sovereignty is designed to provide states the right to execute (or permit) activities on their territory free from intervention by other states. "While monitoring activities in another state may merely constitute espionage, which is not prohibited, emplacement of malware into a system, destruction of data, and hacking into a network to identify vulnerabilities would seem to pierce the veil of sovereignty."[81] CEMA directed at another state violates the principle of nonintervention, and consequently qualifies as an internationally wrongful act, especially when the CEMA is intended to coerce that state. All responses to internationally wrongful acts with coercive actions may not be illegal under the law of state responsibility. There are three types of legal responses available to the injured state: countermeasures, retorsions, and sanctions (sanctions were explained in an earlier chapter and will only be touched on lightly below).

The first response – countermeasure – nests firmly within the law of state responsibility and unquestionably extends to defensive cyber activities. "A remedial measure situated in the law of state responsibility, countermeasures [emphasis added] are state actions, or omissions, directed at another state that would otherwise violate an obligation owed to that state and that are conducted by the former in order to compel or convince the latter to desist in its own internationally wrongful acts or omissions."[82] The Articles on State Responsibility are not a treaty and therefore are nonbinding. "However, they are authoritative in the sense that the International Law Commission (ILC) developed them during a process that took over half a century under the leadership of five special rapporteurs."[83] Once completed, the U.N. General Assembly commended the Articles to all nations. Currently, the Articles are generally characterized as reflecting customary international law. In 2012, the Articles and the accompanying commentary had been cited 154 times by international courts, tribunals, and other bodies.[84]

Countermeasures (once called reprisals) are a legal method of imposing consequences within the international system, which is a system oftentimes lacking in legal options for contending with CEMA.[85] The purpose of a countermeasure is to return the international situation to a condition of lawfulness. Countermeasures provide coercive options (with stringent restrictions) that would otherwise be unlawful if implemented outside the premise of state responsibility.

Countermeasures may be taken only in response to an internationally wrongful act. "Such acts have two components: (1) breach of an international obligation owed to another state, and (2) attributability of the wrongful act to the state in question."[86] As long as these two conditions are met and there is full compliance with the requirements and limitations, countermeasures are allowable, whether cyber or non-cyber in character.

International law imposes accountabilities on every state, the absence of which can qualify as a breach in the law of state responsibility. The Tallinn Manual asserts, "[a] state shall not knowingly allow the cyber infrastructure located in its territory or under its exclusive governmental control to be used for acts that adversely and unlawfully affect other States."[87] States are required to use their "best efforts" to comply with the obligation. Finally, qualification of an act as a countermeasure excludes the wrongfulness of an act.[88] The Tallinn Manual specifies that, a "state injured by an internationally wrongful act may resort to proportionate countermeasures, including cyber countermeasures, against the responsible State."[89] Countermeasures are internationally acceptable actions to re-establish the status quo ante, but cannot be implemented against another countermeasure (one countermeasure cannot be employed against another countermeasure.)

The restrictions and limitations of countermeasures include: no use of force, necessity, and proportionality. The first – use of force – is reserved and defined in the U.N. Charter 2(4) and is outside the scope of this book. The second – necessity – refers to the prerequisite to take action quickly in response to CEMA directed at a state's pressure points. For example, when faced with a situation that brings "grave and imminent peril" to an "essential interest" (whether in the cyber domain or not), a state may implement countermeasures to safeguard those interests.[90] The principle of necessity is clearly applicable in cases of defense of critical infrastructure. The use of force should be executed only as a last resort and in extremis situations, implying that a state should use the other instruments of statecraft first.[91]   The countermeasures may be either virtual or physical, or a combination thereof. Actions based on necessity differ from other limitations in three ways. "First, there need be no underlying internationally wrongful act to justify them. Second, the originator of the precipitating act need not be a state, or indeed, even be identified, a particularly relevant consideration with respect to cyber operations. Third, action based on necessity is only available when the situation is dire; mere international wrongfulness does not suffice to trigger this response option, as it does with respect to other limitations of countermeasures."[92]   In the cyber domain, necessity is an applicable principle to CEMA directed at critical infrastructure. The final limitation – proportionality – refers to using only the scale and intensity needed in relation to the actions of the illegal CEMA to which the injured state is responding. The injured state cannot respond with excessive actions in relation to the state's actual or imminent danger. [93]

The next category of responses available to the injured state under the Articles on State Responsibility is retorsion. Unlike countermeasure, which may involve acts that are otherwise illegal, retorsion refers to the taking of measures that are lawful, but "unfriendly."[94] Retorsion is less robust than countermeasures but offers the ability for a government, whose citizens are subjected to severe and stringent regulation or harsh treatment by a foreign government, to employ measures of equal severity and harshness upon the subjects of the latter government found within its dominions.[95] A state may, for instance, block certain cyber transmissions emanating from another state because the former enjoys sovereignty over cyber infrastructure on its territory.[96] The action would be lawful even if harmful to the interests of the responsible state so long as it did not violate treaty obligations or applicable customary law.[97]

The last category of response under the Articles on State Responsibility is sanction. Voluntary or compulsory sanctions imposed by the U.N. Security Council in accordance with Chapter VII of the U.N. Charter are not countermeasures because of the Council's international right to render sanctions lawful. "For example, Article 41 of the UN Charter describes interruption of communications as a non-forceful measure that may, with Security Council approval, be taken to address a threat to the peace, breach of the peace, or act of aggression. Thus, a Security Council resolution authorizing interference with a state's cyber capabilities by damaging cyber infrastructure located in that state would render the activity lawful, and hence not be a countermeasure, even if doing so would otherwise have infringed on the target state's sovereignty."[98]   Unilateral sanctions are a tool of statecraft that a nation can use to bring another nation that violates international law principles into consonance with those principles.   Unilateral sanctions have been used for centuries, yet their economic and political cost effectiveness continues to be the subject matter of heated debates.   Regardless of their effectiveness, sanction is one of the many responses available to national leaders.   As mentioned earlier, the Obama Order specifying the use of economic sanctions against individuals who engage in CEMA directed at the United States[99] and the Trump threat of tariffs against Mexico to curb the migrant tide facing the U.S. southern border are recent examples of unilateral sanctions.   Sanctions can be used along with the other instruments of national power in order to form a more comprehensive strategy to coerce an adversary.

The last concept that is applicable to our discussion on international law and coercion is the notion of preemption.   Article 51 of the U.N. Charter specifies that "[n]othing in the present charter shall impair the inherent right of individual or collective self-defense if an armed attack occurs against a member of the United Nations."[100]   The United States government has long held that, in accordance with Article 51 and customary international law, a state may use force in self-defense: (1) if it has been attacked, or (2) if an armed attack is legitimately deemed to be imminent.   This interpretation is also consistent with the United States' domestic notion of self-defense as applied in the criminal and tort law contexts.[101]   Within the traditional framework of self-defense, a preemptive use of proportional force is justified only out of necessity. The concept of necessity includes both a credible, imminent threat and the exhaustion of peaceful remedies.[102] In the physical domain, one could imagine an array of enemy tanks or ships as an imminent threat. Doing the same in cyberspace requires a better understanding of what is vital to the defending nation and then defining the "red line" for what would be considered not tolerable if an adversary would cross that red line.

Clarity may be gained, however, by examining how the U.S. government specifies the right of self-defense in cyberspace. In the United States' 2011 International Strategy for Cyberspace, President Obama articulates the objective for defense. "The United States will, along with other nations, encourage responsible behavior and oppose those who would seek to disrupt networks and systems, dissuading and deterring malicious actors, and reserving the right to defend these vital national assets as necessary and appropriate."[103] The strategy further states:

"When warranted, the United States will respond to hostile acts in cyberspace as we would to any other threat to our country. All states possess an inherent right to self-defense, and we recognize that certain hostile acts conducted through cyberspace could compel actions under the commitments we have with our military treaty partners. We reserve the right to use all necessary means—diplomatic, informational, military, and economic—as appropriate and consistent with applicable international law, in order to defend our Nation, our allies, our partners, and our interests. In so doing, we will exhaust all options before military force whenever we can; will carefully weigh the costs and risks of action against the costs of inaction; and will act in a way that reflects our values and strengthens our legitimacy, seeking broad international support whenever possible."[104]

271

Because each case is unique, applying the notion of preemption should also be selective. Although not specifically stated in the President's International Strategy for Cyberspace, the repeated discussion of self-defense would likely be accompanied by the consideration of preemptive responses in situations where the United States considered the stakes sufficiently high. In fact, The New York Times reported that a "secret legal review on the use of America's growing arsenal of cyberweapons has concluded that President Obama has the broad power to order a preemptive strike if the United States detects credible evidence of a major digital attack looming from abroad, according to officials involved in the review."[105] The report also specified what targets were likely the types to warrant such consideration. The targets include the military, the nation's power grids, the U.S. financial systems, and communications networks.[106] Consequently, if the report is accurate, the notion of preemption does apply to cyberspace from the United States' perspective. With the typical tests of necessity and the proof of the presence of an imminent threat, the United States may take preemptive actions to defend those targets the nation deems most vital to its economic and national security.

The above examination of international law provides a preliminary basis for understanding how and when to apply coercion in cyberspace. Outside the law of armed combat, the laws of state responsibility and law of non-intervention provide an already established framework for response options where cases of CEMA fall below an act of war. Given the current realities within cyberspace, countermeasures, retorsion, and sanctions are legal responses to cyber incidents of national significance. Under the correct conditions, preemptive actions may be taken when grave, imminent threats imperil U.S. vital economic and national security centers of gravity.

Conclusions

Coercion is possible and needed in the virtual domain, despite the fact that the United States does not currently possess a national strategy to use it within cyberspace. There are several shortcomings in the government and private sectors' ability to secure critical infrastructure in cases that rise to the level of CINS. Any attempt to identify a proper governmental structure and public-private relationship and strategy should be informed by United States cybersecurity policies. Form should follow function and not lead it. However, and despite the absence of a national cyber strategy, the United States has used cyber as a limited coercive tool in and of itself. For example, in response to Iranian attacks on oil tankers in the Persian Gulf, as well as targeting of Saudi oil facilities, in June 2018 the U.S. conducted covert cyber-attacks on Iran, which wiped out a critical database used by Iran's paramilitary arm to plot attacks against oil tankers and degraded Tehran's ability to target shipping traffic in the Persian Gulf.[107] Additionally, there were several media allegations of the United States conducting retaliatory cyber strikes – one against ISIL's websites in 2016 and another against Russia's election interference infrastructure prior to the 2018 elections.[108] These limited cyber strikes indicate, among other things, that while the United States may not have a proper cyber defense strategy, it is integrating cyber into other strategies to achieve national objectives. Given the growing use of coercive CEMA to achieve national political objectives, the United States is at a crossroad for which it must determine how best to use its vast capabilities alongside private industry to protect U.S. critical infrastructure as part of a more holistic national cyber strategy.

One could then ask how best can the United States create the structure for the defense and vitality of the nation's critical infrastructure. How should the United States properly address the realities of the cyber domain and the threat actors therein? More specifically, to what extent can the United States use coercion to influence the decision making of state or state-sponsored malicious cyber actors in cases where they threaten United States' economic and national security? With appropriate national coercive cybersecurity policy, a coherent national cybersecurity strategy can be created. This national cybersecurity strategy should be made up of the elements of coercion and should employ all the effects of cyber (futility, counter-productivity, and cost imposition), along with the employment of all the instruments of national power available to the United States. An effective coercive cybersecurity strategy will deny the adversary the success of his strategy while influencing his decision making in a way that favors the coercer's aims.

---

[1] Martin Reeves, Knut Haanaes, and Janmejaya Sinha, "Navigating the Dozens of Different Strategy Options," *Harvard Business Review*, June 24, 2015, found at: https://hbr.org/2015/06/navigating-the-dozens-of-different-strategy-options.

[2] Ibid.

[3] Ibid.

[4] Ibid.

[5] Ibid.

[6] Ibid.

[7] Ibid.

[8] Richard L. Kugler, "Deterrence of Cyber Attacks," in *Cyberpower and National Security*, Franklin D. Kramer, Stuart H. Starr, and Larry K Wentz, eds., (National Defense University Press, Washington D.C., 2009), pg. 310.

[9] Ibid, pg. 311.

[10] K. A. Taipale, "Cyber Deterrence," Center for Advanced Studies in Science and Technology Policy, Jan 1, 2009, pg. 19, found at: http://books.ssrn.com/sol3/books.cfm?abstract_id=1336045.

[11] Charles L Glaser, "Deterrence of Cyber Attacks and U.S. National Security," *The George Washington University Cyber Security Policy and Research Institute: Thoughtful Analysis of Cyber Security Issues*, (The George Washington University Press, June 1, 2014), pg. 1.

[12] K. A. Taipale, pg. 37.

[13] See Department of Homeland Security, *National Infrastructure Protection Plan*, 2013, pg. 111, found at: https://www.dhs.gov/national-infrastructure-protection-plan.

[14] John D. Moteff, "Critical Infrastructure Resilience: The Evolution of Policy and Programs and Issues for Congress," Congressional Research Service report, Aug 23, 2012, pg. 1, found at: https://www.fas.org/sgp/crs/homesec/R42683.pdf.

[15] K. A. Taipale, pg. 38.

[16] Symantec, "Know," *Symantec Online*, accessed 12 Mar 16, found at: http://www.symantec.com/page.jsp?id=cyber-resilience. For more on resilience, risks, and assessing both, see the U.S. Department of Homeland Security, U.S. Cert, "Assessments: Cyber Resilience Review," found at: https://www.us-cert.gov/ccubedvp/assessments.

[17] U.S. Department of Homeland Security, "Enabling Distributed Security in Cyberspace: Building a Healthy and Resilient Cyber Ecosystem with Automated Collective Action," March 23, 2011, pp. 8-18, found at: https://www.dhs.gov/xlibrary/assets/nppd-cyber-ecosystem-white-book-03-23-2011.pdf.

[18] Ibid, pg. 8.

[19] Ernst and Young, LLC., "Achieving resilience in the cyber ecosystem," December 2014, pg. 10, found at: http://www.ey.com/Publication/vwLUAssets/cyber_ecosystem/$FILE/EY-Insights_on_GRC_Cyber_ecosystem.pdf.

[20] Critical safety, security and emergency preparedness systems at nuclear energy facilities are isolated from the Internet. They are further protected by cyber security and physical security plans required by the U.S. Nuclear Regulatory Commission (NRC). The NRC ordered the companies that operate nuclear power plants to enhance security in several areas and subsequently codified the new requirements in 2009. As part of this rule, the NRC established new cyber security requirements. Every company operating nuclear power plants has an NRC-approved cyber security program. See the Nuclear Energy Institute, "Policy Briefs: Cyber Security for Nuclear Power Plants," April 2015, found at: http://www.nei.org/Master-Document-Folder/Backgrounders/Policy-Briefs/Cyber-Security-Strictly-Regulated-by-NRC;-No-Addit .

[21] *United States National Military Strategy for Cyberspace Operations*, Defense Cyber Operations as explained by IT WikiLaw, accessed online 8 Nov 2015, found at: http://itlaw.wikia.com/wiki/Defensive_cyberspace_operations.

[22] Charles L. Glaser, pg. 1.

[23] The U.N.'s Advisory Board on Disarmament Matters develops policy on weapons of mass destruction. By adding cyber-weapons to their list of weapons, the U.N. could define a class of CEMA that is not acceptable and thereby impose punishment on those who violate the U.N. mandate. See United Nations Advisory Board on Disarmament Matters at: http://www.un.org/disarmament/HomePage/AdvisoryBoard/AdvisoryBoard.shtml.

[24] K. A. Taipale, pg. 41.

[25] David Talbot, "Exposing Hackers as Deterrent," *MIT Technological Review*, April 13, 2010, accessed 13 Mar 2016, found at: https://www.technologyreview.com/s/418434/exposing-hackers-as-a-deterrent/.

[26] Patrick J. McDonnell and Kate Linthicum, "By turning back caravans, Mexico is acting as Trump's border wall, critics say," *The Los Angeles Times*," Jan 24, 2020, found on-line at https://www.latimes.com/world-nation/story/2020-01-24/in-turning-back-caravans-mexico-becomes-trumps-wall.

[27] For a comprehensive review of the illegalities of unauthorized access to another's computer as it relates to private entities employing such tactics to hackback or retaliate, see the *Computer Fraud and Abuse Act* (1986), the *Identity Theft Enforcement and Restitution Act of 2008*, and the *USA PATRIOT Act*, see U.S. Department of Justice, "Prosecuting Computer Crimes," Computer Crime and Intellectual Property Section Criminal Division, found at: https://www.justice.gov/sites/default/files/criminal-ccips/legacy/2015/01/14/ccmanual.pdf.

[28] In general, sandboxing refers to restricting malware in an isolated computing environment so that a program or file can be executed without affecting any other system of application. See *TechTarget* for more on Sandboxing at: http://searchsecurity.techtarget.com/definition/sandbox.

[29] Byman and Waxman, pp. 148-150.

[30] Byman and Waxman, pg. 42.

[31] Leon Fuerth, "Cyberpower from the Presidential Perspective," in *Cyberpower and National Security*, Franklin D. Kramer, Stuart H. Starr, and Larry K. Wentz, eds. (Washington D.C., National Defense University Press, 2009), pg. 559.

[32] Ernst and Young, "Cyber Threat Intelligence – how to get ahead of cybercrime," Ernst and Young LLC, November 2014, pp. 2-3, found at: http://www.ey.com/Publication/vwLUAssets/EY-cyber-threat-intelligence-how-to-get-ahead-of-cybercrime/$FILE/EY-cyber-threat-intelligence-how-to-get-ahead-of-cybercrime.pdf.

[33] Elizabeth Chamberlain, "Behavioral Influences Analysis - Methodology Description," (Air University, Maxwell AFB, AL), pg. 1, found at: http://www.au.af.mil/bia/documents/methodology1.htm.

[34] Ibid, pg. 1.

[35] NSTAC Report, pg. ES-2.

[36] Ibid, pg. 7

[37] Ibid, pg. 7.

[38] Ibid, pg. 7.

[39] This is a modification of the NSTAC's Notional Unified Risk Assessment Process of Mobilization. NSTAC's framework neglects the geopolitical context, the origins of the CEMA (Adversary's motivations and objectives), and the nature of the cyberspace target and inherent vulnerabilities. NSTAC Report, pg. 7.

[40] Patrick M. Morgan, "applicability of Traditional Deterrence Concepts and Theory to the Cyber Realm" in *Proceeding of a Workshop on Deterring Cyber Attacks: Informing Strategies and Developing Options for U.S. Policy Makers*, (National Academy of Sciences) pg. 61, found at: http://www.nap.edu/catalog/12997.html.

[41] Ibid, pp. 61-62.

[42] Symantec Whitebook, *The Cyber Resilience Blueprint: A New Perspective on Security*, accessed online 24 Apr 2015, found at: https://www.symantec.com/content/en/us/enterprise/white_books/b-cyber-resilience-blueprint-wp-0814.pdf.

[43] For more on the five pillars, see Symantec Whitebook, pp. 2-7.

[44] Forrester Research, Inc., "Introducing Forrester's Targeted-Attack Hierarchy Of Needs," (May 2014, Rick Holland blog) found at: http://blogs.forrester.com/rick_holland/14-05-20-introducing_forresters_targeted_attack_hierarchy_of_needs.

[45] Neil Robinson, Agnieszka Walczak, Sophie-Charlotte Brune, Alain Esterle, and Pablo Rodriguez, "Stocktaking Study of military cyber defence capabilities in the European Union," (RAND, Prepared for the European Defence Agency, 2013), found at: http://www.rand.org/content/dam/rand/pubs/research_reports/RR200/RR286/RAND_RR286.pdf.

[46] RAND makes the assumption of a hierarchy of strategies in order of importance: 1. A national level cyber-security strategy should be a broad national level instrument outlining what strategy the country needs to take in order to become secure in cyberspace and the objectives, role and mandate (if any) of defense in achieving strategic security objectives; 2. A Critical Information Infrastructure

Protection strategy is next down the hierarchy, describing the 'what' of the protection of the critical information infrastructure(s) – those technological elements of cyberspace essential for social and economic well-being; 3. A cyber defense strategy should describe a desired end-state that the defense and armed forces should work toward achieving to contribute to overall national cyber security objectives across the DOTMPLF-I framework; 4. A cyber defense doctrine should outline how this strategy may be achieved through different tools, including Computer Network Operations (CNO) but also Information Assurance; information sharing; co-ordination with other government departments and the private sector; 5. A CNO doctrine can be thought of as the handbook governing the conduct of various types of CNO □ We assume that a national cyber-security strategy and a national CI Information Protection strategy are the two most important building blocks to have in place to move from non-existent level of maturity to initial. RAND assume that the presence of a cyber deterrence doctrine and defining cyber-attacks as armed attack are indicative of the most mature level. Ibid.

[47] Although RAND does not include "experience" this researcher concludes through extensive interviews that experience in operations cannot always be taught and must be learned on the job. Consequently, experience is equally important with "training" and is included here.

[48] Ibid.

[49] The White House, The 2019 Presidential Budget, Section 630 of the Consolidated Appropriations Act, 2017," Washington D.C., Fiscal Year 2019, found on-line Mar 22, 2019, at: https://www.whitehouse.gov/wp-content/uploads/2018/02/ap_21_cyber_security-fy2019.pdf.

[50] Danny Vinek.

[51] Ibid.

[52] Ibid.

[53] John Markoff, David E. Sanger, and Thom Shanker, "In Digital Combat, US Finds No Easy Deterrent," *The New York Times*, Jan 26, 2010, available at: http://www.nytimes.com/2010/01/26/world/26cyber.html?_r=0. See also Danny Vinik, "America's Secret Arsenal," *Politico, The Agenda*, Dec 9, 2015, found at: http://www.politico.com/agenda/story/2015/12/defense-department-cyber-offense-strategy-000331 and Steven Aftergood, "US Cyber Offense is "The Best in the World," *Secrecy News*, Aug 26, 2013, found at: http://fas.org/blogs/secrecy/2013/08/cyber-offense/ .

[54] Ibid.

[55] Office of Management and Budget, "Report on Federal Information Security: Agencies Need to Correct Weaknesses and Fully Implement Security Programs GAO-15-714," Published: Sep 29, 2015, Publicly Released: Sep 29, 2015, found at: http://www.gao.gov/products/GAO-15-714.

[56] NSTAC Report, pg. 7.

[57] Thomas Schelling, pg. 135.

[58] Or the unacceptable behavior should be clearly articulated in international law, norms, or the United Nations Charter.

[59] NSTAC Report, pg. 7.

[60] Ibid, pp. 7-8.

[61] Ibid, pg. 2.

[62] This is the author's definition but is drawn from several sources. See World Bank blog authored by Sina Odugbemi and titled "Whose Will Constitutes 'Political Will'?" found at: http://blogs.worldbank.org/publicsphere/whose-will-constitutes-political-will , and Lawrence Woocher, "Deconstructing 'Political Will': Explaining the Failure to Prevent Deadly Conflict and Mass Atrocities," (Princeton University Press, Oct 2001) found at: https://www.princeton.edu/jpia/past-issues-1/2001/10.pdf .

[63] Kenneth Geers, *Strategic Cyber Security*, (NATO Cooperative Cyber Defence Center of Excellence, Tallinn, Estonia, June 2011), pg. 397.

[64] Derived from an interview conducted by the author on 12 May 2016 with a senior FBI agent in the Cyber Division.

[65] Derived from an interview conducted by the author on 5 May 2015 with a mid-level executive on the United States National Security Council staff.

[66] Nicole Bitette, "Titanic: Three ways the disaster changed laws and safety on the seas," *New York Daily News,* Sept 1, 2015, found at: http://www.nydailynews.com/news/world/titanic-3-ways-disaster-changed-sea-travel-article-1.2344573.

[67] Lawrence Freedman, pg. 9.

[68] Michael A Vatis, "The Council of Europe Convention on Cybercrime," pg. 208.

[69] Joseph Biden, "Vice President Biden Announces $25 Million in Funding for Cybersecurity Education at HBCUs," (The White House, Washington DC, Jan 15, 2015), found at: https://www.whitehouse.gov/the-press-office/2015/01/15/vice-president-biden-announces-25-million-funding-cybersecurity-educatio.

[70] National Science Foundation Press Report, "NSF awards $74.5 million to support interdisciplinary cybersecurity research," Oct 7, 2015, found at: https://www.nsf.gov/news/news_summ.jsp?cntn_id=136481.

[71] CenturyLink is a global communications, hosting, cloud and IT services company enabling millions of customers and offers network and data systems management, Big Data analytics and IT consulting, and operates more than 55 data centers in North America, Europe and Asia. The company provides broadband, voice, video, data and managed services over a robust 250,000-route-mile U.S. fiber network and a 300,000-route-mile international transport network. For more info see: http://www.centurylink.com/Pages/AboutUs/CompanyInformation/.

[72] For a few see: Tom Gjelten, "Pentagon Strategy Prepares For War In Cyberspace," *National Public Radio News Online,* Jul 15, 2011, found at: http://www.npr.org/2011/07/15/137928048/u-s-military-unveils-cyberspace-strategy; David Alexander, "U.S. reserves right to meet cyber-attack with force," *Reuters News,* Nov 15, 2011, http://www.reuters.com/article/us-usa-defense-cybersecurity-idUSTRE7AF02Y20111116; and Mark Pomerleau, "How might the US respond to cyber-attacks?" *Defense Systems,* Jun 10, 2015, found at: https://defensesystems.com/articles/2015/06/10/us-response-scenario-cyber-attack.aspx. Also reference U.S. Department of Defense Cyber Strategy (Washington D.C., 2015) found at: http://www.defense.gov/Portals/1/features/2015/0415_cyber-strategy/Final_2015_DoD_CYBER_STRATEGY_for_web.pdf.

[73] U.N. Charter art. 51. An "armed attack" is the textual condition precedent set forth in Article 51 for the exercise of the right of self-defense. On the customary nature of the right of self-defense, see Military and Paramilitary Activities in and Against Nicaragua (Nicar. v. U.S.), 1986 I.C.J. 14, see Michael N. Schmitt, "'Below the Threshold' Cyber Operations: The Countermeasures Response Option and International Law," *Virginia Journal of International Law,* Vol. 54:3, Aug 1, 2014, pg. 698, found at: http://www.vjil.org/assets/pdfs/vol54/Schmitt-v7-JRN_FINAL_TO_PUBLISH.pdf.

[74] Oona A. Hathaway, Rebecca Crootof, Philip Levitz, Haley Nix, Aileen Lowlan, William Perdue, and Julia Spiegel, "The Law of Cyber-Attack," (Yale Law School, Yale Law School Legal Scholarship Repository, Jan 1, 2012), pg. 5, found at: http://digitalcommons.law.yale.edu/cgi/viewcontent.cgi?article=4844&context=fss_books.

[75] Much of this section follows the legal framework and logic espoused in the *Tallinn* Manual and by Michael N. Schmitt, in "The Law of Cyber-Attack," The Virginia Journal of International Law, Vol. 54:3.

[76] Responsibility of States for Internationally Wrongful Acts, art. 1, G.A. Res. 56/83, Annex, U.N. Doc. A/RES/56/83 (Jan. 28, 2002); referred to as *"Articles on State Responsibility,"* found at: http://legal.un.org/ilc/texts/instruments/english/commentaries/9_6_2001.pdf.

[77] Michael H. Schmitt, pg. 700.

[78] "REPORTS OF INTERNATIONAL ARBITRAL AWARDS: Island of Palmas Case" (Netherlands vs the United States), Vol. II, pp. 829, 838 (Perm. Ct. Arb. 1928), found at: http://legal.un.org/riaa/cases/vol_II/829-871.pdf .

[79] *The Tallinn Manual,* supra note 1, at pp. 15–16.

[80] Michael N. Schmitt, pg. 704.

[81] Ibid, pg. 704.

[82] Ibid, pg. 700, supra note 15.

[83] Ibid, pg. 700, supra note 15.

[84] United Nations Legislative Series, "Materials on the Responsibility of States for Internationally Wrongful Act," U.N. Doc. ST/LEG/SER.B/25 (2012).

[85] The older concept of reprisals was broader than that of countermeasures and included both non-forceful and forceful actions. Currently, forceful reprisals have been subsumed into the U.N. Charter's use of force paradigm, which allows nations to resort to force in response to armed attacks. One must not confuse countermeasures with *belligerent reprisals.* Belligerent reprisals are actions taken during an "armed conflict that would violate international humanitarian law but for the enemy's prior unlawful conduct." See U.N. Charter articles. 2(4), 39, 42, 51. For a discussion of this paradigm and its customary nature, see THE CHARTER OF THE UNITED NATIONS: A COMMENTARY 200, 211–13 (Bruno Simma et al. eds., 3d ed., 2013).

[86] In the law of State responsibility, the State breaching the obligation is known as the *"responsible state,"* whereas the State to which the obligation is owed is styled the *"injured state." Articles on State Responsibility,* Article 2, pg. 75.

[87] The *Tallinn Manual,* supra note 1, rule 5. The accountability applies when state entities (or entities under governmental control) can take the remedial action. Furthermore "if a remedial action could only be performed by a private entity, such as a private Internet service provider, the state would be obliged to use all means at its disposal to require that entity to take the action necessary to terminate the activity," pg. 28. Note: the *Tallinn Manual* is a non-binding document and used primarily for informational purposes.

[88] Ibid, Article 22.

89 Ibid, supra note 1, rule 9, which is based on Articles 22 and 49–53 of the *Articles on State Responsibility*.

90 *Articles on State Responsibility*, supra note 13, art. 25(1)(a).

91 Hathaway, et al, pg. 36.

92 James Crawford, "The International Law Commissions Articles on State Responsibility: Introduction, Text and Commentaries," (2002), pp. 178–86.

The Cambridge University Press publication reprints the official International Law Commission's Articles and accompanying commentary. See also the *Tallinn Manual*, supra note 1, at 39–40.

93 Ibid, pg. 36.

94 Thomas Giegerich, "Retorsion," *Max Planck Encyclopedia of International Law*, Vol. 8, (2012), pg. 976.

95 The Law Dictionary, (Black's Law Dictionary Free Online Legal Dictionary 2nd Ed.), found at: http://thelawdictionary.org/retorsion/.

96 The *Tallinn Manual*, supra note 1, rule 2.

97 Michael N. Schmitt, pg. 702.

98 Ibid, pg. 702. See also U.N. Charter Article 41.

99 For more on the Executive Order: "Blocking the Property of Certain Persons Engaging in Significant Malicious Cyber-Enabled Activities", see, President Barak Obama, Executive Order 13694, (Washington D.C. 2015), found at: https://www.whitehouse.gov/the-press-office/2015/04/01/executive-order-blocking-property-certain-persons-engaging-significant-m. For a complete list of U.S. Sanctions, see the U.S. Department of the Treasury, Resource Center Online, found at: https://www.treasury.gov/resource-center/sanctions/Pages/eolinks.aspx.

100 See U.N. Charter Article 51.

101 William H. Taft, IV, Legal Advisor, U.S. Department of State, "The Legal Basis for Preemption," *Council on Foreign Relations*, Nov 18, 2002, found at: http://www.cfr.org/international-law/legal-basis-preemption/p5250.

102 Ibid.

103 Barak Obama, *2011 International Strategy for Cyberspace: Prosperity, Security, and Openness in a Networked World*, (Washington D.C., May 2011), pg. 12, found at: https://www.whitehouse.gov/sites/default/files/rss_viewer/international_strategy_for_cyberspace.pdf.

104 Ibid, pg. 12.

[105] David E. Sanger, and Thom Shanker, "Broad Powers Seen for Obama in Cyberstrikes," *The New York Times*, Feb 3, 2013, accessed online 6 Mar 2016, found at: http://www.nytimes.com/2013/02/04/us/broad-powers-seen-for-obama-in-cyberstrikes.html?_r=0.

[106] Ibid.

[107] Julian E. Barnes, "U.S. Cyberattack Hurt Iran's Ability to Target Oil Tankers, Officials Say," *The New York Times,* April 28, 2019, found on-line at: https://www.nytimes.com/2019/08/28/us/politics/us-iran-cyber-attack.html.

[108] For more on the ISIL attack, see "Joint Task Force ARES and Operation GLOWING SYMPHONY: Cyber Command's Internet War Against ISIL," *National Security Archive," George Washington University, published Aug 13, 2018, found at:* https://nsarchive.gwu.edu/briefing-book/cyber-vault/2018-08-13/joint-task-force-ares-operation-glowing-symphony-cyber-commands-internet-war-against-isil. For more the counter Russia cyber operation, see: Ellen Nakashima, "U.S. Cyber Command operation disrupted Internet access of Russian troll factory on day of 2018 midterms," *The Washington Post*, Feb 27, 2019, found online at: https://www.washingtonpost.com/world/national-security/us-cyber-command-operation-disrupted-internet-access-of-russian-troll-factory-on-day-of-2018-midterms/2019/02/26/1827fc9e-36d6-11e9-af5b-b51b7ff322e9_story.html.

CHAPTER SIX

APPLYING COERCION IN CYBERSPACE: USING THE FINANCIAL SECTOR AS A TARGET DEMONSTRATION

"Repeated cyber intrusions into critical infrastructure demonstrate the need for improved cybersecurity. The cyber threat to critical infrastructure continues to grow and represents one of the most serious national security challenges we must confront. The national and economic security of the United States depends on the reliable functioning of the Nation's critical infrastructure in the face of such threats. It is the policy of the United States to enhance the security and resilience of the Nation's critical infrastructure and to maintain a cyber environment that encourages efficiency, innovation, and economic prosperity while promoting safety, security, business confidentiality, privacy, and civil liberties. We can achieve these goals through a partnership with the owners and operators of critical infrastructure to improve cybersecurity information sharing and collaboratively develop and implement risk-based standards."

President Barack Obama

2013 Executive Order - Improving Critical Infrastructure Cybersecurity[1]

P rior to September 11, 2001, the United States government's primary attention, when it came to protecting the homeland, was on national missile defense.[2] Following the 9-11 attacks, America refocused its national defense on the terrorist threats and the transportation industry. Eighteen years later, the United States faces multiple asymmetric threats, both physical and virtual, that threaten America's economic and national security. The United States also is a nation that is dependent upon its global financial, communications, energy, and transportation infrastructures to carry out the daily essential activities of its citizens and to maintain its position on the world economic and political stage. Those vital infrastructures, unfortunately, are vulnerable to attack and difficult to defend. In a hyperconnected world, malicious cyber actors exploit vulnerabilities and gain access to data for the purpose of exploitation, theft, disruption, or destruction. Those nefarious actors seek to embarrass their victims, steal data or money, commit espionage, or inflict damage, now or at a later time of their choosing. Across the spectrum of CEMA, the effects are not restricted or confined to just the intended victim – there are second and third order effects and collateral damage that affect other systems and entities. For example, CEMA directed at Manhattan's power grid affects not just the citizens of Manhattan, but also affects the national economy via the financial sector by crippling the New York Stock Exchange, banks, trading houses and credit card agencies through the loss of power. Across all critical infrastructure sectors, the cyber threat trend is rising, and with it, so too are the risks to the United States security and vitality. Now, as directed in the 2019 National Defense Authorization Act, Congress shifted the focus of national defense away from terrorism and toward nation-sponsored threats. Although the 2017 "Cyber Security Strategy of the United States of America" lays the foundation for developing a coercive cyber strategy to address the threats that face the nation, America still does not adequately defend its critical infrastructure from such threats. More specifically, despite the advancement of United States cyber policy, the cyber threat trend rises while malicious actors continue to successfully target critical infrastructure to reap their bounty without fear of retribution from the Federal government.

Why is the United States, arguably as the most powerful nation on the planet, so vulnerable and its homeland remains at risk? The U.S. Constitution is clear that providing national defense is the priority of, mandatory for, and exclusive responsibility of the Federal government; however, the United States struggles to manage and mitigate risk in such a way that deters aggression in cyberspace. One of the reasons, as national security experts Jim Talent and the Honorable Jon Kyl suggest, is "a lack of clarity on a strategic level – an escalating failure over time to define the interests that together give meaning to the term 'national security,' to identify the threats to those interests, and to define the basic strategy and operating principles of a foreign policy that will effectively defend America over time."[3] The authors opine that the United States once had the necessary clarity in the decades following World War II when the threat was high and the United States could not play a secondary role in world affairs outside the Western Hemisphere. At that time, the United States had three priority national interests within its strategy: defend the American homeland, protect the common areas of the world through which Americans traded and traveled, and preserve the political equilibriums in parts of the world vital to the United States security and prosperity, and particularly in Europe and Asia.[4] That strategy proved valuable to the United States' economic and national security through several decades, despite some tactical and operational failures over the years. By returning once again to strategic clarity, the United States should now develop the necessary national strategy to effective secure of the nation's critical infrastructure against cyber-attacks.

This chapter develops a clear national coercive cybersecurity strategy for the United States critical infrastructure sectors. As the strategy is developed below, we will focus on just one sector – the Financial Services Sector (FSS) – for ease and simplicity in explaining a national coercive cybersecurity strategy; however, the strategy is applicable and modifiable to all sectors. The FSS was selected for several reasons. First, negative impacts in the financial sector can significantly impact not just that sector, but the entire nation as well as the global economy. CEMA directed on the financial sector may have second and third order effects on the other sectors, which make the FSS one of the more significant sectors (similar to the energy, transportation, and communications sectors). For example, destroying the nation's ability to transfer money would severely degrade every sector and industry reliant upon funds transfer. Second, the FSS is currently the sector with the greatest increase in CEMA directed at it over the last few years – and in need of governmental involvement to reverse that trend.[5] Furthermore, the financial sector topped the list of 26 different industries that cyber-criminals most targeted, and the sector remains the "most susceptible to malicious email traffickers, as consumers are seven times more likely to be the victim of an attack [CEMA] originating from a spoofed email with a bank brand versus one from any other industry."[6]

Although "defending the American homeland" appears straightforward, it is not specific enough for the development of a national coercive cybersecurity strategy. By elaborating on the United States' homeland defense interests and the threats that place those interests at risk, a clearer set of objectives may be developed for the protection of the United States Financial Services Sector (and more broadly all of the critical infrastructure sectors). The sections below are not intended to be the complete strategy, but rather present a foundation for which United States strategists and policymakers can build a national coercive cybersecurity strategy that influences malicious cyber actors who threaten United States economic and national security. This chapter demonstrates that coercion can be used along with the other instruments of power to impose substantial consequences on malicious cyber actors and change the United States' paradigm for national cybersecurity.

National Strategy Development

Noted strategist, Colin Gray once wrote, "[t]rue wisdom in strategy must be practical because strategy is a practical subject. Much of what appears to be wise and indeed is prudent as high theory is unhelpful to the poor warrior who actually has to do strategy, tactically and operationally."[7] Strategy development is quite complicated; and in a hyperconnected world, it is extremely perplexing. The number of malicious actors, methods of attack, vulnerabilities, and risks are numerous. No longer are industrial-aged thought, organization, and processes sufficient for the digital-age environment. With the advent of cyber conflict arise chaos and complexity, through which strategy must chart a clear path. There are no silver bullets and no technical solutions in national cyber strategy. Effective national strategy is the conceptual bridge between policy and operations.[8] Conflict is a perilous endeavor; and effective strategy provides direction through the alignment of campaigns and policy objectives, and through the application of all of the instruments of national power. Most importantly, effective national strategy must properly account for not only the fog and friction of conflict, but also "the will, skill, and means of an intelligent and malevolent enemy."[9] A useful national strategy accurately aligns the nation's goals, means, and ways within the geopolitical context of the conflict and successfully opposes a thinking, determined adversary. Coercion is a particularly important tool for the strategist to influence the foe's decision making.

Crafting the Strategy Using Operational Design

The methodology for developing the strategy below was guided by the theoretical underpinnings of *military operational design*, which combines the aspects of military theory, systems theory, writings on the nature of problems and problem solving, and the challenge of critical and creative thinking in order to help understand and develop effective solutions for complex, ill-defined national problems. Operational design's initial focus is on helping visualize the environment, understanding the problem that must be solved, and developing a broad conceptual approach that can achieve the desired end state(s).[10] Below is the product of the application of military operational design. Understanding the environment is the first step; United States critical infrastructure sectors will be expounded upon below.

The Financial Sector Defined

The private organizations that make up the Financial Services Sector constitute the foundation of the United States' financial system and are a vital component of the global economy. "These organizations are tied together through a network of electronic systems with innumerable entry points. An incident, whether manmade or natural, impacting these systems could have detrimental effects on the entire economy."[11] Large-scale power outages, recent natural disasters, and a rise in the number, frequency, and sophistication of CEMA reveal the wide range of potential risks facing the FSS. According to the Department of Homeland Security, the FSS "includes thousands of depository institutions, providers of investment products, insurance companies, other credit and financing organizations, and the providers of the critical financial utilities and services that support these functions.

Financial institutions vary widely in size and presence, ranging from some of the world's largest global companies with hundreds of thousands of employees and many billions of dollars in assets, to community banks and credit unions with a small number of employees serving individual communities.[12] Broadly stated, FSS entities, whether small or large, allow customers to deposit funds and make payments to other parties, provide credit and liquidity to customers, invest funds for both long and short periods, and transfer financial risks between customers.

According to the Federal Reserve Bank of New York, on the average day, more than \$14 trillion of dollar-denominated payments is routed through the banking system. Essential to a well-functioning economy are the timing and smooth flow of dollars for large-value transactions and the infrastructure that enables that monetary flow. Several nightmare scenario worry the financial leaders and three of them are: "physical attacks that shut off or damage some aspect of critical services, financial attacks that spin out of control and lead to bank runs, and hackers changing data in a way that erodes trust in the economy and critical institutions."[13] The financial market infrastructure provides essential economic services—"plumbing" for the economy—and is made up of a variety of entities.[14] The various financial transactions occur within and between financial entities and financial market utilities (FMU). Transfer of funds (or value) occurs when balances are shifted between entities that both have accounts with the same financial institution, and the transactions are settled when the transfer is complete. "The Federal Reserve Banks provide this service for United States depository financial institutions, settlement banks provide a similar service for their bank and FMU customers, and clearing banks do so for government securities dealers."[15] Given the interests at stake, the risks involved, the number of entities that transfer funds, and the sheer magnitude of money moved daily, any CEMA targeting this capability could rapidly rise to the level of CINS for the United States. Moreover, given the impact a CINS in the FSS could have on the nation, an effective national coercive cybersecurity strategy to defend against such a CINS is crucial to achieving securing this critical infrastructure.

Financial Services Sector Threats

According to a recent Mandiant cybersecurity report, it is difficult to overstate how quickly cybersecurity has gone from a niche technology issue to a consumer issue to boardroom priority. Now corporate executives know what seasoned security professionals have long been aware of: there is no such thing as total security. Security breaches will continue to occur, because determined malicious cyber actors will always find a way to exploit vulnerabilities in cyber defenses.[16] This is to say that cyber threat actors will always find the opportunity to harm. Importantly, they will also have the willingness to harm given the powerful lure of prizes they seek. Cyber threats were discussed in general in previous chapters; however, the specific threats to the FSS, are worth elaborating on and include: hacktivists, cybercriminals, and state-sponsored cyber actors. In general, cyber threats to the FSS grow in frequency and severity every year. VISA's Chief Executive Officer, Charles W. Scharf, described the cyber threat as a result of four broad factors: first, financial cyberspace provides larger targets given the breadth and criticality of the data it controls; second, the amount and value of the data financial service entities produce and store expands continually – the data is a gold-mine for cyber-criminals; third, hyperconnectivity makes it easier for more people to steal from or disrupt FSS organizations; and fourth, malicious cyber actors are more sophisticated, better organized, better funded, and harder to bring to justice that ever before.[17]

Hacktivists targeting the FSS often seek to garner fame for their hacks or damage the reputation of an FS organization as was the case in October 2015, when the online hacktivist group "Anonymous" launched Operation Black October through a YouTube video. This cyber campaign was designed to identify and highlight the allegedly corrupt attitudes within the FSS.[18] The public smear campaign was intended to damage the character of financial institutions. Hacktivists recently shifted their campaign away from government organizations to the FSS. The actual brand name damage is difficult to quantify; however, financial entities are now taking the threat seriously. A loss of brand name or reputation effects the financial institution's ability to retain or gain customers and clients. Many larger financial institutions are expanding their information security perspective (focus on data) to a broader cybersecurity program that include brand protection as part of their remit. In the spectrum of cyber threat activity, hacktivism is the least impactful to the Sector.

Cybercriminals constitute the majority of the threats faced by the Financial Sector currently. Mandiant reported for companies across multiple sectors, the median number of days attackers were present on a victim network before they were discovered was 229 days, while only 33% of the organizations had discovered the intrusion themselves.[19] Cyber-criminals typically identify and exploit financial intuitions vulnerabilities, gather information required to breach the most sensitive of networks and systems, and then navigate the complex systems, establish covert presences, and execute sophisticated CEMA in order to steal valuable data (and identities) and funds. Cyber-crime directed at financial institutions continues to be a growth industry with high payoffs and almost no consequences. In a recent cyber-attack on Bangladesh's central bank, hackers stole over $80 million from the institutes' Federal Reserve bank account, which was reportedly caused by malware installed on the bank's computer systems.[20] Although the FBI indicted the cyber-criminals, they remain at large. In a different type of CEMA incident, hackers stole user contact information for 76 million households and 7 million small businesses from JP Morgan Chase in 2015.[21] Theft of customer's personally identifiable information (PII) and money are lucrative targets for cyber-criminals targeting the FSS. Stolen PII leads to identity theft, which becomes a life-long issue for the victims. More recently in 2018, allegedly North Korean cyber-criminals successfully executed the cyber theft of $10 million from Banco de Chile through the exploitation of the SWIFT system.[22]

The process for which a cyber-criminal acquires his ill-gotten gains (such as credit card data) progresses along a typical path. For credit card theft, a cyber-criminal usually first infects a financial institution's computer with malware or a

Trojan often through a spear phishing scheme, and then the hacker identifies the high-value target and upgrades the backdoor to one that is not detectable by antivirus software. Next the hacker sells the backdoor access to a cyber-criminal specializing in cardholder data theft. Finally, another cyber-criminal from a more sophisticated criminal organization buys the backdoor access, uploads additional utilities to move laterally, and establishes supplementary backdoors to maintain unauthorized access.[23] Systems that hold large quantities of cardholders' data are lucrative targets and cyber-criminals will expend substantial effort to steal or use that information. Elaborate cyber enterprises are established now to seize the profitable proceeds. Cyber-criminals can "convert stolen data into cash or cash equivalent benefits, leading to lost sales, strategic partner hijacking, counterfeit products, patent infringement, negotiation advantage and so forth. A typical breach could impact an organization's public reputation and stakeholder confidence, its market share, revenue and profit, and reduce return on capital and R&D investments."[24]

The most significant new threats to the FSS are cyber extortion and company insiders acting as free-agents for crime. Cyber-criminals now are embarking upon a relatively new form of CEMA – cyber extortion – against financial institutions and other sectors. Large financial institutions encounter cyber extortion CEMA and several cover up these extortions by paying out as much as $100 for every $5's worth of anticipated damages. A cybercriminal tactic, known as Distributed Denial of Service For Bitcoins (DD4BC), uses a combination of ransomware schemes with traditional DDoS attacks against a number of financial institutions.[25] According to a recent DDoS Threat Report, while 90% of ransomware DDoS attacks lasted less than 30 minutes, one particular attack lasted 70 hours. This shorter attack strategy is being used to advance the nature of the attack as well as distract the attention of cyber-defenders away from the actual intent of an attack: deploying malware and stealing data.[26] These CEMA indicate that today's attackers are becoming smarter and more sophisticated. The second rising trend in cyber-crime is the company insider who operates as a free agent cybercriminal. This malicious cyber actor is an individual, either current or former employee, who is trained in specific industries to steal and profit from the sale of customer data on the "dark web."[27] The recent 2019 Capitol One data breach was an example of that.[28]

The final type of FSS cyber threat is the state or state-sponsored malicious cyber actor. State or state-sponsored actors direct their CEMA at financial institutions for several reasons – and the first is cyber espionage. State or state-sponsored organizations are extremely well organized and mechanized, with considerable resources. They strive to improve the strategic capabilities of their host state by providing them with information about products, processes, current strategies, and other data, which can lead to long-term strategic losses for the financial entity.[29] Additionally, some financial organizations experience CEMA because a state wishes to exert political influence on the organization simply because of where the financial institution conducts its business. For example, a bank that executes daily business in a country where the attackers might not desire the bank to conduct business, can become a target just because the company has a "business relationship" in that country.

Cyber threats to the FSS constitute a grave risk to the nation simply because of the vast data, funds, and processes necessary for proper function of daily financial business in the United States. CINS directed at the Sector can have substantial effects on the organizations involved, the entire sector, and the United States and global economy. The cascading second and third order effects on the other sectors can negatively impact the economic and national security of the United States. No single financial institution can possibly match the resources (physical and financial) and tactics of the sophisticated malicious cyber actors that chose to target the FSS. "Threat actors are constantly inventing new tools and techniques to enable them to get to the information they want and are getting better at identifying gaps and unknown (zero-day) vulnerabilities in an organization's security. Discouragingly, attackers often fund their new tools and vulnerability research with money taken from the very organizations victimized before."[30] A national coercive cybersecurity strategy is needed to impose substantial consequences on the malicious cyber actors in order to change their cost-benefit calculus. Next in the development of a national strategy, it is important to comprehend and assess the issues involved with the current FSS cybersecurity.

Financial Organizations' Cybersecurity Efforts

Financial industry cybersecurity reports routinely highlight the rise from year to year in CEMA directed at the organizations within the sector. Based upon the escalation of malicious cyber activity, national financial firms invest heavily in cybersecurity enterprises to protect their organization, customers, firm's reputation, and data through the use of cloud-based cybersecurity services, Big Data analytics, and advanced authentication and biometrics.[31] According to one survey of financial cybersecurity executives, the most significant cybersecurity challenges facing FSS organizations are: security protocols/standards of third-party vendors; rapidly evolving, sophisticated, and complex technologies; cross-border (international) data exchanges; increased use of mobile technologies by customers; and heightened information security threats from outside the country.[32] The top targets of malicious cyber actors are: employee and customer data and intellectual property (IP), with the theft of IP rising 183% in 2015.[33] "While employees remain the most cited sources of compromise, incidents attributed to organized crime jumped 45%."[34]

In 2017, banks lost $16.8 billion to cyber-criminals.[35] United States FSS organizations lost on average $23.6 million from CEMA breaches in 2013,[36] which represent the highest average loss across all sectors. To accentuate the rise in CEMA, this figure is 43.9 percent higher than in 2012, when the FSS was ranked third, after the defense and utilities and energy sectors.[37] While this trend is substantial, the actual damages sometimes are not meaningful to firms' income statements. "The potentially greater impact from cyber-crime is on customer and investor confidence, reputational risk, and regulatory impact that together add up to substantial risks for financial services companies."[38] Unfortunately, not all organizations are developing their cybersecurity enterprises at the same pace and with a level of quality necessary to effectively protect their firms. One report noted that CEMA success (time taken to compromise a victim) was less than one day 88% of the time, and discovery success (time from compromise to discovery of the CEMA) was less than a day only 21% of the time and often took months or years to notice 39%of the time.[39] Additionally, restoration success (time from discovery to containment of the CEMA effects) took less than a day 40% of the time, leaving the rest of recovery period (60%) in days, weeks, and months.[40] The swiftness of the CEMA initiation, the delay in discovery rates, and lengthy restoration time amplifies the challenges that the FSS organizations have in detection and response to CEMA. Several firms are simply not prepared to contend with the magnitude of the threat and the sophistication of the CEMA seen currently. Worse yet, most executives stated that they expect the cyber threat to increase in frequency, impact, and intricacy in the coming years.

The various FSS organizations range in size and capability to contend with the cyber threat. In one survey across all sectors and which represented the state of FS Sector organizational cybersecurity enterprises, 74% of executives indicated their cybersecurity enterprise only partially met their needs, 42% did not possess a security operations center, 25% did not have a vulnerability identification program, and 16% did not possess a data breach program.[41] In a different survey focused solely on the FS Sector, 65% had a cybersecurity strategy, 56% conducted threat assessments, 59% had security baseline/standards for third-parties, and 54% used active monitoring/analysis of security intelligence.[42] For organizations that operate in the most vulnerable CI sector, a great number of organizations are not prepared for the cyber threat they face, now or in the future.

According to a 2019 joint Accenture and Ponemon study, the global financial sector, "banks, capital market firms and insurers grapple with a per-firm average of $18.5 million annually to combat cybercrime, over 40 percent more than the average cost ($13 million per firm) across all industries surveyed."[43] The Accenture study goes on to state that malware, phishing and social engineering, botnets, and malicious code are among the major issues with which the financial sector contends. Further, "web-based attacks increased the most, with an 8 percent rise from 2017 to 2018...and banks stand to lose $347 billion, insurers $305 billion and capital markets $47 billion."[44] Unfortunately, not all of the FSS organizations have the profit margins required to markedly improve their cybersecurity enterprises. To improve this condition and mitigate the risks to financial industry, the FSS works to raise the level of cybersecurity awareness and capability across the sector and nation. This data points to one important fact, as critical as the FSS is to the United States' economy, a great number of America's financial institutions admit they are not properly prepared to defend their firms, leaving doubt as the overall impact to the United States economy should CINS strike the sector. This must be a wake-up call for U.S. policymakers to take a more proactive and deliberate role in protecting the sector against threat that will commit CINS.

Financial Services Sector's Cybersecurity Efforts

From an FSS perspective, collaboration across organizations aids in reducing the overall risk that the sector and nation faces. By working together, these FSS organizations seek to reduce the physical and cybersecurity risks through several sector initiatives and sector-wide entity activities. Foremost in activities is the *Financial Services Sector-Specific Plan 2015* undertaken by the Sector in cooperation with the Department of Homeland Security. The security and resilience of the FSS depends on close collaboration among a broad set of partners, including sector companies and trade associations; government agencies; financial regulators; State, local, tribal, and territorial governments; and other government and private sector partners in the United States and around the world. "Responding to a broad set of risks in a complex environment requires a shared and flexible strategic framework to inform decision-making among individual stakeholders, each of whom maintains their own distinct approach to risk management."[45] The 2015 Sector Specific Plan (SSP) provides an overview of the FSS and the risk it faces, establishes a strategic framework to guide the prioritization of the sector's work, and describes the key mechanisms through which the strategic framework is executed and assessed. The mission of the FSS SSP is stated below:

"Continuously enhance security and resilience within the Financial Services Sector through a strong community of private companies, government agencies, and international partners that establishes shared awareness of threats and vulnerabilities, continuously enhances baseline security levels, and coordinates rapid response to and recovery from significant incidents as they occur."[46]

In order to improve its security and resilience and advance its mission, the sector works to advance four primary goals:

1. Implement and maintain structured routines for sharing timely and actionable information related to cybersecurity and physical threats and vulnerabilities among firms, across sectors of industry, and between the private sector and government.

2. Improve risk management capabilities and the security posture of firms across the Financial Services Sector and the service providers they rely on by

encouraging the development and use of common approaches and best practices.

3. Collaborate with the homeland security, law enforcement, and intelligence communities; financial regulatory authorities; other sectors of industry; and international partners to respond to and recover from significant incidents.

4. Discuss policy and regulatory initiatives that advance infrastructure security and resilience priorities through robust coordination between government and industry.[47]

The four goals above emphasize the importance of collaboration (both across the sector and with government entities) for effective cybersecurity. This realization acknowledges the necessity to partner with other organizations in order to provide greater capability and capacity directed at the sector's cyber threat. Furthermore, that collaboration should be in the form of shared threat intelligence, best practices for risk mitigation, and incident response activities. Several FSS exercises helped to highlight and recommend areas for improvement for the attainment of the four goals.

Exercises for the FSS typically are accomplished as a table-top discussion with various leaders from across the sector and government, and are based upon an unfolding scenario which forces the FS Sector to describe the respective organizations' response(s) to a particular threat. The general observations and recommendations for six different Sector exercises are summarized below.[48]

The FSS Specific Plan is improved, but has areas for enhancement, namely in understanding each organization's capabilities, response mechanisms, technical cybersecurity operations, and ability to integrate response activities with the broader sector.

Information sharing has improved; however, the process still lacks sufficient speed and context to full facilitate an effective response. Oftentimes, the threat information passed to private FS organizations is too general and late to be actionable, while the majority of threat intelligence is classified too high to be disseminated. All agree that more should be done to improve threat intelligence sharing.

Both the government and FSS have response processes; however, they are not well understood, coordinated, or integrated. More should be done to integrate the regulators, law enforcement, homeland security and the intelligence community in order to create a whole of nation response plan. Furthermore, there is no single entity (currently there are many) within the government that private firms may turn to that possess the requisite authority, resources, and capabilities to effectively partner with the FSS in the attainment of sector-side cybersecurity.

Private FS organizations would rather use private third-party cybersecurity companies for aiding in their response plans than the government since FS organizations routinely work with the third-party companies. Part of the reason has to do with the legal hurdles of working with the government as compared to private cybersecurity companies. Better cybersecurity response would benefit from improved research and development partnerships between third-party firms, government research labs, and academic institutions.[49]

FSS exercises continue to advance the dialogue between organizations within the sector as well as with government and other sector entities. With the rise of CEMA inside and outside the Sector, senior executives are motivated to improve their organization's and the sector's capabilities and processes to become more resilient to CEMA, mitigate the risks, and advance the response activities of all involved. Government-private collaboration was repeatedly highlighted as a topic of great import as well as one of need for significant improvement. In an interview with the author,[50] one executive emphasized several areas that hinder full collaboration by private organizations with the government. Those hindrances include: fiscal vulnerability (Private Board members have fiduciary responsibility to their shareholders if the decisions they make by partnering with the government negatively affect stock prices), brand reputation (also known as the Edward Snowden effect – where by a corporation can be exposed in the press for partnering with the government in cases where the government is not seen as wholly scrupulous), Sherman Anti-Trust Act[51] (corporations are limited in what information they can share with each for fear of conspiring to create an unfair market condition), fear of penalty or fines when allowing governmental regulators access to cybersecurity information within private networks (in accordance with regulatory policy), and the Sarbanes-Oxley Act of 2002[52] (which imposes audit requirements on corporate executives who are supposed to protect investors by improving the accuracy and reliability of corporate disclosures). Given that the financial organizations and the FSS have limited ability to contend with CEMA directed at them, one should then examine what the United States government does to protect the sector and the nation's economy from CEMA.

The United States Government's Cybersecurity Support to the FS Sector

As was mentioned earlier, the President directed through Executive Order the protection of United States critical infrastructure from CEMA. Specifically, the "Federal Government shall work with critical infrastructure owners and operators and [State, local, tribal, and territorial] SLTT entities to take proactive steps to manage risk and strengthen the security and resilience of the Nation's critical infrastructure, considering all hazards that could have a debilitating impact on national security, economic stability, public health and safety, or any combination thereof. These efforts shall seek to reduce vulnerabilities, minimize consequences, identify and disrupt threats, and hasten response and recovery efforts related to critical infrastructure."[53] The government's efforts are intended to improve the security and resiliency of CI in an integrated, holistic manner. Three "strategic imperatives" articulate how the government is supposed to strengthen critical infrastructure security and resilience: "1) refine and clarify functional relationships across the Federal Government to advance the national unity of effort to strengthen critical infrastructure security and resilience; 2) enable effective information exchange by identifying baseline data and systems requirements for the Federal Government; and 3) implement an integration and analysis function to inform planning and operations decisions regarding critical infrastructure."[54]

Observation of the Current Capabilities to Defend United States Financial Industry (Hindrances)

To fully comprehend where the United States and the Financial Services Sector should evolve, one must understand their current hurdles to success and the topics that hinder the respective government and private entities' ability to overcome those hurdles. In the recent past, several governmental organizations conducted multiple series of cybersecurity exercises to explore the state of government-private capabilities to defend the nation against CEMA. One of those cyber exercises series was designed and implemented by the United States Air Force (USAF) Wargaming Institute for the USAF Cyber College. In that wargame series, the government inter-agencies and private CI sector representatives explored cybersecurity at the national level in an effort to better determine the hurdles to reversing the negative cyber threat trend while investigating when and how the DoD might participate in CI cybersecurity.[55]

Several findings and observations can be drawn from the USAF Cyber College Wargames After Action Reports and the above brief explanation of the financial organizations. A number of findings and observations along with the comments from interviews conducted with mid and senior government and private leaders are presented here related to the current capabilities to defend against CEMA targeting the FSS. First, no single entity, either in the FSS on in government, possesses the requisite capabilities, capacities, and authorities to effectively ensure the defense of the FSS and the vitality of the plethora of critical functions that the FSF organizations perform. Each entity discussed (either private or government) conducts cybersecurity activities that contribute to the overall security of the sector; however, neither individually nor collectively do those contributions effectively deter malicious cyber actors. Second, despite the Presidential direction to DHS to ensure the unity of effort across the governmental departments and agencies, each government department and agency executes its mission individually and with only marginal understanding of what the other entities are doing.[56] Currently there are a great many number of substantial cybersecurity initiatives occurring across the U.S government inter-agency. However, without unity of effort (and a national cybersecurity strategy), the individual efforts are not integrated or synchronized to improve effects for the sector or nation. Furthermore, those individual initiatives are not developed concurrently and therefore cannot achieve a synergistic effect.

Third, although the NIST Framework provides a guideline for an effective cybersecurity enterprise, it is only a voluntary framework. More importantly, only those entities with the sufficient profit margins to devote to building and adhering to the standards can implement the framework. Furthermore, the NIST Framework provides individual organizations with guidelines, but does not address entire sectors or interconnectedness of companies across the sector where other vulnerabilities exist. Fourth, the importance of the government-private partnership repeatedly was emphasized by both government and private leaders, and further stressed in cyber exercises; however, there are major hurdles to full collaboration. Private partners are hesitant to share proprietary data (privacy concerns along with reputational costs of doing so) and to participate while the government struggles with to how to share classified threat intelligence for private enterprises' defense. Overcoming the hurdles to full collaboration is essential to a whole of nation approach to FSS cybersecurity.

Fifth and closely related to the fourth, the government must determine how to share classified cyber threat intelligence or declassify it quickly enough for private firms' use. The government has specific information on threats or mitigation measures, which private entities might find useful. Private institutions that are preparing to defend against an impending CEMA, or recently experienced a cyber incident, may have specific information that could help identify potential vulnerabilities, induce other firms to make new investments in security technologies, or aid them in taking additional actions to reduce the risk of cyber events. However, the existence of certain legal and regulatory measures can prevent the public and private sectors from sharing information that could yield security benefits.[57] The type, frequency, and number of threat intelligence reports past to private industry leaves private firms with the sense that they are left to defend themselves and they will have to rely on their own means to develop cyber threat intelligence. Several cyber exercises have highlighted that some classified information should be shared with private firms in a legally responsible way. The potential costs of disclosure should be carefully assessed and the circumstances and means of disclosure delineated when applicable. With the above understanding of the FSS environment and the assessment of the sector and the nation's ability to contend with CEMA, the next section will develop the national coercive cybersecurity strategy to defend the United States Financial Services Sector.

Finally, the multitude of cyber exercises reinforced a point made in previous chapters, despite all of the work accomplished in private and government organizations, the cyber threat is increasing. The reason noted by most experts for this increase was primarily because there are no substantial consequences being imposed on the malicious cyber actors who perpetrated CEMA against the FSS –

the benefits outweigh the costs/risks for cyber threat actors. Any new strategy developed for CI or FSS protection must change the paradigm of malicious cyber actors by raising their costs to an unacceptably high level.

Strategy

With an adequate understanding of the FSS environment, which includes the threats facing the sector, the ability to defend it by all relevant actors, and the hurdles that prevent success, this section will describe what is required in a national strategy that utilizes coercion as part of that strategy. This operational design process results in a coercive national strategy that wields all instruments of national power to effectively influence cyber actors who threaten United States national and economic security in and through cyberspace. At the most basic level, a national strategy must establish its *aims*, its *means*, and its *ways* in which the nation shall dominate each adversary. A *coercive strategy* should integrate the use of threats and/or punishments directed at the adversary's strategy and/or pressure points along with inducement to influence his decision making. An effective national coercive cybersecurity strategy should create advantages in relation to an adversary, across the spectrum of national security effects (resilience/redundancy, defense, coercive diplomacy, forceful coercion). In order to develop a national coercive cybersecurity strategy to defend the United States Financial Services Sector, one must establish the appropriate *aim* first.

National Coercive Cyber Strategy Goal

In light of this, the **goal** of the United States' national coercive cybersecurity strategy is to defend the United States homeland and critical infrastructure from cyber incidents of national significance (CINS) in accordance with American values, interests, and international law. To achieve this goal, the United States government, in partnership with its CI private entities and international allies, will employ dominant cyberpower (**means**) in conjunction with the other instruments of national power, at the appropriate time and **ways**, to create United States advantages in relation to an adversary, across the spectrum of national security effects (resilience/redundancy, defense, coercive diplomacy, forceful coercion). When faced with a grave, imminent CINS threat, the United States will exercise the inherent right to self-defense in an effort to disrupt/mitigate the **risks** to the nation's CI or degrade/defeat the threat. For the Financial Service Sector, one can substitute FSS for CI above in order to clarify and elaborate on details necessary to explain the strategy further.

The Desired End States

Having now explained the context of the current cybersecurity paradigm of the United States Financial Services Sector along with articulating the national goal of the coercive cybersecurity strategy, the next step in the strategy development process (operation design) is to articulate the desired end state that the strategy is meant to achieve. Again, strategy is the bridge between policy and operations. By using the above FSS observations, one may develop the strategy's desired end state. Below is the suggested *strategy statement*.

The desired end state for the Financial Service Sector is:

One multi-disciplinary (joint public/private) team with the decision authorities and resources necessary to build and execute a "whole of nation" cyber strategy that influences malicious cyber actors (through deterrence and compellence), by ensure key FSS cyber terrain is defended from meaningful cyber-attacks and U.S. and world consumer confidence in the U.S. FSS remains strong.

The ways and means to achieve those desired ends states would include: the establishment of national *unity of effort* by fusing all means of credible disciplines, resources, and capabilities from across United States government departments and agencies, while fostering *full collaboration* between government and private FSS organizations to coerce potential foes to choose not to attack. That coercion can occur in three ways: 1) through effective cyber defense of key FSS terrain by raising the costs to successfully achieve the foe's objectives; 2) through effectively deterring strategies to deny the adversary his objectives through proactive defense; and 3) through targeted coercive punishment actions meant to impose substantial costs on the threat by targeting what he values when he crosses the threshold of CINS. Since resources are finite, the strategy should focus the United States defense on the most vital portions of the FSS first – the financial sector's key pressure points (or key cyber terrain). The national coercive cybersecurity strategy should *impose real consequence* on malicious cyber actors based upon a new threshold definition that clearly specifies what constitutes CINS in the FSS. Finally, the strategy should integrate and synchronize all the domestic FSS cybersecurity efforts with international efforts by incorporating our allies to help build capability and capacity to place even greater pressure and costs on the malicious cyber actors.

The Specifics of the National Coercive Cybersecurity Strategy

The following sections will elaborate on the above strategy statements and objective in order to provide the necessary details for the creation and execution of a whole of nation effort to achieve the strategy's goal. Elements of coercion (see Figure 6.1 below) and the foundations of a successful coercive strategy will be utilized to help clarify the specifics of the strategy needed to defend the United States Financial Services Sector. Having already explained the actors involved (in defining the FSS and government players) and the interests at stakes/risks involved, the next element to discuss is the notion of what to protect – the pressure points within the US FSS for which credible capabilities must be arrayed against.

307

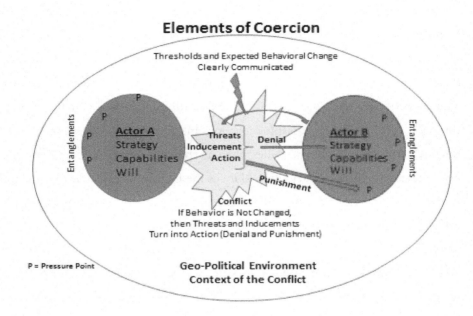

Figure 6.1 – Elements of Coercion

The Financial Services Sector's Key Cyber Terrain (Pressure Points)

The United States Financial Services Sector is literally made up of thousands of institutions and companies that hold, move, and trade money and securities (Stocks, Bonds, Mortgages, and Insurance). Defending the entirety of the sector is not realistic nor desired – each company has the responsibility to defend their firm, albeit with varying degrees of ability. Determining which pressure points to defend for this strategy should be undertaken with the close cooperation of the United States Justice Department, United States Federal Reserve Bank, FS-ISAC, and other major financial institutions. It is not my intent to fully define the Pressure Points, but to offer a starting point for a deeper analysis by more qualified experts.

Furthermore, the strategy should not be designed to defend the institutions themselves, but rather the key functions they implement and which "drive" the United States economy. There may be some cases where the entire institutions may constitute a pressure point and may require protection beyond what the private firm's cyber team can provide. This was the motive behind EO 13636, Section 9's definition of Globally Significant Financial Institutions[58] that are, by function, "too big to fail" and therefore require special consideration in defining key cyber terrain. These Section 9 entities, which include other sectors as well, are defined as "critical infrastructure where a cybersecurity incident could reasonably result in catastrophic regional or national effects on public health or safety, economic security, or national security."[59]

The FSS's key cyber terrain includes several broad and critically important components that include but are limited to:

- The Financial Markets (New York Stock Market, the NASDAQ, etc.);
- The Financial Institutions that hold, trade, and move money and securities (to include the financial clearing and money movement functions mentioned earlier (i.e., banks such as JPMorgan Chase & Co., Wells Fargo & Company, Bank of America Corporation, and Citigroup Inc, etc.);
- Insurance companies (i.e., American International Group and Chubb Limited, etc.);
- The Federal Regulatory Bodies (key functions of the Justice Department and Secret Service); and
- The United States Federal Reserve Bank (the Central Bank).

To better understand how a malicious cyber actor might target the key cyber terrain of these components, we can examine an example of just a single critical function (high-value payment and settlement systems) of the sector's key cyber terrain and its impact on the US economy. In January 2020 the New York Federal Reserve highlighted how a cyber-attack on a major U.S. bank could have a catastrophic impact on the entire U.S. banking system. Given that the banking system is hyperconnected, an attack on the high-value payment and settlement systems presents a "key vulnerability for cyber-attack." If one of the five most active banks suddenly lost access to these systems, the issue would not be isolated to that bank, but would cascade throughout the financial sector. Potentially, payments from one bank moving into the "affected" bank would not be able to move on to other financial institutions, and therefore "by accumulating payments from its counterparties, the attacked institution would soak up liquidity, effectively acting as a liquidity black hole." Consequently, this would have the effect of denying other financial institutions the liquidity they rely on throughout the day in order to facilitate transactions, and would mean that approximately six percent of institutions would not meet their end-of-day reserve threshold (the amount of funds a financial institution must hold in reserve against specified deposit liabilities). Subsequently, the spillover effect of a cyber-attack of this type on one of the five largest banks could be devastating and impact approximately 38 percent of affected banks' assets, excluding the attacked institution. "This reflects the high concentration of payments between large institutions, and the large liquidity imbalances that follow if even one large institution fails to remit payments to its counterparties." This CEMA situation could result in major uncertainty and initiate liquidity hording, similar to what was seen in the 2007-2008 financial crisis. Despite the fact that an individual bank might not be directly affected by the CEMA, that financial institution could still stop sending and receiving liquidity. The Federal Reserve report stated that this scenario would mean a large number of payments will fail to settle "as a consequence of banks' strategic hoarding behavior." The scale of these unsettled payments was estimated to be from one-third to over 2.7 times daily U.S. GDP, or 35 percent of total daily payment value. This example highlights the possible significance CEMA targeting the financial sector could have on the U.S. economy. By defining a threshold of attack on the FSS's key cyber terrain, strategists may better understand how to define those pressure points for which cyber strategies may be designed.

Threshold of Attack Definition for Key Cyber Terrain

Crafting a definition for what constitutes a CINS on the FSS's key cyber terrain must be sufficiently precise to trigger the initiation of cyber operations to defend the nation (both reactively and proactively), while being adequately broad enough to incorporate all the appropriate agencies of the Federal government. One of the reasons why the United States government struggles to synchronize and integrate cyber operations is that they each work under different authorities (or United States Legal Codes/Titles). As stated in earlier chapters, the FBI acts under United States Code Title 18 to conduct operations in Federal Law Enforcement and Counter-Intelligence responsibilities. Regarding cyber operations, the FBI deals primarily with cases of fraud and theft and their threshold for action is clearly specified in the federal statutes of United States Code. The National Security Agency and Central Intelligence agency follow statutes within United States Code Title 50 (amongst others), which describe responsibilities for foreign intelligence operations. The United States Department of Defense falls under Title 10 and is primarily driven by war/combat operations. DoD has been primarily based upon defending against a cyber operation, whether offensive or defensive, that is reasonably expected to cause injury or death to persons or damage or destruction to objects. The Department of Homeland Security operates under United States Code Title 5 and is responsible for the coordination among federal, state, and local governments to advocate for cybersecurity while sharing cyber threat information. Each respective interagency undertakes cyber operations, oftentimes in isolation of the other agencies. Consequently, there exists a "grey area" in thresholds for action that is between criminal activities (LE) and what constitutes a cyber act of war (DoD). There should be some intermediate threshold that allows for United States action short of war that adequately accounts for today cyber realities.

For a holistic national coercive cyber strategy to be effective, a single definition that allows all agencies to jointly operate within established code while also allowing for the integration and synchronization of their respective capabilities and authority is required. The following definition of CINS on the FSS is the threshold for action and allows for joint operations.

The cyber-enabled malicious activity that actually or potentially (a grave imminent threat) results with the intended effect of destroying or debilitating the essential functions of the FSS's key cyber terrain (either singularly or in conjunction with other key pressure points), which would in turn negatively affect the United States economy, national security, and public confidence.

This short-of-war attack definition provides the specificity and significance necessary for joint proactive United States Federal government operations while aligning to each of the United States Code for appropriate actions.[60] In this definition, Law Enforcement, the Military, the Intelligence Community, and DHS can operate within their authorities, but now be focused and unified by one singular CINS definition and mission. Furthermore, because private organizations are the primary entities defined within "key cyber domain," they too are integral to the definition and the strategy. With this definition, one team may operate jointly to ensure the defense and vitality of the United States Financial Services Sector's key cyber terrain for CEMA that rise to the level of CINS (CyberCon Orange and Red).

Credible Capabilities

To be effective, coercive strategies must employ substantial capabilities for which the adversary believes can credibly carry out any deterrent or punitive action.

From the coercer's perspective, those capabilities must span the spectrum of resiliency/redundancy to defense to offensive coercive operations. For the United States, that would include the cyber capabilities of the NSA, DoD, CIA, FBI, Secret Service, and DHS – arguably some of the world's most formidable assets. As noteworthy as the government cyber capabilities are, however, they are not enough for the strategy. Given that private industry owns and operates key cyber terrain along with the Internet backbone that cyber capabilities must traverse, their cyber capabilities also are necessary. Optimally, several technology companies that operate software, routers, and fiber optics capabilities would be essential as well. Furthermore, the Internet Services Providers are critical to carrying out this strategy since they own and operate much of the virtual backbone of the Internet. Private industry possesses exceptional intelligence gathering and response capabilities that round out the government's substantial resources. With a robust partnership of government and private entities focused on one unifying mission, the coercive strategy has the potential to achieve its goals and objectives. Of note, these cyber capabilities already exist within the respective organizations...no new capabilities are required to develop and implement the proposed coercive cyber strategy. Effectively bringing these entities together in way that overcomes the issue of classification of cyber intelligence and capabilities is a hurdle that will be rectified in a later section.

Thresholds and Expected Behavior Clearly Communicated to Would-Be Adversaries

For this coercive strategy to be effective, the threshold for what constitutes unacceptable behavior worthy of a substantive response by the above-mentioned credible capabilities must be clearly communicated publicly to all would-be adversaries. Any CEMA that breaks the law should be investigated and prosecuted by local, state, and federal law enforcement. CINS that crosses, or potentially (clear imminent threat) will cross the threshold of the FSS CINS definition will be investigated and acted upon by the credible joint team described above. Furthermore, both the definition and the existence of the joint cyber team should be publicly communicated around the world so that would-be foes understand the intent and mission of this team. Their known existence contributes to the overall deterrence value of the strategy. Finally, the repercussions of crossing the defined CINS threshold should also be communicated. Specifically, this joint team will defend, disrupt, and defeat any attempt to target the Sector's key cyber terrain. If an adversary attacks the FSS, then the joint cyber team will proactively and legally (International law of state responsibility and principle of non-intervention) strike at the foe's pressure points in a way that imposes substantial consequences in order to return the situation to the status quo ante (countermeasures, retorsion, and sanctions). This proactive cyber action provides the teeth to the strategy.

Political Will

Next, the United States government – more specifically, the President and his Administration – must possess the political will to implement this coercive cyber strategy. As was demonstrated in earlier chapters, political will was often lacking in cases where malicious cyber actors attacked the United States. This book clearly presents numerous cases in recent history in which the United States did not act. Furthermore, state-sponsored cyber thieves absconded with a treasure trove of intellectual property that allowed nations to forego research and development and leap frog to near-peer status with and at the expense of the United States. Political will was lacking because the United States did not possess a clear threshold of attack, did not have the credible cyber team, and did not have a national cyber strategy. With a robust coercive cyber strategy along with the necessary elements, a joint cyber team can train and exercise to demonstrate to the Administration that proactive deterrence and compellence are possible. By repeatedly executing coercive operations, confidence is gained and political will grows. Proving the ability to achieve the desired effects while minimizing collateral damage allows political elites to be reassured and political will to more effectively influence nefarious state and state-sponsored actors in ways that may change the cost/benefit calculus of malicious cyber actors, thus reversing the negative cyber threat trend. Furthermore, by including inducements and factoring the entanglements of the various malicious actors, all the facets of statecraft can be applied to magnify the desired effects, namely, to convince adversaries that launching a cyber-attack would not serve their interests and objectives and that the costs and risks would outweigh any sensible calculation of benefits.

The Foundations of the FSS Coercive Cyber Strategy

To properly implement a national strategy using coercion, the United States must possess the unified operational decision-making organizational structure and processes that allow the government to analyze the global environment, comprehend the actors and issues involved, and then act decisively and appropriately at a pace quicker than the adversary. Only through and by a unified operational organizational structure can the United States, along with the FSS, begin to have the appropriate footing to dominate the enemy. This unified operational structure has been allusive for the United States. However, by dominating the decision cycle (action/reaction cycle between the coercer and the foe) with an effective unified operational cyber organization, the coercer may be able to control the events as they occur rather than be control by them…that can only occur with a new, joint cyber organization.

A successful coercive strategy should not rely on existing cyber organizations' operations centers that operate under independent and different authorities and disciplines. The NSTAC recommended a unified organization should be able to describe mutual priorities and objectives for national protection, prioritization, and/or recovery, and to define the actions, options, authorities, statutory provisions, indemnifications, information flow, waivers, and other processes specific to requesting resources from both government and industry for those circumstances. Having thus defined the United States' priorities and objectives, the organization should be able to identify the key functions and related stakeholders required to support them, and the specific events, conditions, circumstances and/or actions which will serve to trigger the protections defined above.[61]

As was described earlier, the current government cyber architecture is made up of multiple departments and agencies with specific cybersecurity responsibilities. The result is that vulnerabilities can arise in the seams between organizations when one organization presumes another should respond; and functional redundancies can exist across organizations such as during the dissemination of cyber threat intelligence or counter-threat operations. Throughout my research, I participated in several cyber exercises for the financial sector and more broadly for the nation, all of which highlighted this fact. Exercise participants often commented that the United States government cyber organizational structure is complicated and complex, not only from a government point of view, but also from the private industry's perspective.[62] A key observation from the Hamilton Series exercises summed up the United States government cyber response groups this way: "[i]t was unclear what the composition of those groups were [the Cyber Response Group and the UCG], how they interacted to coordinate action with the private sector and what criteria was used by these groups to evaluate actions they may take or resources they bring to bear."[63]

To achieve the necessary unity of effort, the principal United States government cyber organizations should integrate and synchronize their intelligence, law enforcement, economic, security, information, and defense disciplines together in such a way so that a coherent national joint team could develop and execute enemy-dominating plans across the spectrum of action (resiliency/redundancy, defense, coercive diplomacy, and forceful coercion). None of the United States government cyber guidance documents adequately address how to accomplish the fusing and synchronization of government disciplines, let alone integrate them with the private sector. In the physical domain, there are mission areas and teams across the United States government that fused disciplines, capabilities, resources effectively and can provide a template for this coercive cyber strategy.

Notably, Joint Inter-Agency Task Force – South (JIATF South) is one such effective example. Its mission: "JIATF South conducts interagency and international Detection & Monitoring operations and facilitates the interdiction of illicit trafficking and other narco-terrorist threats in support of national and partner nation security. JIATF South is the center of excellence for all-resource fusion and employment of joint, interagency, and international capabilities to eliminate illicit trafficking posing a threat to national security and regional stability."[64] JIATF South fuses the capabilities, resources, and authorities of Customs and Border Patrol, CIA, the Drug Enforcement Agency, DoD, Defense Intelligence Agency, FBI, Immigration and Customs Enforcement, NSA, and the National Geospatial-Intelligence Agency (NGA).[65] The JIATF South model is a proven construct for multi-jurisdictional and multi-disciplinary integration of whole of government for which national cyber integration could emulate. Using JIATF South as a model, a **National Cyber Center** (NCC) should be assembled to be the nucleus of credible United States capabilities for this coercive cyber strategy. Once created, the NCC would need to evolve beyond the JITAF South model to also integrate key private industry partners.

The NCC, a whole of government cyber organizational structure should must fuse government intelligence and actions with private industry cyber situational awareness and activities. Currently United States government cyber entities do work with private industry, but in a limited fashion; consequently, the level of collaboration between public and private sectors has room for improvement. In the 2015 Quantum Dawn 3 financial cyber exercise, the public-private relationship problem was highlighted as an area for improvement. The consensus from exercise participants was the cyber threat intelligence passed to them from the DHS NCIIC was often old, too general to be actionable, and of little value. The recommendations for interactions between firms and the public sector (e.g., government agencies, regulators, law enforcement) included: "Strengthen communication with regulators and government agencies, and raise awareness concerning government resources and capabilities available to assist the Sector; promote information sharing standards and processes to allow market participants to share various cyberattack data, such as threat actors, common vulnerabilities, and mitigation strategies; and establish criteria and thresholds jointly between the private sector, government agencies and regulators, that will be used to trigger contact and action between them."[66]   The necessary first step to achieving the needed public/private partnership as described above is to overcome the classification hurdle mentioned previously.

For the NCC to succeed, the information and capabilities must remain at current Top-Secret level of classification, given the nature and methods used to gain that intelligence. Ensuring all United States government participants are cleared for this classification level is relatively easy and normal. For the private sector, it is more challenging; however, not impossible. Currently, the United States government already grants security clearances to select private partners on a limited basis. For the NCC, this process should be extended to a select set of private cyber experts from each of the Section 9 companies based upon the criticality of their function to national and economic security. In this way, all participants within the NCC would be cleared to same classified information. For those private industry partners within the NCC, they could still pass relevant unclassified information (indicators of compromise (IOCs) and adversary tactics, techniques, and procedures (TTPs)) to their trusted agents back at their parent firm in times of crisis. The exact process and procedures for this dissemination can be worked out, and is not insurmountable.

When presented with this public/private partnership concept during several cyber exercises, private industry partners were supportive but intimated some reservation. The three top concerns are as follows. First, private partners did not want to be openly associated with an organization that conducted offensive operations – they wanted their participation anonymized so as to alleviate any potential concerns their customers and clients might have of such an involvement, especially if those customers were in other countries. Second, because of how Edward Snowden exposed several corporations' sensitive involvement with the NSA (insider data breach in 2013) in the hunt for terrorists' activities, those companies' reputation was damaged. Again, participation must be anonymized with assurance. Third, private corporations are highly regulated and there is fear that if a corporation shared sensitive information about what was occurring in their network, United States government regulators might penalize them for this new-found fact.

To address these concerns, three provisions must be enacted. First, the security clearances must be granted to the private partners without association to the NCC. When the private partners traveled to the NCC, they should do so under concealed pretense (hide the travel to the NCC and use some other reason). There can be no association of the private firm to the NCC when applying for the security clearance. Second, the NCC's network and facility access databases must be segregated (partitioned) off of any other networks and maintained at a classified level. Lessons learned by the NSA's Edward Snowden breach must be applied here to ensure there is no unauthorized access to the data of who has access to and participates in the NCC. Third, government regulators are not permitted within the NCC. Only elements of U.S. government agencies (e.g., Treasury) that are charged with the defense mission can be members of the coercive cyber strategy team. United States governmental leaders must assure their private partners that anything a corporation brings to the discussion, remains confidential and within the NCC team. When private industry partners were presented with these stipulations during the exercises I participated in, each of the private industry participants opined their belief that these additional steps were essential for their company's involvement in the NCC.[67]

For the United States government team members on NCC, there should be additional training to ensure the joint operations are truly joint. Currently, each interagency member only trains, is qualified, and operates within their respective United States Code and Title (i.e., 10, 50, 18, etc.). Typical military members are not permitted to conduct law enforcement actions (with certain exceptions). Similarly, the FBI cannot execute military combat operations. Actions and operations with the NCC would have to be different in order to be effective and overcome existing siloed missions and outcomes. Operations within the NCC must span all the disciplines and Titles of the agencies mentioned. The members of the NCC should, therefore, be able to implement operations seamlessly. Currently United States Air Force Office of Special Investigations (OSI) possesses agents who are trained, qualified, and execute cyber operations under Titles 18 (Law Enforcement), 50 (Intelligence Gathering), and 10 (Military Operations)...one agent covers the spectrum of actions needed to gather intelligence, conduct investigation, make arrest, and if needed, take offensive action. The USAF OSI model is the precedent and benchmark for the necessary training and certification required for all NCC government members.

NCC membership from relevant U.S. government agencies is a point necessary of further clarification. Unlike existing government cyber operations centers where interagency participation is through "Liaisons" sent to that Ops Center (i.e., DHS' NCIIC, FBI's NCIJTF, etc.), NCC would have forces with their full capabilities and authorities deployed to the NCC to conduct joint operations. Although laudable in the conceptual "partnership" and "transparency," existing Ops Centers fall well short of coordinated actions against persistent, sophisticated cyber threats. As an example, membership in the NCC should at a minimum include two United States Cyber Command National Mission Force teams[68] (one for defense and one for offense), elements of USAF OSI Cyber, a detachment of FBI Cyber Division agents, Analysts from NSA and CIA, Agents from the Secret Service Cyber division, United States Treasure Cyber experts, and DHS NCIIC experts. As the NCC matures, members from key U.S. government and international cyber teams should be added to increase cyber capabilities and international legitimacy. Commanding and controlling the NCC should follow the JIATF South model, but with one suggested modification. Given that several U.S. government departments and agencies would be members of the NCC, there should be a rotation of leadership every two years to a have a different U.S. government organization leader head the NCC. The rotation of leadership allows for greater "buy-in" from each organization because they know that they will be afforded an opportunity to lead the team. Additionally, the NCC should take strategic direction from the National Security Staff for overall guidance, but the operational and tactical operations should remain within the NCC structure. Any time-sensitive coercive cyber operations and permission should be orchestrated similarly to how the U.S. Cyber Command operates (Secretary of Defense has authority to approve operations in extremis situations) in accordance with political direction and the national strategy.

Now with the core aspects of the national coercive cyber strategy defined, let us consider how the NCC could manage the seven foundations of a successful coercive strategy: decision cycle dominance, escalation dominance, adversary intelligence, defense, coercion, offense, and strategy assessment. The first step is to ensure the defense and resiliency/redundancy of the FSS's key cyber terrain in order to increase the futility of attacking them. This is one of private industry's principal roles in the NCC. The joint national team must conduct an analysis of the financial sector to properly identify the pressure points within the Section 9 organizations and then "harden" them against exploitation. As was described in previous chapters, NIST provides the framework for what the essential security measures are and must be in place. Furthermore, corporations must ensure the key cyber elements have robust business continuity and disaster response plans established to provide the redundancy and resilience to ensure a graceful degradation of critical functions while providing for rapid restoration when defense fails. Each participating private corporation should join and follow the Sheltered Harbor processes for added resiliency. Sheltered Harbor is the Financial Sector initiative to protect its "customers, financial institutions, and public confidence in the financial system if a catastrophic event like a cyber-attack causes an institution's critical systems - including backups - to fail."[69] The government NCC teammates should help by providing the "Red Teams" to test the defense of the key cyber terrain as the threat would attack them while also providing private partners with the latest classified IOCs and TTPs that threats may use to target those pressure points.

A successful coercive cyber strategy that accurately achieves decision cyber dominance (OODA Loop) is one that effectively develops the procedures and framework for global intelligence gathering, cyber plan development, and cyber operations at the tactical level in a fashion quicker than the adversary. In the timelines of digital battles, that requirement is a challenge. Despite the fact that CINS executes at near light speed, even adversaries must take time to develop their plans and set the conditions where they can execute them. For the NCC, outpacing would-be malicious cyber actors is about establishing repeatable and regular routines that execute pre-developed "playbooks" or can capitalize on pre-existing capabilities and tools that will thwart the adversary's plan and objectives. The regular routines should follow existing operations center protocols like what the United States Air Force employs in its Air Operations Centers (AOCs). Namely, teams that regularly conduct intelligence gathering that then feed other team's planning and execution cycles. AOCs execute iterative procedures that can operate on a near-real time perspective needed when crises arise.

Gathering the necessary adversary intelligence for the NCC's success means developing extensive adversary profiles and maintaining global cyber awareness through every source available (public and private). The key to that success is gathering intelligence and then sifting through it to discover the pertinent data that affects the FSS's key cyber terrain. As good as the NSA, CIA, FBI, and DoD's sources are, they are not enough. With private industry embedded in the JIATF, they can significantly enhance the global cyber intelligence gathering effort. Imagine what the NCC could assemble related to the threat if one could combine the U.S government's cyber picture with what corporate firms were capturing in their network, along with what other cybersecurity firms gathered. Then add in what the technology companies and Internet Service Providers could provide regarding what traversed their networks. This new level of intelligence would be an unparalleled view of the cyber landscape upon which the NCC could gain and maintain cyber situational awareness dominance over the threat. The NCC's intelligence team must be extremely knowledgeable with what the key cyber terrain is and how it works if they are to understand how the threat can exploit that terrain and create CINS.

To create escalation dominance, the NCC must have the command and control structure, routines, and procedures in place that allows for rapid and effective dialogue with senior leaders above the NCC. For national decision-makers within the National Security Staff and private key cyber terrain leaders to make appropriate decisions, the NCC must possess the secure means to quickly present the facts, which include: the nature and target of the CINS, how this event nests within other related global political and economic factors, attribution of threat, and potential response options to disrupt, deny, or defeat that foe. Having preapproved "playbooks" of possible response options not only speeds up the decision timeline, but also instill confidence in the NCC, since those playbooks would become familiar to senior decision-makers over time. Moreover, it is critical to have a designated leader (like the Secretary of Defense) who possesses emergency approval authority for extremis situations where clear and imminent threats do not allow for normal approval routines with the National Security Staff.

NCC cyber response options that align to international law include: working with private firms to bolster defenses of the key cyber terrain; disrupting or defeating the CINS before it commences (proactive defense); coercive diplomacy, sanctions, information/disinformation campaigns and when necessary, offensive operations (virtual or physical) that target the foe's pressure points (forceful coercion). Response options may include private firms in certain situations and with appropriate legal direction (and with indemnification for the firm). Those instances where private corporations may be involved include times when threats use that firm's network, hardware, or software to execute the CINS. In those cases, it is vital to have the partnership of private industry. Furthermore, some response options may only be executed by other United States government entities because they fall outside the purview of the NCC. For example, sanctions or diplomacy would happen through State and Treasury Department protocols. Therefore, the NCC must possess robust relations with other governmental bodies as well. The actual details of how to build and execute cyber response options are beyond the scope of this book and much more is available on that topic from other authors.

The last foundation of the coercive cyber strategy is assessment. For the strategy to be effective and the NCC to mature, the team should continually assess its progress and capture the lessons learned in order to incorporate improvements into their planning, processes, and operations. The assessment must also include an iterative mechanism to determine if and to what extent coercion is working on adversary behavior. A dedicate small team focused on assessments is essential to providing this function.

Conclusions

Although not all-inclusive, this chapter elucidates a national coercive strategy to secure the United States Financial Services Sector from the current cyber storm. This strategy's *aim* is to ensure the defense and vitality of the FSS's key cyber terrain for CEMA that rise to the level of CINS (CyberCon Orange and Red). The *means* would include all the necessary instruments of national power along with credible government and private industry's capability to defend the FSS's key cyber terrain. The *ways* would include gaining and maintaining United States initiative to dominate the adversary's decision cycles, integrate and synchronize cyberspace capabilities (resiliency and redundancy, defense, coercive diplomacy, and forceful coercion) across the whole of nation (which is whole of government alongside whole of private industry) to achieve the stated national aim while working closely with international partners, where needed, to create the effects of futility, counter-productivity, and cost imposition in order to influence malicious cyber actors' decision making, and assess and manage the strategic risk to the nation. For each specific threat to FSS, a distinct and deliberate plan must be constructed and executed to coerce that adversary…there are no cookie-cutter approaches. With a coercive strategy such as articulate above, the United States could more effectively protect one of its core sovereign functions – its financial sector – which in turn would help protect the nation's economic and national security. Although focused just one sector of U.S critical infrastructure, this coercive strategy is modifiable and applicable to all sectors…and applicable to other likeminded nations.

---

[1] Barack Obama," 2013 Executive Order - Improving Critical Infrastructure Cybersecurity," (The White House, Washington DC, Feb 12, 2013), found at: https://www.whitehouse.gov/the-press-office/2013/02/12/executive-order-improving-critical-infrastructure-cybersecurity.

[2] Stephen E. Flynn, "America the Vulnerable," *Foreign Affairs*, January/February Issue, found at: https://www.foreignaffairs.com/articles/2002-01-01/america-vulnerable.

[3] Jim Talent and Honorable Jon Kyl, "A Strong and Focused National Security Strategy," *National Security and Defense*, Special Report #135, Oct 31, 2013, found at: http://www.heritage.org/research/reports/2013/10/a-strong-and-focused-national-security-strategy.

[4] Ibid.

[5] Mandiant, "M-Trends Beyond the Breach," (Mandiant – A FireEye Company, 2014), pg. 2, found at: https://dl.mandiant.com/EE/library/WP_M-Trends2014_140409.pdf.

[6] Deloitte, "Transforming Cybersecurity: New approaches for an evolving threat landscape," (Deloitte Center for Financial Cybersecurity, 2014), pg. 3, found at: http://www2.deloitte.com/content/dam/Deloitte/global/Documents/Financial-Services/dttl-fsi-TransformingCybersecurity-2014-02.pdf.

[7] Colin S. Gray, "Strategy is Difficult," in *Joint Forces Quarterly*, Summer 1999 (Air University Press, AL), pg. 7, found at: http://www.au.af.mil/au/awc/awcgate/jfq/1434.pdf.

[8] Ibid, pg. 9.

[9] Ibid, pg. 10.

[10] For more on military operational design, see the Department of Defense, Joint Staff J-7, *Planer's Handbook for Operational Design*, Version 1.0, (Joint Staff J-7, Suffolk, VA, Oct 7, 2011), found at: http://www.dtic.mil/doctrine/doctrine/jwfc/opdesign_hbk.pdf.

[11] "Financial Services Sector-Specific Plan 2015," (Financial Services Sector Coordinating Council and the Financial and Banking Information Infrastructure Committee in coordination with the Department of Treasury and the Department of Homeland Security), pg. vii, found at: https://www.dhs.gov/sites/default/files/publications/nipp-ssp-financial-services-2015-508.pdf.

[12] The Department of Homeland Security website, "Financial Services Sector," accessed 9 Apr 2016, found at: https://www.dhs.gov/financial-services-sector.

[13] Kate Fazzini, "Power outages, bank runs, changed financial data: Here are the 'cyber 9/11' scenarios that really worry the experts," CNBC Markets Online, Nov 18, 2018, found at:

https://www.cnbc.com/2018/11/18/cyber-911-scenarios-power-outages-bank-runs-changed-data.html.

[14] For more information on how money is transferred in the FS sector, see the Federal Reserve Bank of New York, "Liberty Street Economics," Aug 12, 2012, accessed 9 Apr 2016, found at: http://libertystreeteconomics.newyorkfed.org/2012/08/intraday-liquidity-flows.html#.Vwl3aZUo7j0.

[15] Ibid.

[16] Mandiant, "M-Trends Beyond the Breach," (Mandiant – A FireEye Company, 2014), pg. 1, found at: https://dl.mandiant.com/EE/library/WP_M-Trends2014_140409.pdf.

[17] Charles W. Scharf, Foreword in "Navigating the Digital Age," Matt Rosenquist, ed., (Georgia Tech University, Institute of Information Security and Privacy, sponsored by Paloalto Networks, Oct 2015), pg. v.

[18] Waqas, "Anonymous Starts Operation Black October To Target Banking Sector," *Hackread: Security is a Myth*, Oct 7, 2015, accessed 9 Apr 2016, found at: https://www.hackread.com/anonymous-operation-black-october-against-banks/.

[19] Mandiant, "M-Trends," pg. 1.

[20] Swati Khandelwal, "Here's How Hacker Stole $80 Million from Bangladesh Bank," *The Hacker News*, Mar 14, 2106, accessed online 9 Apr 2016, found at: http://thehackernews.com/2016/03/bank-hacking-malware.html.

[21] Marcie Geffner, "Hacker attack! Could bank hackers steal your money?" *Bankrate.com,* Feb 19, 2016, accessed online 9 Apr 2016, found at: http://www.bankrate.com/finance/savings/could-bank-hackers-steal-your-money-1.aspx.

[22] Reuters News, "Bank of Chile trading down after hackers rob millions in cyberattack," Jun 11, 2018, found at: https://www.reuters.com/article/us-chile-banks-cyberattack/bank-of-chile-trading-down-after-hackers-rob-millions-in-cyberattack-idUSKBN1J72FC.

[23] Mandiant, "M-trends," pg. 12.

[24] Ernst and Young, LLC., "Cyber threat intelligence – how to get ahead of cybercrime," Nov 2014, pg. 2, found at: http://www.ey.com/Publication/vwLUAssets/EY-cyber-threat-intelligence-how-to-get-ahead-of-cybercrime/$FILE/EY-cyber-threat-intelligence-how-to-get-ahead-of-cybercrime.pdf.

[25] The Information Protection & Recovery Company International, "Top IT Security Threats Facing Financial Institutions in 2015," *IPRSecure.com*, accessed online 9 Apr 2016, found at: http://iprsecure.com/top-it-security-threats-facing-financial-institutions-in-2015.

[26] Ibid.

[27] The Dark Web is a term that refers specifically to a collection of websites that are publicly visible, but hide the IP addresses of the servers that run them. Thus, they can be visited by any web user, but it is very difficult to work out who is behind the sites. And you cannot find these sites using search engines. Almost all sites on the so-called Dark Web hide their identity using the Tor (The Onion Router) encryption tool. See Matt Egan, "What is the Dark Web? How to access the Dark Web. What's the difference between the Dark Web and the Deep Web?" *PC Advisor*, Mar 3, 2016, accessed online 9 Apr 2016, found at: http://www.pcadvisor.co.uk/how-to/internet/what-is-dark-web-how-access-dark-web-deep-joc-3593569/.

[28] For more information, see Julia Carpenter and Bourree Lam, "The Capital One Hack: Life in the Time of Breach Fatigue," *The Wall Street Journal*, Aug 4, 2019, found on-line at : https://www.wsj.com/articles/the-capital-one-hack-life-in-the-time-of-breach-fatigue-11564824600.

[29] Ernst and Young, pp. 2-3.

[30] Ernst and Young, pg. 3.

[31] PwC, "Turnaround and transformation in cybersecurity: Financial services," 2015, found at: www.pwc.com/gsiss.

[32] Ibid.

[33] PwC, "Turnaround and transformation in cybersecurity: Financial services."

[34] Ibid.

[35] Bhakti Mirchandani, *Forbes Magazine*, "Laughing All The Way To The Bank: Cybercriminals Targeting United States Financial Institutions," Aug 28, 2018, found at: https://www.forbes.com/sites/bhaktimirchandani/2018/08/28/laughing-all-the-way-to-the-bank-cybercriminals-targeting-us-financial-institutions/#5e342bf46e90.

[36] "2013 Cost of Cyber Crime Study: United States," Ponemon Institute (sponsored by HP Enterprise Security), October 2013.

[37] "2012 Cost of Cyber Crime Study: United States," Ponemon Institute (sponsored by HP Enterprise Security), October 2012.

[38] Deloitte, pg. 1.

[39] Ibid, pg. 5.

[40] Ibid.

[41] Ernst and Young, pg. 4.

[42] PwC, "Turnaround and transformation in cybersecurity: Financial services."

[43] Based upon the "Ninth Annual Cost of Cybercrime Study," conducted jointly by Accenture and the Ponemon Institute, LLC, Chris Thompson, "What will cybercrime cost your financial firm?" July 15, 2019, found on-line at: https://www.accenture.com/us-en/insights/financial-services/cost-cybercrime-study-financial-services.

[44] Ibid.

[45] *Financial Services Sector-Specific Plan 2015*, (Financial Services Sector Coordinating Council (FSSCC) and Financial and Banking Information Infrastructure Committee (FBIIC), 2015), pg. 3, found at: https://www.dhs.gov/sites/default/files/publications/nipp-ssp-financial-services-2015-508.pdf .

[46] Ibid, pg. 3.

[47] Ibid, pg. 3.

[48] These generalize observations and recommendations are consolidated from three Hamilton Series and three Quantum Dawn financial sector exercises.

[49] Ibid.

[50] Author's interview with FS-ISAC President Bill Nelson on May 6, 2015 in Reston, VA.

[51] For more on the Sherman Anti-Trust Act see: the Federal Trade Commission website at : https://www.ftc.gov/tips-advice/competition-guidance/guide-antitrust-laws/antitrust-laws .

[52] For more on Sarbanes-Oxley Act of 2002 see: http://www.soxlaw.com/.

[53] Barack Obama, PPD-21.

[54] Ibid.

[55] For more information on the Cyber College Wargame, see "Cyber Wargame 2015 and 2016 for the Air Force Cyber College After Action Reports", filed on record at the Air Force's Wargaming Institute at Maxwell AFB, AL.

[56] This was one of the primary observations of the Cyber College Wargaming Series and was reiterated to the author by several senior leaders during the course of interviews undertaken for this book.

[57] Department of the Treasury, "Report to the President on Cybersecurity Incentives Pursuant to Executive Order 13636," pg. 5, found at: https://www.treasury.gov/press-center/Documents/Supporting%20Analysis%20Treasury%20Report%20to%20the%20President%20on%20Cybersecurity%20Incentives_FINAL.pdf.

[58] EO 13636, Section 9 institutions are not publicly defined given the sensitive nature of their import to the United States economy. The individual institutions are told by the United States government, but are told not to disclose that information.

[59] See EO 13800 at: https://www.dhs.gov/sites/default/files/publications/EO-13800-Section-9-Report-Summary-20180508-508.pdf.

[60] This definition was "socialized" with legal teams from the NSA, DoD, United States Cyber Command, Treasury, Secret Service, and DHS…and in every case, each legal team supported the sufficiency of the wording to allow for their respective organization to act in accordance with United States Code. Further, this definition was used in the two USAF Cyber War Games to exercise this strategy.

[61] NSTAC Report, pg. ES-4.

[62] Paraphrased observations from exercise participants, "USAF Cyber Wargame 2015 for the Air Force Cyber College," 2 Nov 2015.

[63] Hamilton Alliance, "Hamilton Alliance After Action Report," Dec 9, 2014, pg.13.

[64] See Joint Inter-Agency Task Force – South website at: http://www.jiatfs.southcom.mil/index.aspx.

[65] Ibid.

[66] Deloitte & Touche, working with SIFMA, "Standing together for financial industry cyber resilience Quantum Dawn 3 after-action report," Nov 23, 2015, slide 8, found at: http://www.sifma.org/uploadedfiles/services/bcp/quantumdawn-3-after-action-report.pdf?n=07980.

[67] Private industry partners participation in the JIATF-C was a theme raised repeatedly in the Hamilton Series Exercises and the Cyber War Games in which this authored played. Through several exercises and months of discussion with key corporate leaders, these stipulations were worked out as suitable measures to protect corporate involvement. Furthermore, government leaders who participated were confident that the information provided to the JIATF-C team by private firms would be held in confidence and not passed to their regulator counterparts in their organization.

[68] "The cyber mission force is Cybercom's action arm, and its teams execute the command's mission to direct, synchronize and coordinate cyberspace operations in defense of the nation's interests. Cyber national mission teams defend the nation by identifying adversary activity, blocking attacked and maneuvering to defeat them. The cyber national mission force plans, directs and synchronizes full-spectrum cyberspace operations to deter, disrupt and if necessary, defeat adversary cyber actors to defend the nation." See: Department of Defense News, "Cyber Mission Force Achieves Full Operational Capability," May 17, 2018, found at: https://dod.defense.gov/News/Article/Article/1524747/cyber-mission-force-achieves-full-operational-capability/.

[69] More than 100 FS institutions participate on a regular basis, to make a copy of the consumer's account data in a standard format, which enables the restoration of accounts in the event of a major outage. The account data is archived in a secure data vault that is protected from alteration or deletion. The data will stay intact and accessible if needed — exactly as when it was archived. All participating institutions update their adherence reviews to ensure that the Sheltered Harbor standards are exercised consistently and in accordance with Sheltered Harbor specifications. For more on Sheltered Harbor, see: https://shelteredharbor.org/about.

CHAPTER SEVEN

CONFRONTING THE CYBER STORM

Conclusions

This book helps to explain the complexities surrounding national cybersecurity and coercion in the virtual domain. The ever-evolving cybersecurity threat landscape is complex and presents substantial challenges to the United States and other modern nations. Cyber-enabled malicious activities directed at national critical infrastructure has already occurred across the globe and with varying degrees of success. Both academics and policymakers alike have struggled over the past decades to adequately understand and apply traditional political and military concepts in an effort to solve the national problem of how to secure the country's critical infrastructure against CEMA and conflict in and through cyberspace. Despite the shortage of empirical evidence surrounding CINS, this book demonstrates that coercion is relevant and is an essential element to a definitive solution to confronting the cyber storm that the United States faces. Furthermore, this monograph shows how and when policymakers may use coercion in the development of a national cybersecurity strategy to influence adversaries and events at the global level.

CEMA and CINS are likely to continue at an increasing frequency if nothing different is done to thwart their threat. For being such a technically advanced nation, it is disappointing to see how unprepared the United States is to contend with cyber threats. Despite the emphasis by numerous Presidential Administrations, the Federal government has done little to actually curb the cyber threat trend over the last three decades. Throughout my research on cybersecurity strategy development, it was evident that a significant shift in the conceptual approach to national strategy is required to alter the paradigm of United States national cyber policy making, organizational archetypes, and cyber operations. Now, not only is the United States' critical infrastructure being threatened by state and state-sponsored threats, but also our democratic electoral processes as was evident in the 2016 and 2018 national elections.

The evidence presented in this book clearly demonstrates that the United States does not adequately use coercion to influence malicious cyber actors who threaten the United States' economic and national security due to three primary reasons: the United States does not possess the necessary political will; the United States has a dearth of national cybersecurity strategy; and the United States lacks an effective cybersecurity organization/framework to integrate and synchronize all of the government disciplines together with the vital private critical infrastructure owners and operators. If a nation is to be successful in the application of coercion as part of the effective defense of its critical infrastructure, then it must manage all three deficiencies. Through exhaustive research, I present solutions to the decades-old quandary of when and how the Federal government should act against cyber threats at the upper end of the spectrum. Now there is a feasible concept for how the United States can use a coercive strategy to influence the decision making of state or state-sponsored malicious cyber actors in instances of CINS.

Technology is important, and yet there is no silver bullet to fighting the global cyber threat. To effectively develop a national coercive cyber strategy, United States policymakers must have an understanding of the domain, use a common and accurate vernacular to describe the malicious cyber events, comprehend the context of playing field and players, and the recognize the nuances of cyber competition on the global stage. Concepts – more importantly – properly applied concepts of political power—matter more in national-level cybersecurity strategy development and implementation than does the technology used to defend, deter, dissuade, and defeat a potential cyber foe.

The last decade witnessed an evolution of thought on the subject of national cybersecurity along with a growing desire to see an improvement in the relationship and partnership between public and private leaders responsible for protecting national critical infrastructure. The concepts and strategy presented in this book represent a quantum leap in defining a more mature and effective public-private partnership for national cybersecurity for this decade. In fact, throughout the socialization of the concepts in this book across the financial, energy, telecommunications, technology and retails sectors of United States critical infrastructure, I witnessed significant public and private enthusiasm for this concept, its organizational structure, and coercive strategy. Public-private partnerships are critical to any effective ability to impose consequences on malicious cyber actors and defend the nation in the virtual domain. Now is the time to apply the lessons and concepts of this book to change the United States' approach to defending its critical infrastructure and securing its future. U.S. national leaders must transform their thinking on cyber defense and coercion if the United States is to remain the global leader and adequately protect its citizenry. The United States (and every nation) has the obligation to effectively ensure the continued functioning of its society – in and through every domain. Furthermore, success in national cybersecurity cannot occur just by one nation…it is a global effort…an effort that must align like-minded countries in concept and action in order to curb the growing cyber storm.

Major Findings

Words matter. A proper vernacular expresses the abstract by defining its context, meaning, and background. "The power and meaning of labels come not only from the choice of words but also from how those words are said."[1] Too often, media portrays CEMA as something more significant than what it really is, through use of words that do little to convey the true sense of the situation. For example, the use of "cyber war" by the media and authors in situations that are not actual a cyber war desensitizes the public and inaccurately conveys the realities of the situation. No doubt, a useful lexicon should describe a spectrum of malicious activity so that students, policymakers, and practitioners may explain where CINS fits as a part of a broader explanation of conflict. It is also important to point out that CEMA and CINS, in almost all cases, is not war...but so too is it not peace. The proper vernacular is critical to understand the domain, the actors, and their motives, as well as to develop a national coercive cyber strategy.

Effective cybersecurity at the national level is extremely complex. Breaking down the nature of national cybersecurity highlights the fact that there are multiple actors involved, to include private entities and corporations, and a plethora of government agencies and departments. These entities have varying (and sometimes competing) interests, capabilities, responsibilities, authorities and jurisdictions. Additionally, there are wide array of threats with contrasting goals/objectives, capabilities, and means. Further, given the relatively new and markedly different domain of cyberspace, traditional notions of physical defense and deterrence are not always easily understood or applicable in the virtual domain, and therefore, not implemented. Additionally, if legislators or governmental leaders are waiting for a catastrophic cyber 9/11 before they act, the nation will have already lost its initiative, as it will be too late to begin the actions necessary to secure the United States' critical infrastructure…let alone develop a national coercive cyber strategy. Now is the time to apply the necessary intellectual capital to define the objectives, concepts, and capabilities of a cyber strategy that will outpace the ever-growing cyber threat and protect the nation's future from cyber-attacks.

CEMA is growing in significance and sophistication. The nature and impact of CEMA and CINS have and are evolving, largely because the cyber threat goes unchecked and there is the growing lure of enormous profits from cyber-crime. That cyber threat continually reinvests its financial gains in itself, while growing in capability to be able to penetrate any network and gaining access to unauthorized data and technology to achieve the desired effects of the malicious cyber masters. This book's analysis and strategy definitively describe how the United States should progress to curb that threat.

Cyber defense is largely civilian focused. As a result of the current United States government's paradigm of relegating cyber defense of United States critical infrastructure to private entities, corporate America is left dealing with and defending against CEMA and CINS. Those private industries and critical infrastructure operators are not postured fiscally or legally to contend with those threats. There is little a private corporation or entity can do to impose consequences on or deter malicious cyber actors. They are largely defensive in nature, reacting to cyber threats because of their limited authority to wage counterattacks in the international arena (the business of governments), beholding to the government to offensively create problems for malicious cyber actors and enforce laws. The United States Government, in turn, should not have a defensive-only mindset for national cybersecurity and, furthermore, should not relegate that effort to the private entities responsible for securing United States critical infrastructure. The imposition of consequences (e.g., law enforcement, counter-espionage, or offensive cyber actions) remains the purview of governments.

Insufficient consequences for malicious cyber actors. For various reasons, the United States has done little to influence malicious cyber actions. To date, the greatest contributions to curbing the threat have come from Federal law enforcement, which have largely been in the form of indictments. Those indictments infrequently lead to arrests, since most indicted malicious cyber actors remain at-large today because United States' jurisdiction does not reach into the necessary countries. The U.S. struggles to gain assistance from states that sponsor malicious cyber actors. Currently, there is insufficient deterrence against, and consequences for, malicious cyber actors given that even law enforcement cannot prosecute them. However, there exists far greater cyber capability within the Federal government (beyond law enforcement) that may be brought to bear to alter the malicious cyber actors' nefarious actions. To be effective, the United States must go beyond law enforcement operations.

There is a threshold for Federal Government cyber involvement and leadership. Despite the past inactivity and lack of political will by the United States related to national cybersecurity, there is a responsibility to ensure the proper functioning of its society and critical infrastructure. In fact, international law provides the United States with the clarity for its responsibility to act in cases of CINS. The international law of non-intervention specifies that every nation possesses the right and obligation to protect its citizens and the functioning of essential societal activities (such as critical infrastructure) against any other state's illegal interference in those functions. The threshold for action presented in this book defines when the United States should and can proactively respond to any nation or entity that plans to deliberately cross that threshold. Therefore, when it is probable that an adversary intends to deliberately and substantially interfere in, degrade, deny or destroy the nation's ability to provide for an essential societal function, the Federal government must proactively defend against and ensure such actions do not occur…and if those actions do occur, then take necessary actions to restore the status quo ante through all legally acceptable means (e.g., countermeasures, retorsions, and sanctions).

Coercion has a place in national cyber strategy. Coercion is the use of threats or punishments directed at the adversary's strategy and/or pressure points along with inducement to influence his decision making. The case studies presented demonstrate that CEMA directed at a target state can pressure and/or manipulate that state's leadership's decision making. Coercion is about influence and it can occur in the virtual domain just as it does in the physical. To implement coercion adequately as part of a national cyber strategy, strategists and policymakers should comprehend and properly implement all nine elements of coercion: national political strategy, actors involved, interests at stake and risks, credible capabilities, pressure points, thresholds and expected behavioral changes clearly communicated, will, inducements, and entanglements. Furthermore, a successful coercive cyber strategy should take a multidimensional approach by considering the seven foundations of a successful coercive strategy: decision cycle dominance, escalation dominance, adversary intelligence, defense, coercion, offense, and strategy assessment. This book explicitly defines each of the elements and foundations to show how coercion may be applied, albeit with varying levels of effectiveness depending on the situation.

There are limits to the use of coercion in state-on-state conflict. My research also elucidates the current realities and limitations of coercion in recent cases of CINS to influence national decision makers. In the cases presented, coercion was used to degrade a target's national critical infrastructure and the target's ability to cope was often ill-prepared and/or ill-equipped. The cases also highlight that rarely did coercion actually compel the target to acquiesce, largely because the contextual circumstances of the conflict did not escalate the CEMA to a point where compellence would occur. Past CINS have been designed to steer politics, propel agendas, and gain competitive advantage/economic power by targeting the nation's critical infrastructure, such as banking, communications, power, and government services. If an adversary is able to gain the right access to a state's critical infrastructure, that foe may then influence how the victim state may act or respond in an international situation. This is especially true when an aggressor state has an advantage of possessing sophisticated cyber capabilities or there are significant vulnerabilities within a protagonist's critical infrastructure.

CINS may be used to limit escalation or it may be a prelude to physical war. In the case studies presented, there are two broad conclusions we may draw with regard to escalation or de-escalation of conflict. In some cases, the protagonists used CEMA as part of a larger clandestine campaign whereby they revealed their cyber prowess along with their intentions in an effort to manage the conflict. In these cases (Estonia and China), the attacker used CEMA for espionage and to message the target state. Similarly, Stuxnet is another clear example and message to the world demonstrating what a powerful nation or group is capable of, as a warning to all who might challenge it.[2] In these cases, the coercer limited CEMA to ensure the events did not escalate or cross the physical threshold of an act of war (equal to an armed attack or use of force). This use of CEMA below the threshold of war represents the vast majority of the CEMA that targets national critical infrastructure as witnessed over the last three decades, and it points to the likelihood that malicious cyber actors will continue to operate this way in the virtual domain.

Alternatively, in two other case studies (Georgia and Ukraine), the cyber conflict was a prelude to conflict in the physical domain. In extremis situations, CEMO may be executed prior to and during a physical conflict in which a target state possesses the modern, sophisticated weapons and infrastructure that are vulnerable to cyber-attack. Hybrid warfare, as the Russians label it, allows the attacker the synergistic effects of degradation and destructions of key targets simultaneously in the virtual and physical domains. Hybrid warfare will likely be the future of modern warfare. Consequently, the presence of nefarious state-sponsored cyber actors in the United States' critical infrastructure portends a grave imminent threat, which if not rectified, could produce a significant leverage against the United States in future conflicts.

Coercion in cyberspace is more effective when used along with other instruments of national power. The case studies also highlight the fact that strategy is more effective when multiple instruments of statecraft (military, information, diplomatic and economic) are combined to coerce would-be foes. In the Estonia case, Russia could not have pressured Estonia with just ethnic riots and was not likely to escalate the tensions by resorting to military force without fear of NATO invoking Article V of the NATO treaty (escalation to war). Consequently, CEMA was used to pressure Estonia leadership without external physical force. In the Georgia and Ukraine cases, Russia could have achieved its objectives without CEMA given its overwhelming military might compared to Georgia or Ukraine. However, by using CEMA in conjunction with military force (and sometimes unilaterally), Russia achieved improved effects by synchronizing and integrating virtual and physical effects against its adversaries while ensuring attainment of its objectives, which included controlling the international narrative to downplay its aggression in those two countries. CEMA was not always necessary, but proved advantageous in achieving national objectives. In the Chinese cyber-espionage case, it would have been exponentially more difficult to rely solely on human intelligence (physically gaining access to American facilities and stealing the documents) to achieve its espionage goals. CEMA continues to be an invaluable method for extracting terabytes of data with ease and over a prolonged period of time. Finally, in the Stuxnet case, the perpetrators could have attempted a military air strike to achieve a delaying effect on Iran's nuclear enrichment operation; however, that may have escalated tensions in the region to the point of military hostilities and war.

Using CEMA as the means and method provided an alternative way of achieving the perpetrator's goal in a less aggressive fashion while denying attribution (at least making attribution ambiguous).

Coercive cyber strategies require private partners. State-on-state conflict does not often include private corporations; however, conflicts in cyberspace show just how critical partnerships with private critical infrastructure operators and cybersecurity entities can be. Even sophisticated cyber nations must rely on the corporations under attack as well as private cybersecurity firms to fully understand what is occurring in the virtual domain and how to contend effectively with the CEMA. Conflict in cyberspace, unlike the physical domain, will rely upon the public-private partnership to achieve national success. Effective national cybersecurity is not possible without that partnership with private industry…as good as United States' national cyber capabilities are, national cyber organizations still cannot see into private corporate cyber landscapes, and therefore, they need the assistance of private partnership to build the requisite cyber situational awareness to anticipate and proactive respond to sophisticated cyber threats that threaten CINS. It behooves the United States to embrace this reality fully and create the habitual relationships with private industry necessary to succeed in future cyber conflicts.

Recommendations

To resolve the current national cybersecurity enigma and secure the United States' future, the Federal government must develop a comprehensive coercive cyber strategy to impose consequences on the malicious cyber actors. In the current security paradigm, there is very little deterrence that would reduce the frequency and impact of today's CEMA trend. We cannot block all credible attacks on our critical infrastructure…we must convince malicious actors to choose to abandon their opportunity to attack. This reality of the current cyber archetype necessitates a change in perspective, lexicon, and strategies for cyber conflict. No matter how well critical infrastructure owners and operators build their organization's defensive cyber perimeter (network architecture and cybersecurity protocols), malicious cyber actors will discover new ways to exploit vulnerabilities. Therefore, innovative strategies and organizations must be created to thwart the malicious cyber actors' strategies and means of attacking the United States' key critical infrastructure cyber terrain while simultaneously influencing adversary decision making in such a way as to induce a change in their behavior.

The Path to Confronting the Cyber Storm and Securing the Nation's Future

Shape the National Cyber Dialogue – The United States must take positive steps to properly quantify the cyber threat in terms of impact on national and economic security, and then define a course for America that is free from negative influence of foreign threat actors. As was highlighted in Chapter Four, disinformation campaigns have been effective at shaping national narratives in favor of foreign actors. As more facts are uncovered related to Russian social media successes to influence the 2016 U.S. presidential election and other national dialogues, more aspects of Russia's approach to its disinformation campaigns are coming to light. A steady flow of new disclosures is revealing a complex combination of "hacking, public disclosures of private emails, and use of bots, trolls, and targeted advertising on social media designed to interfere in political processes and heighten societal tensions."[3] Consequently to control the national cyber narrative and shape it in a way that benefits America, the United States must first acknowledge that it exists, then develop a 'metric of damage that acknowledges a range of objectives', and finally work with tech and social media companies to denounce the false narrative and set the facts straight.[4]

Focus on a Unifying Vision – Embrace the United States government's obligation and leading role in national cybersecurity as the foundational responsibility to its citizenry. The opening lines of the United States Constitution state: "We the People of the United States, in Order to form a more perfect Union, establish Justice, insure domestic Tranquility, provide for the common defence [sic], promote the general Welfare, and secure the Blessings of Liberty to ourselves and our Posterity…"[5] Although our Founding Fathers did not envision the virtual domain, they nonetheless understood the need to protect the nation against adversaries, both foreign and domestic. National cybersecurity is a twenty-first century phenomenon that necessitates the Federal government provide for the common defense, promote general welfare, and secure the blessing of liberty. Consequently, only the Federal government (President and Congress) can put forth a unifying vision to effectively secure the United States from CINS. Furthermore, the unifying vision should embrace coercion as part of the development of a national cyber strategy. The President and Congress must unite public and private stakeholders in both vision and strategy development.

Establish a National Operational Cyber Center. Both the President (through policy) and the Congress (through the Legislation) should establish a National Cyber Center (NCC) under the single leadership of one department (rotated bi-annually between Departments) along with the necessary capabilities and authorities of all the appropriate Departments and Agencies of the United States government (e.g., DHS, FBI, DoD, NSA, CIA, State, Treasury, Secret Service, etc.). Joint Interagency Task Force – South (JIATF-South) provides an existing precedent for how best to organize for interagency operations. As in JIATF-South, the NCC would have each departmental and agency "deploy" with the full complement of their cyber capabilities, authorities, and resources to operate within a single unified mission to develop and implement the strategy necessary to secure the United States' critical infrastructure from CEMA. Finally, it is imperative that the NCC be a new stand-alone entity (drawn from existing cyber capabilities), outside of existing USG departments or agencies' cyber organizations in order to establish a neutral and non-bias operating environment in which the USG organizations would contribute equally. Placing the NCC under an existing government cyber organization would bias and limit the NCC's potential for success.

Ratify essential authorities. Congress must ratify the necessary authorities in NCC to ensure the task force's mandate remains within international law and that NCC possesses the necessary emergency powers to act quickly and decisively against "grave imminent threats" that intend to degrade, deny, or destroy United States critical infrastructure. Additionally, it is recommended that NCC develop, ratify, and publish cyber vernacular and attack definitions as described in this book in an effort to standardize the lexicon of cyber-enabled malicious activity. Through a standardized vernacular will come a greater acceptance of the ways to discuss actions and responses in and through the virtual domain. Finally, Congress should work to declassify cyber threat intelligence (as the Israelis do) while still protecting sources and methods, so that more timely cyber intelligence may be shared with private industry and the United States public.

Incentivize a robust and collaborative public/private partnership. Success in the virtual domain can only occur through a robust public-private partnership. In order to instill trust between partners, private industry must be afforded the protection, anonymity, and indemnification for their participation in NCC. Specifically, cyber intelligence that private partners bring to NCC must be protected from regulatory oversight, scrutiny, and fines. Currently, when governmental regulators observe vulnerabilities within private industry networks, regulators are quick to enforce expensive fines and remediation efforts at a pace private industry struggles to keep up with. Yet it is these private industry vulnerabilities and subsequent exploitative activities by malicious cyber actors that must be shared with the NCC in real-time to allow for the NCC's exploitation of the threat and the development of a coercive cyber campaign to defend United States critical infrastructure. Therefore, the Federal government must incentivize private participation through formal agreements with and fiscal incentives for critical infrastructure owners and operators. Moreover, knowing that not all cyber threat intelligence may be declassified, private partners must be allowed to earn Top Secret clearances to participate in NCC intelligence gathering activities so that they may observe real-time cyber threat intelligence and help understand the threat's intentions. Although private industry will not be able to share the classified intelligence with their company, they can pass more timely redacted unclassified information with better context of the threat, which is far better than what the United States government now shares. Through this new trust-based partnership, private industry may better understand the threat, proactively harden their networks against attacks, and then assist with the required unity of action to secure the critical infrastructure.

Fully develop and execute a global, coercive cyber campaign. A national coercive strategy to defend the United States Critical Infrastructure Sectors must be developed and implemented as soon as possible. This strategy's *aim* is to ensure the defense and vitality of the Critical Infrastructure Sector's key cyber terrain from CINS (CyberCon Orange and Red). The *means* would include all the necessary instruments of national power along with credible government and private industry's capability to defend the critical infrastructure's key cyber terrain. The *ways* would include gaining and maintaining United States initiative to dominate the adversary's decision cycles, integrate and synchronize cyberspace capabilities (resiliency and redundancy, defense, coercive diplomacy, and forceful coercion) across the whole of nation to create the effects of futility, counter-productivity, and cost imposition in order to influence malicious cyber actors' decision making, and assess and manage the strategic risk to the nation. To be effective, coercive strategies must focus on influencing the decision-maker leading the CINS. As my research elucidates, coercion should not be directed at organizations, but rather at the key humans behind the nefarious actions. Their minds are the targets. Furthermore, a coercive cyber strategy must also consider options and actions in the physical domain to be fully effective. Understanding what those malicious decision makers value forms a list of targets against which the United States may apply pressure. Finally, for each specific threat, a distinct and new plan must be constructed and executed to coerce that adversary. The Financial Services Sector strategy example provides the modern nation with an effectively template to properly secure its core sovereign functions, which in turn would help ensure the nation's future.

Establish key international allies in which to partner and execute the coercive strategy. No one nation alone can effectively coerce and reduce the global cyber threats present today. Therefore, the United States must engage its allies and partners to develop and implement similar strategies, organizational constructs, and capabilities in order to work in unison with the United States to thwart the sophisticated and complex foes who operate in and through the virtual domain. International law and governing bodies must be leveraged to help perpetuate acceptable international norms and behaviors, along with the lawfully appropriate responses to illicit cyber activities. Furthermore, partnerships with entities such at the United Nations, Interpol, and European Union would also be necessary to expand the coercive strategies against malicious cyber actors and to propagate the legitimacy of the cybersecurity strategy.

Further Research

The modelling of the coercive cyber effects directed at decision-makers is an area ripe for additional research. Although there has been a great number of cyber exercises and war-games conducted on the subject of national cybersecurity over the last decade, they do not dive deeply into the psychological effects of coercion on the humans involved. Further research is needed to more accurately determine the mental machinations decision makers undertake when coercion is used against them in and through the virtual domain, especially in cases of CINS. Early work in deterrence and coercion relied on game theory to forecast responses. Now, more research must be conducted to shed light on how the actions and responses of national-level political competition would play out on human behavior when cyber is the leading or primary method of influence.

Another area of further required research falls in the category of political control and direction for national cyber actions as described in this book. For the physical defense of the nation, there are extensive organizational structures and processes in place. Much has been written on that subject, both about conventional and nuclear command and control. The subject is well researched and is not debated, in part because physical defense of the nation is implemented primarily by just the Federal government (DoD and DHS with support from a few other agencies). Conversely, for national cybersecurity command and control with the vast number of United States government departments and agencies that have responsibilities in the virtual domain, plus the need to incorporate the private owners and operators of United States critical infrastructure, the command and control structure and procedures are complex and complicated…and have not been fully debated. I believe that an entire book could be devoted to flushing out the issues, challenges, and suggestions for national-level decision-making along with the execution of coercive cyber operations across the Federal government. As was presented earlier, JIATF-South presents one model for deeper exploration as a possible starting point for this topic for research.

Finally, and closely related to the last topic, research is required on how best to evolve the public-private partnership. Previously mentioned cyber table-top exercises and war-games often cite a robust public-private partnership as a key aspect to success when implementing national cybersecurity. In October 2018, a group of government and private industry leaders conducted a cyber table-top exercise. The recent report from the Foundation for Defense of Democracies (FDD) and consultant firm The Chertoff Group, the hosts of the cyber table-top exercise, set about to determine what could happen in the event of a major cyberattack that impacted United States critical infrastructure. The exercise after-action report stated, "the most important finding from the discussion is that unless government and private sector decision makers begin developing specific procedures and trust now, the United States will find itself flat-footed during a major cyber event."[6] The cyber war-games in which I participated came to the identical conclusion. What is lacking in the plethora of exercise reports is a detailed explanation of exactly how to establish that robust partnership in a way that protects and incentivizes private partners' participation in a meaningful manner. Private industry leaders wish to participate, but find the relationship lacking on many accounts. Further research is required to explore the challenges and concerns and then develop practicable recommendations for overcoming the current hurdles to full and robust private sector collaboration in national cybersecurity.

The Most Likely Future CINS Scenarios

In reality, it is impossible to definitively predict future political competition in and through cyberspace. Each adversary is different with alternative motives and pressure points. Each situation possesses different leaders who value different things. Coercion in and through cyberspace will therefore be unique depending on the contextual elements of the protagonists, the political landscape, and the entanglements each side possesses. Much more research is needed to fully understand the singular variables of each state when attempting to predict how and to what level a particular state may choose to use coercion in future cases of CEMA and CINS. However, there are some generalities that may be presented in an effort to categorize the protagonists.

When examining the research on CINS across the global stage, states will likely use cyber coercion in line with their established political motives and national interests. The most powerful nations, outside of major physical wars, will likely use CEMA (and not CINS) to achieve less than vital interest objectives and therefore attempt to maintain the status quo (not escalate a situation) with their peers. These major powers are unlikely to instigate CINS, but may "test" how far they may push interstate competition in the virtual domain in order to promote their national interests. Russia's recent nefarious cyber actions to meddle in United States' 2016 and 2018 elections are examples of that.[7] The United States has yet to respond in any meaningful way, and therefore, has not imposed any consequences on the Russian's for their activity...thereby signaling Russia that this sort of CEMA is tolerable. Conversely, as part of significant competition between major powers or between a major power and a lesser power, coercion may be used to avoid war. It is plausible that a major power may use CINS as a way to deliberately signal the intentions of political leaders in attempt to de-escalate tensions. CEMA may also be used to raise costs on a personal level for the political elites of the target state. In times of war, major powers may conduct CINS in conjunction with physical military and economic actions (hybrid wars) in an effort to quickly gain the upper hand in a conflict. By commencing CINS simultaneously with physical military actions, a major power may coerce or even compel an adversary in effective ways.

For lesser states or nations on the rise on the global stage, it is unlikely they would use CINS against a peer or major power since it may be challenging to control the escalation and risks associated with instigating CINS. For these states, directly confronting the more powerful states through a cyber-attack on critical infrastructure is not probable. Consequently, less powerful states will likely rely primarily on cyber espionage as China did during the Byzantine-Hades series of operations or attacking non-critical infrastructure private entities. Regardless, it is safe to predict that CEMA will become a more significant tool in use of influencing other states actors and we will likely see an increase in its use across the globe.

Final Thoughts – Leadership

On May 25, 1961, President John F. Kennedy addressed the nation and articulated the hurdle that lay before the United States with regard to placing a man on the moon within the decade. He stated, "I believe we possess all the resources and talents necessary. But the facts of the matter are that we have never made the national decisions or marshaled the national resources required for such leadership. We have never specified long-range goals on an urgent time schedule, or managed our resources and our time so as to insure their fulfillment."[8]

Interesting enough, the United States is in a similar position today, but related to securing its future against the pending cyber storm. Resolving the national cybersecurity enigma does not require additional laws, fresh talent, new funding, or different cyber capabilities. All of the necessary elements exist now and are in place for use by the United States. What is missing however, is the leadership and the unified vision to direct the necessary coercive cyber strategy development and organizational constructs to secure the nation's future against CINS.

Both public and private leaders, each with widely different responsibilities, represent varied views within the complex national and economic cybersecurity conundrum. Each stakeholder takes a perspective that most directly affects them, as would be expected. Consequently, given the unrelenting nature of the cybersecurity threat, each leader adopts a stance that limits their exposure and responsibility for mounting effective remedies. Given the involvement of state actors and cyber-criminals, the private sector expects the Federal government to play a protective intermediary role. Because the cyber infrastructure is largely owned and operated by the private sector, the government expects the private sector to protect its networks and firms.[9] This is clearly problematic when actors attack from beyond borders, let alone from within borders. Private industry can only do so much. Imposing consequences on the malicious cyber actors who perpetrate CINS is neither a simple nor linear task, but requires strong leadership across government and private industry to see through the morass of conflicting agendas and promote a joint vision for defending the nation.

Leadership is the key ingredient to set the joint goals, marshal the resources, and ensure all obstacles are overcome in order to reach the stated national goals. This book breaks down the complexities of the problem facing United States in national cybersecurity and presents an alternative and decisive path to securing the nation's future. It is my hope that others join my call to push our national leaders to action. The time is long overdue to secure the United States' future against the impending cyber storm.

---

[1] "Holocaust and Human Behavior," in Facing History and Ourselves, accessed on Mar 10, 2019, found at: https://www.facinghistory.org/holocaust-and-human-behavior/chapter-1/words-matter.

[2] Unfortunately, since the cyber-attack on Iran, Stuxnet has been reverse engineered and now any cyber actors possess the tools to attack the critical infrastructure of a nation with debilitating effect.

[3] Kier Giles, "Countering Russian Information Operations in the Age of Social Media," Council on Foreign Relations, Nov 21, 2017, found at: https://www.cfr.org/report/countering-russian-information-operations-age-social-media.

[4] Ibid.

[5] "The Constitution of the United States of America," United States Government Archives, accessed Mar 16, 2019, found at: https://www.archives.gov/founding-docs/constitution-transcript.

[6] The Foundation for Defense and Democracies, "United States Government and Private Industry Must Prepare for Cyber-Enabled Economic Warfare Escalations", The FDD Organization On Line,

Feb 5, 2019, found on line at: https://www.fdd.org/analysis/2019/02/05/government-and-private-industry-must-prepare-for-cyber-enabled-economic-warfare-escalations/.

[7] Kathleen Hall Jamieson, a professor of communications at the University of Pennsylvania, explored the available evidence of the 2016 United States national election and determined that Russia's meddling had a decisive impact in 2016. In her book, "Cyberwar: How Russian Hackers and Trolls Helped Elect a President—What We Don't, Can't, and Do Know," she presents the forensic analysis of the available evidence and concludes that Russia very likely delivered Trump's victory. Reported by Jane Mayer, "How Russia Helped Swing the Election for Trump -

A meticulous analysis of online activity during the 2016 campaign makes a powerful case that targeted cyberattacks by hackers and trolls were decisive," *The New Yorker*, Oct 1, 2018, found on line at: https://www.newyorker.com/magazine/2018/10/01/how-russia-helped-to-swing-the-election-for-trump.

[8] President John F. Kennedy, " Moon Shot - JFK and Space Exploration," John F. Kennedy Presential Library and Museum on line, accessed on Mar 17, 2019, found at: https://www.jfklibrary.org/visit-museum/exhibits/past-exhibits/moon-shot-jfk-and-space-exploration.

[9] Leonard J. Marcus, Ronald L. Banks, Eric J. McNulty, Richard Serino, and Lisa B. Flynn, "National Leadership

Dialogue on Cyber Security: Key Themes and Recommendations," A collaboration between the USAF Cyber College and the National Preparedness Leadership Initiative, Dec 2, 2016, National Preparedness Leadership Initiative Harvard School of Public Health, found on line at: https://cdn2.sph.harvard.edu/wp-content/uploads/sites/88/2016/09/National-Leadership-Dialogue-on-Cyber-Security.pdf.

INDEX

Made in the USA
Las Vegas, NV
09 February 2022

43513337R00203